# MEDIA AND SUICIDE

# MEDIA AND SUICIDE

International Perspectives on
Research, Theory, and Policy

Thomas Niederkrotenthaler
and Steven Stack, editors

Routledge
Taylor & Francis Group

LONDON AND NEW YORK

First published 2017 by Transaction Publishers

Published 2017 by Routledge
2 Park Square, Milton Park, Abingdon, Oxon OX14 4RN
711 Third Avenue, New York, NY 10017, USA

*Routledge is an imprint of the Taylor & Francis Group, an informa business*

Library of Congress Catalog Number: 2016048821
ISBN: 978-1-4128-6508-1 (hbk)

Library of Congress Cataloging-in-Publication Data

A catalog record for this book has been requested

# Contents

# Preface

This work is based on the unique contribution of experts who are active members in the International Association for Suicide Prevention's Media and Suicide Special Interest Group (SIG). In addition to many local and national activities in the area of suicide prevention in the media, the IASP SIG Suicide and the Media is dedicated to facilitating research and prevention activities in the area of suicide and the media globally. Initiated by Jane Pirkis from Australia in 2005, the SIG currently has forty-seven members from sixteen countries and is cochaired by Dan Reidenberg from the United States and Thomas Niederkrotenthaler from Austria. The provision of an interdisciplinary, international platform for suicide prevention experts from across the globe who discuss their findings on the impact of suicide awareness and education campaigns using media as a tool has rarely been more important than today, where we are increasingly living in a globalized, connected media-world. Exchange of experiences from different countries is therefore crucial to help inform more evidence-based approaches on how to work effectively with the media to prevent additional suicides and raise awareness about suicidality and how to cope with it.

A shift that has had a great impact on task force activities recently reflects ongoing changes in suicide-related media use, with an ever-increasing relevance of online media.

The SIG has the following goals:

- To improve linkages between suicide experts and media professionals;
- To systematically review research about suicide and the media (including evaluations of media guidelines), to identify gaps in knowledge, to develop a research agenda to address these gaps, and to encourage relevant research;
- To identify, collect, and collate media guidelines which have been developed around the world, and examine and report on their content, development, and implementation;

- To work collaboratively with media professionals to develop recommendations for developing and implementing media guidelines;
- To work collaboratively with media professionals to promote media guidelines to journalists, editors, and other stakeholders;
- To work on prevention of suicide using online media; and
- To provide an international body of experts that can provide authoritative comment on issues regarding suicide and the media, including issues surrounding media guidelines.

For more and up-to-date information on the SIG activities, please visit https://www.iasp.info/suicide_and_the_media.php

# 1

# Introduction

*Thomas Niederkrotenthaler and Steven Stack*

## Significance of Suicide

Recent data from the World Health Organization report that suicide took the lives of approximately eight hundred and four thousand people in 2012, representing a global suicide rate of 11.4 per 100,000 (15.0 for males and 8.0 for females). Put another way, there is a suicide someplace in the world every forty seconds. In addition, it is estimated that for every death by suicide there are more than twenty additional persons who attempt suicide. Globally, suicides account for 50 percent of all violent deaths among men and 71 percent of such deaths for women. Among youth, persons aged 15–29, suicide is the second leading cause of death. Younger persons are considered to be the most susceptible to media impacts, including copycat suicides. While there is a high level of suicidality in the world, of the over two hundred nations only twenty-eight are known to have national suicide prevention strategies. Promoting responsible media reporting of suicide is part of many strategies for the reduction of suicide (World Health Organization, 2014).

Female suicide rates are highest in South Korea (23.4/100,000), a nation with evidence of sensationalism in its suicide reporting (Lee et al., 2014). Male suicide is highest in South Korea (49.9/100,000), Lithuania (59.5/100,000), and Guyana (50.8/100,000). Little is known about the frequency or quality of suicide reporting in the latter two nations.

Focusing on the United States, suicide is one of top ten causes of death. There are now more deaths from suicide than motor vehicle accidents; in 2013 the respective numbers were 41,149 and 35,369 (Xi et al., 2016). Generally, many Americans fear death by homicide more than death by suicide. However, the chances of such deaths are much lower for homicide, with 5.1 homicides per 100,000 population, than for suicide, with 13.0 suicides per 100,000 population (Xi et al., 2016). There is evidence of possible cohort effects such as that for the postwar baby boomer generation. While the suicide rate in the United States increased by 19.2 percent between 1999 and 2013, the increase was much larger for baby boomer cohorts: 41.7 percent for ages 45–54 and 48.3 percent for ages 55–64 (Xi et al., 2016). With suicides rates being the highest for the elderly, it is anticipated that as this cohort continues to enter its retirement years, suicide rates will trend higher for that demographic group, perhaps reaching all-time records for those over 65. For example, the suicide rate for 55–64-year-olds (18.1/100,000) already exceeds that of those aged 65–74 (15.0/100,000). Available evidence notes that the elderly are susceptible to media suicide stories, especially if the story is about an elderly celebrity (Stack, 2005).

In the United States and many nations of the world the suicide rate is increasing or remaining stubbornly high. This is in spite of the efforts of suicide prevention programs, psychological therapy, and pharmacological treatments. For example, the accelerated reliance on pharmacological treatments, including the widespread use of anti-depressants (Maris, 2015), has not been sufficient to stem the tide of suicide in the United States. In this context, interventions through the media are gaining attention as a possible low-cost and far-reaching partial solution to the suicide problem. Web-based help outlets such as suicide prevention blogs are among the possible prevention strategies being discussed and researched (World Health Organization, 2014).

## Brief Review of the Literature on Media Impacts on Suicide

Research has often indicated that communications in the media can alternatively increase or decrease suicidality in at-risk individuals (Niederkrotenthaler et al., 2010; Stack, 2005). Much research and public attention has been drawn to documenting increases in suicide due to the "copycat" effects of the media. Over 150 studies to date have explored media influences on suicide. Many have often found evidence of a rise, and a few evidence of a fall, in suicide after widely publicized suicide stories. This body of evidence has resulted in several additional scholarly themes: (1) what are the specific mechanisms and contexts accounting for a copycat or "Werther" effect (Phillips, 1974), or (2) a "Papageno" effect in cases of a decline in suicide (Niederkrotenthaler et al., 2010), and (3) the development of media guidelines for the reporting of suicide in order to minimize copycat effects. Of the three streams of research, the study of possible copycat or "Werther" effects has attracted the most attention.

The first systematic study of the Werther effect analyzed thirty-three nationally publicized American suicide stories that occurred between 1947 and 1968. On average, there were 39.3 additional or excess suicide stories in the month following the suicide story (Phillips, 1974). Substantially greater increases have been recorded in high-risk contexts. One such context involves the reporting of the suicides of well-known celebrities, especially entertainment celebrities (Stack, 2005).

The largest known reported copycat effect involved the suicide of the popular Korean actress, Jin-Sil Choi in October, 2008. Controlling for socio-demographic factors, there were 429 additional suicides during the massive media publicity concerning her suicide. In comparison, although also a marked high increase in suicide, the widely publicized suicide of American actress Marilyn Monroe in 1962 was associated with an additional 197 suicides in the month after her death. South Korea has a population less than a fourth of the United States, but the suicide of a popular actress was followed by twice as many suicides. Such findings suggest the presence of factors that condition the size of copycat effects. These may include the amount and type of media publicity concerning the suicide and cultural differences in the susceptibility of audiences to suicide stories. Even in the case of high-risk stories concerning the suicides of well-known actresses, the size of copycat effects can vary across cultures (Lee, Lee, Hwang, & Stack, 2014).

In general, research based on media coverage of celebrities is the most apt to uncover copycat effects. The largest quantitative review of 419 findings from 55 studies found that findings based on the suicides of entertainment or political celebrities are 5.27 times more likely to report a copycat effect than findings based on other types of stories (Stack, 2005).

As we shall see in this book, the association between media and suicide is complex and not fully understood. It is important to note that media coverage of suicide is often not associated with increases in suicide rates (Stack, 2005). Further, in contrast to findings of a copycat effect, there is also growing evidence of a "Papageno effect." Sometimes media stories concern a once suicidal individual who mastered their personal angst and troubled environment. After the media's presentation of such positive role models, there is evidence that suicide rates decline (Niederkrotenthaler et al., 2010).

In most research, exactly why there is or is not an association between exposure to suicidality in the media and suicidality in the audience is not well understood. A lot depends on specifying the conditions under which a link may or may not be found. Mediators include the characteristics of the audience, including the extent to which they are marked by suicidal predispositions and how exposure affects audience mood. Work has been progressing at the concrete level of individual reactions to media-based suicidal stimuli. Laboratory experiments, many carried out in Austria, have been shedding light on how different categories of the audience react differently to different modalities of suicidal media stimuli (e.g., Till, Niederkrotenthaler, Herberth, Vitouch, & Sonneck, G., 2010; Till, Niederkrotenthaler, Herberth, Voracek, Sonneck, & Vitouch, 2011; Till, Strauss, Sonneck, & Niederkrotenthaler, 2015). The present volume contains the recent contribution by this cutting-edge group to the understanding of the mechanisms operating between media and suicidality.

Given that under certain conditions media stories on suicide can increase suicide risk, researchers and policy makers have been developing suicide guidelines for the reporting of suicide (e.g., Fu, Chan, & Yip, 2011; Jamieson, Jamieson, & Romer, 2003; Pirkis et al., 2006). Such guidelines have been available for distribution and implementation by the media for several decades. However, there have been many challenges in finding the most effective ways for communicating recommendations for the reporting of suicide to media officials and frontline reporters. Media representatives are not always enthusiastic in implementing such guidelines. There are many issues that sometimes prevent implementation. These include freedom of the press issues as well as concerns to give the public what they presumably want—newsworthy stories, stories which may need to actually violate some of the guidelines that prevent copycat effects. Other issues in guideline implementation include the mode of communication between suicide prevention groups and media professionals. Modalities have included merely mailing the guidelines to media officials, to engaging media representatives in long-term meaningful dialogs. Nevertheless, there is evidence that when the media effectively complies with such guidelines, suicide rates fall. However, there is much more work to be done in securing the trust and cooperation of the media in many nations. These challenges are discussed in the final section of the present volume.

## Overview of This Book

The book presents recent developments in research, theory, and policy. Its nineteen chapters are written by members of the Media Task Force of the International Association for Suicide Prevention (IASP).

The volume is an international, multidisciplinary collection of new developments. Disciplines include sociology, psychiatry, journalism, mass communications, literature, and law. Chapters include several systematic literature reviews, quantitative analyses, qualitative work, historical analyses, theoretical or conceptual contributions, and case studies of policy initiatives in six nations.

The book is broken down into three parts. Part I deals with eight new contributions to the research on media and suicide. These include research studies on traditional media, emergent media, and historical analyses. Part II is a critical review of the state of theories of media impacts on suicide. Much of the discussion deals with the Werther and the Papageno effects. Depending on contexts, including story characteristics, the media can alternatively be expected to increase or decrease suicide risk. Finally, Part III is composed of a series of chapters on efforts to influence the responsible reporting of suicide in the national media. These chapters include work by renowned suicide prevention specialists in a variety of different nations including Austria, Germany, Hong Kong, Ireland, Switzerland, the United Kingdom and the United States.

*Part I: Research on Media Impacts on Suicide*

This section of eight chapters is divided into three modalities of media: traditional, emergent, and historical.

*Traditional Media.* Traditional media include film, as well as news coverage in newspapers and television. This section provides two new research works on these media. In addition, there is an innovative structural review of selected works on the media coverage of tragic mass shootings/suicide.

Recent work has shown that traditional media play an important role in the selection of suicide methods. For example, research on persons who have attempted suicide has found that 77 percent reported getting their information on methods of suicide from the movies (Biddle, Gunnell et al., 2012). The second chapter suggests that the gendering of the choice of suicide methods in society is related to the gendering of suicide method portrayed in the movies.

Compared to news stories, there has been relatively little work on film impacts and even less on how the presentation of cinematic suicides shift over a century of film. Stack and Bowman's chapter links a century of exposure to the gendered portrayal of gun suicides in film to the "gender paradox." While the level of psychological distress among women is equal to or exceeds that of men, women have a much lower incidence of suicide. The central question is: is the 4 to 1 American male to female ratio related to the gender differential in use of guns in the suicide movies? Data are drawn from 1,191 suicides in American films from 1900 to 2014. The results of a multivariate logistic regression analysis show that, controlling for the other predictor variables, men were 3.9 times more apt than women to use firearms in their cinematic suicides. The cinema provides cultural scripts to reinforce the gendering of lethal suicide methods and the resulting gender differential in suicide.

Newspaper depictions of suicide have been the main focus of content analyses. These analyses generally show the extent to which the news stories depart from suicide reporting guidelines, departures which presumably increase suicide risk. Placing suicide in the headline, failing to give information on sources of help (e.g., a hotline number), and sensationalizing suicide are story characteristics thought to increase copycat effects. However, most of the research on the content analysis of suicide news stories is done outside of the United States (e.g., Machin, Pirkis, & Spittal, 2013).

The third chapter by Canetto and Tatum provides the first rigorous study of the relative frequency of suicide versus homicide stories in the American press. Of 2,528 media stories on violent deaths analyzed, only 5 percent of the stories focused on suicide, while 95 percent involved homicides. In contrast, 64 percent of violent deaths in the United States are suicides, only 36 percent are homicides. The large overrepresentation of homicide stories in the United States may help to distract public attention from suicide and, hence, minimize resources available for suicide prevention. In addition, the analysis found that suicide stories misrepresented suicide by failing to connect it to mental illness 93 percent of the time and giving disproportionate attention to rare forms such as homicide followed by suicide.

The fourth chapter by Gould and Olivares explores suicidality among the perpetrators of mass killings. Fourteen studies met the criteria for inclusion in the systematic review. A large study of fifty-five rampage killings found that fully 46 percent ended with a suicide. Eight of twelve school rampage shooters themselves referred to the classic reported case of the Columbine murder-suicides and five imitated aspects of that event. Five studies focused on copycat effects after a widely publicized mass-murder/suicide event. Four found at least some evidence of a copycat effect after the event.

*Emergent Media.* New media channels, such as the Internet and Facebook, can act as both risk and protective factors for suicide. While there are many studies of the impacts of traditional bullying on suicidality, there are few to date on cyber bullying. The Internet provides technological resources for new forms of bullying. The degree of shame involved in cyber-based bullying can be multiplied by the sheer size of the audience reached by way of the Internet.

The question of whether the exposure to Internet-based bullying may act as a key additional stress factor in generating suicides is raised in the fifth chapter by Stack. An analysis of data from the 2013 Youth Risk Behavior Survey on 13,583 students determined that fully 52.2 percent of those who attempted suicide reported having been victims of Internet bullying compared to 15 percent of the total sample. Further, even after controlling out the influence of socio-psychiatric confounding variables such as an eating disorder and major depression, Internet bullying was 50 percent more common among attempters than persons just considering suicide. The results suggest that suicide prevention efforts should be enhanced for those at-risk students experiencing Internet bullying. This is the first systematic investigation suggesting that Internet bullying is a pathway from suicide ideation to a suicide attempt.

The sixth chapter deals with the emergent phenomenon of cyber-based memorials to the dead. Bell and Bailey report the results of in-depth interviews with nine persons who have had the experience of creating, maintaining, and utilizing the social media platform Facebook as an online memorial page for a significant other who suicided. They discuss how Facebook is an important part of the therapeutic process of managing trauma in the aftermath of a death by suicide. However, negative aspects of memorialization are noted including several subsequent suicide attempts among the friends of the deceased, unwanted requests from unknown persons to join the memorial group, and the page manager's return to loneliness as the number of hits on the memorial page grind down to near zero.

Pirkis, Mok, and Robinson provide a systematic literature review of thirty-four studies on the effects of the Internet-based media on suicidality. The research is mixed. Some Internet-based materials can do "good" by providing resources for those seeking help. Other sites are "the bad" through promoting suicidality by offering detailed information on methods of suicide, with some emphasis on reporting methods that minimize pain and disfigurement. The "googly" sites are ones that include both positive and negative content simultaneously.

The chapter synthesizes the findings from these studies and discusses where future research is heading.

*Historical Artistic Media.* Two chapters follow on historical work on the portrayal of suicide in art and plays. The eighth chapter by Krysinska and Andriessen traces how the meanings and visual representations of suicide have been changing over centuries. The changes reflect the evolving cultural and philosophical understanding of the behavior and attitudes toward it. However, frequently there are coexisting contradictory meanings and representations. To better understand the links between suicide, the arts, and the broader socio-cultural context, this chapter presents three partially overlapping issues: the semantics of suicide, the gender of suicide, and the aesthetics of suicide. It concludes by presenting some ideas regarding possible ways in which semantics, gender, and aesthetics of suicide might impact the suicidal behavior of individuals.

In chapter 9 Krysinska describes an Eastern art form from the seventeenth-century Japan, the Kabuki play. Suicide is a recurrent theme in these plays. Some depict double suicide between troubled lovers. These include one based on a true story, *The Love Suicides at Sonezaki* (1703), which was reportedly linked to a wave of copycat suicides. The plays were banned for a time in the 1720s. In an effort to deter copycat suicides, the authorities hung the bodies of persons copying the suicide on public display for three days. Importantly, this "Kabuki effect" actually predated the Western-based similar phrase the "Werther Effect." Johann Wolfgang von Goethe's novel, *The Sorrows of Young Man Werther* (1774), appeared over a half century later. The double suicide in the Japanese play has been memorialized at the Shinto shrine *Tsuyu no Tenjinja* built on the place where the double suicide took place centuries ago.

## Part II: Theories of Media Impacts

Research on suicide-related media effects has often been criticized for a lack of theoretical foundation. This section comprises four chapters related to an integration of theoretical concepts and novel research dedicated to the understanding of media effects in suicide and suicide prevention.

Charles E. Notredame and colleagues provide an update on theories used to explain the Werther effect. They argue that, in spite of the accumulated evidence of and epidemiological meaning of the Werther effect, namely the temporal correlation between mortality by suicide and media reporting, the exploration of the causal underlying mechanisms continues to suffer from severe methodological issues. Multiple theoretical concepts including contagion, identification, social learning, modeling, copycat, and imitation have frequently been presented as synonyms, but their notions refer to distinct frameworks, from social psychology, to infectiology, going through sociology, cognitivism, or behaviorism. This semantic confusion reveals the necessity to stabilize an epistemological nomenclature to empirically explore the psychosocial mechanisms at work in the Werther effect. The authors make an effort to disentangle the theoretical concepts and to integrate them into a novel model that can serve future research in the topic area.

While research on harmful media effects has had a long history in suicide prevention, research on protective effects (Papageno effect) has only been emerging recently. Thomas Niederkrotenthaler provides an update on current research in the area of protective media effects.

The description of a potentially suicide-protective Papageno effect in 2010 has been an important milestone for the acknowledgment of protective potentials of media reporting that addresses how people can cope with suicidality and adverse circumstances. New research from randomized controlled trials (RCTs) supports the potential of media reporting on personal lived experiences to help prevent suicide. In particular, a recently conducted RCT showed that individuals exposed to a newspaper report on coping with suicidality decreased suicidal cognitions in the audience. In another RCT, it was found that fictional films featuring a young man mastering his crisis by falling in love was associated with a short-term decrease in suicide risk factors. New evidence for suicide-protective potentials is also emerging for the Internet: exposure to educative suicide-prevention websites resulted in a sustained reduction in suicidality in individuals from the general population with above-average suicidality scores, supporting the hypothesis of a suicide-protective Papageno effect online.

Research using qualitative designs to analyze media effects is scarce but needed to better understand media impacts. Benedikt Till presents findings from focus group interviews on the impact of suicide portrayals in fictional films.

Ten focus groups of three to four non-suicidal adults each were randomly assigned to one of five test conditions. Four focus groups watched original or censored versions of the film *It's My Party* (USA, 1996), four groups watched the film *The Fire Within* (France/Italy, 1963), and two focus groups watched the film *Phenomenon*

(USA, 1996), which concludes with the protagonist's non-suicidal death. Data were collected with group discussions and analyzed with the "Documentary Method." Three major categories of emotional impact of the films were identified: (1) Some participants experienced a slight deterioration of mood due to the film screening, while (2) others reported concurrent positive and negative emotional reactions or (3) avoided discussing the impact of the film on their emotions. Participants across all groups showed psychological defense mechanisms such as humor, denial, or rationalization when discussing topics related to suicide or death, indicating that coping is a key factor in processing of suicide and death portrayals in fictional films.

In their chapter, Scherr and Steinleitner analyze ambiguous findings in the area of suicide research on media impacts. Their literature review focuses on equivocal studies ($n = 25$) on copycat suicides that were systematically analyzed based on theoretically derived criteria. The results of the systematic analysis of all identified studies imply that media effects on suicidality are better understood and discussed as a continuum between the two extremes that were introduced as either a damaging Werther effect or a beneficial Papageno effect. Future studies must clarify what factors contribute to a shift from ambiguous findings to harmful media effects on individual suicidality.

*Part III: Policy Issues*

The promotion of safe and responsible reporting that enhances a shift in media conversation toward preventive styles of reporting is a public health priority and part of many national suicide prevention programs. The sharing of information regarding experiences in the implementation of related interventions is crucial for others. This section comprises five chapters related to experiences from Austria, the United States, French-speaking Switzerland, the United Kingdom, and Hong Kong.

In their chapter, Sonneck and Etzersdorfer discuss their seminal study on the prevention of subway suicides in Vienna, Austria. After the opening of the first parts of the Viennese subway system in 1978, it became increasingly acceptable as a means for suicide and suicide attempts, with a sharp increase beginning in 1984. This and the fact that the press reported about these events in a very dramatic way led to the formulation of media guidelines which were launched to the press in mid-1987. The media reports changed immediately and markedly and the number of subway suicides and suicide attempts decreased by more than 80 percent from the first to the second half of 1987, remaining at a rather low level since. This intervention has been a model for many other countries to develop and adopt media recommendations for suicide prevention.

*Development of American Media Guidelines.* Following the release of the first media recommendations for reporting on suicide in 1994 and an updated version in 2001, a comprehensive and collaborative approach was undertaken to develop the current US recommendations. Using the best science available on the media's impact on suicide, including research from around the world, as well as the ethical guidelines for journalists, an international task force was convened to develop what would become the first US best practice-endorsed Media Recommendations. The process included various tiers of involvement and professional backgrounds both within the field of suicide prevention and the field of journalism. Over a two-year period there were several meetings held, nearly twenty drafts completed and edited to arrive at what was the best practice consensus statement on reporting on suicide. This article reviews the participants involved, the timeline, project components, and release of the US Media Recommendations.

*Stop Suicide.* Irina Inostroza from Stop Suicide describes the implementation of a program is to raise awareness about the risk and the benefits of reporting on suicide in the media in French-speaking Switzerland. Stop Suicide works on four main axes: press review and analysis; awareness-raising; informing media professional; training young media professionals and building partnerships with young media makers. In this chapter the implementation of these four areas of the program are described and thoughts about what works and what doesn't work are presented; reasons of such successes and failures are discussed; and some best practices are suggested.

*The Samaritans.* Lorna Fraser and colleagues report on the activities of The Samaritans, a suicide prevention charity in the United Kingdom and Republic of Ireland, and the recognized lead expert on the subject for UK media. The authors describe a number of proactive initiatives to raise awareness and educate the industry, at all levels: lobbying for change in media regulation, careful and ongoing monitoring and analysis of media reports of suicidal behavior, and extensive work with the media and key stakeholders to improve coverage, not least in relation to high-profile stories and programs. Drawing on case examples, it is illustrated what can be achieved through this strategy, highlighting key challenges and successes, as well as emerging concerns for research, policy and practice.

*Hong Kong.* In comparison to many Western countries, where individual suicide is often left unreported, a large proportion of suicides are reported in the Hong Kong media. Qijin Cheng and Paul Yip describe the implementation process of the first set of media recommendations in 2004 and compare their experiences to their revised implementation process in 2015. Suicide news in Hong Kong was found to be generally sensational, frequently publishing bloody photos, private information of the deceased and family, and details of suicide methods and locations. However, over the years, positive changes are afoot in Hong Kong.

In the final, nineteenth chapter, we relate the work in this volume to dominant issues in the broader suicidology and media literature. We also offer suggestions for points of departure for new work. These include suggestions on the specific problems raised by the present authors, as well as related issues.

The chapters collectively present a set of new works on the subject of media and suicide. They include many by leading international authorities on the subject, researchers who have contributed many articles, chapters, and books in the past. They are among the most cited authorities on the subject around the globe. There are also chapters by relatively new researchers in the field.

## References

Biddle, L., Gunnell, D., Owen-Smith, A., Potokar, J., Longson, D., Hawton, K . . . Donovan, J. (2012). Information sources used by the suicidal to inform choice of method. *Journal of Affective Disorders, 136,* 702–709.

Fu, K. W., Chan, Y. Y., & Yip, P. S. (2011). Newspaper reporting of suicides in Hong Kong, Taiwan and Guangzhou: compliance with WHO media guidelines and epidemiological comparisons. *Journal of Epidemiology and Community Health, 65*(10), 928–933.

Jamieson, P., Jamieson, K. H., & Romer, D. (2003). The responsible reporting of suicide in print journalism. *American Behavioral Scientist, 46,* 1643–1660.

Lee, J., Lee, W., Hwang, J. S., & Stack, S. (2014). To what extent does the reporting behavior of the media regarding a celebrity suicide influence subsequent suicides in South Korea? *Suicide and Life Threatening Behavior, 44,* 457–472.

Machin, A., Pirkis, J., & Spittal, M. J. (2013). Which suicides are reported in the media – And what makes them "newsworthy?" *Crisis, 34,* 305–313.

Maris, R. W. (2015). *Pillaged: Psychiatric medications and suicide risk.* Columbia, SC: University of South Carolina Press.

Niederkrotenthaler, T., Voracek, M., Herberth, A., Till, B., Strauss, M., Etzersdorfer, E. . . . Sonneck, G. (2010). The role of media reports in completed and prevented suicide – Werther versus Papageno effects. *British Journal of Psychiatry, 197,* 234–243.

Phillips, D. (1974). The influence of suggestion on suicide: Substantive and theoretical implications of the Werther effect. *American Sociological Review, 39*, 340–354.

Pirkis, J., Blood, R. W., Beautrais, A., Burgess, P., & Skehan, J. (2006). Media guidelines on the reporting of suicide. *Crisis, 27*, 82–87.

Stack, S. (2005). Suicide in the media: A quantitative review of suicide based in non fictional stories. *Suicide & Life Threatening Behavior, 35*, 121–133.

Till, B., Niederkrotenthaler, T., Herberth, A., Vitouch P., & Sonneck, G. (2010). Suicide in films: The impact of suicide portrayals on non-suicidal viewers' well-being and the effectiveness of censorship. *Suicide & Life-Threatening Behavior, 40*, 319–327.

Till, B., Niederkrotenthaler, T., Herberth, A., Voracek, M., Sonneck, G., & Vitouch, P. (2011). Coping and film reception: A study on the impact of film dramas and the mediating effects of emotional modes of film reception and coping strategies. *Journal of Media Psychology, 23*, 149–160.

Till, B., Strauss, M., Sonneck, G., & Niederkrotenthaler, T. (2015). Determining the effects of films with suicidal content: a laboratory experiment. *British Journal of Psychiatry, 207*, 72–78.

World Health Organization (2014). *Preventing suicide: A global imperative.* Geneva: author.

Xi, J., Murphy, S. L., Kochenek, K. D., & Bastian, B. (2016). Deaths: Final data for 2013. *National Vital Statistics Reports, 64*(2): 1–118.

# Part I

## Research on Media Impacts on Suicide

# 2

# Why Men Choose Firearms More than Women: Gender and the Portrayal of Firearm Suicide in Film, 1900–2013

*Steven Stack and Barbara Bowman*

A key pattern in the American etiology of suicide is based on gender: American men generally have a suicide rate three to four times higher than that of women. The greater risk among men is also found in nearly all nations of the world (Lester, 2000; Mergl, Koburger, Heinrichs et al., 2015; Stack, 2000; Wasserman & Stack, 2009). In the contemporary United States, the male suicide rate (20.0/100,000) is actually almost four times that of women (5.2/100,000). Men account for approximately 80 percent of all suicides (Murphy et al., 2013; Proquest, 2014). While much has been written on the gendered nature of suicide risk, there has been little systematic work on the possible role of the media in generating high risk for males. This chapter focuses on a new possible risk factor: the gendered nature of the presentation of a highly lethal suicide method, firearms, in a popular media channel: American feature films.

## Background

The high rate of male suicide is not what would be expected from a psychiatric perspective on suicide. The incidence of severe mental disorders linked to suicide is often about the same for men and women, while for some disorders females are at greater risk. For example, a recent meta-analysis found that men are 63 percent less apt than women to develop depression, a strong predictor of suicide risk (Abate, 2013). Hence, the gender ratio in suicide is something of a puzzle or a gender paradox (Canetto & Sakinofsky, 1998). This chapter briefly reviews highlights of the existing explanations for the gender paradox and suggests a new one based on cinematic depictions of suicide methods.

While there have been a series of possible explanations for the gender paradox, including gender differentials in religiosity, strength of social support in social networks, and help-seeking (Moller-Leimkuhler, 2002; Schnabel, 2015; Stack, 2000), an important explanation has been centered on the choice of suicide method. American men are more apt than women to choose a highly lethal method: firearms. Fully 95 percent of suicide attempts by firearms lead to death (Shenassa et al., 2003). In contrast, women are more apt than men to select methods that are low in lethality such as poisons. While 95 percent of suicide attempts by firearms lead to death, only 2 percent of attempts by poison are followed by death (Shenassa et al., 2003). Nevertheless, the reasons why women choose less lethal methods than men are not well understood.

The choice of suicide method has often been said to follow cultural scripts (Canetto & Sakinofsky, 1998; Lester & Stack, 2015). In the United States the script for men involves firearms whereas the script for women involves poisons. However, the sources of these cultural scripts are unclear. It is often correctly argued that men may choose guns since a higher percentage of men are more apt to have served in the military and police forces, groups where individuals are socialized into the use of firearms. These and other male-dominated activities such as hunting do provide males with a familiarity with firearms. However, these groups constitute a minority of males. Other areas of society may also serve to pressure males into suicides utilizing firearms. In particular, cultural narratives about suicide and suicide methods that reach larger audiences may also promote the gendering of suicide methods. For example, feature films, in particular, are assumed to affect much larger audiences than those involved in at-risk occupations, such as the military (0.44 percent adult population) and police (0.31 percent adult population), which directly involve firearms. Further only 9.1 percent of those 18 and older are veterans (Proquest, 2014). Indeed, watching movies is the number one leisure pastime of Americans (Stack & Bowman, 2012). Nearly everyone watches movies, but only less than 10 percent of the population has served in the armed forces.

The present analysis assesses the extent to which American feature films provide differentially more male role models in their portrayals of suicide with firearms. The movies may both reinforce and reflect firearmsas the scripted method for suicide for men.

## Social Learning of Suicide Methods

While there is relatively little work on the extent to which the media shape cultural scripts for methods of suicide, available work suggests the media play a role in the selection of suicide methods. Persons learn about suicide and suicide methods used by others through exposure to news stories, the Internet, films, books, and other channels of mass communication (e.g., Biddle, Gunnell, Owen-Smith et al., 2012; Schmidtke & Hafner, 1988; Stack, 2009). For example, a study of a German six-part television series, *Death of a Student,* found a strong link between the method of suicide in the film and subsequent suicides by the same method, jumping in front of trains (Schmidtke & Hafner, 1988). The increase in train suicides among persons most similar to the age of the student suicide in the film was substantial. Among 15–19-year-old males, suicide on the rails increased by 175 percent after the film. Among females aged 15–19 the increase was also large, 167 percent.

Recent qualitative work interviewed suicide attempters to find out what information sources influenced their selection of a suicide method. The main source of information was from film and television. Fully 77.2 percent of the respondents reported that their information on suicide methods came from films and television. Specific films were mentioned. These included the *Shawshank Redemption* (a film that features suicides by hanging and handgun) and *Full Monty*, a film that demonstrates a suicide attempt by CO poisoning inside a car (Biddle, Gunnell, Owen-Smith et al., 2012).

It is beyond the scope of the present analysis to track the incidence of suicides by firearms after the portrayal of over 1,000 cinematic suicides. Data on firearm suicides are not available for most of the 114 years under analysis. This study is limited to the assessment of the gendering of suicide method in a large sample of American films. It is concerned with the extent to which the cinema produces a cultural script which may help us understand the large gap in suicide between males and females. This is the first systematic, historical study on the gendering of suicide method in the United States.

## Methodology

The sample of films to be included was based on an extensive search taking over ten years. Lists of suicide films were obtained from six web-based filmographies including the *Internet Movie Data Base* and the catalog of the *American Film Institute* (Stack & Bowman, 2012). For a film to be included in the study it needed to meet the following six criteria: (1) produced by the American film industry (non-US films excluded), (2) contains a completed suicide (attempts excluded), (3) film refers to real life (animated films, horror films excluded), (4) feature length (sixty minutes or more), shorts were excluded, (5) shown in theaters in the United States, and (6) the film provides information on suicide method. Films where the suicide of a character is reported, but information on the method is not provided, are deleted. Over a period of ten years, copies of most of these films were obtained and reviewed by the authors. Films meeting the criteria contained a total of 1,145 suicides. They span the period from 1900, the year of the first American feature film with a suicide, through 2013, 114 years of film history.

The dependent variable in this study is firearm suicide. This is coded as a binary variable where 1 = suicide by firearm and 0 = suicide by any other method. Suicide by firearm refers to suicide by handguns as well as long guns. Long guns refer to rifles and shotguns. There were no cases of suicide by other categories of firearms including machine guns, mortars, and cannons.

A control is incorporated in the analysis for time. This is meant to capture any trend in change in the incidence of firearm suicides in the cinema. It is anticipated that firearm suicides in the cinema increased over time given an upward trend in such suicides in society. From scattered available data, for example, the percentage of suicides carried out with firearms increased from 30 percent in 1910 to 50 percent in 2010 (US Department of Commerce, 1913; Murphy et al., 2013). Since the dependent variable (cinematic firearm suicide, 0,1) is a dichotomy, logistic regression techniques are appropriate (Pampel, 2000).

## Results

During 1900–2013 there were a total of 386 firearm and 759 non-firearm suicides. Males were portrayed in 329 of the firearm suicides while females accounted for 57 firearm suicides.

Table 2.1 lists selected male firearm suicides involving major film stars. These can serve as major role models for suicidal men. Such stars would be expected to promote identification in the audience and influence attitudes and behavior more than the suicides of minor characters.

**Table 2.1.** Selected contemporary major male stars who suicide with firearms in their cinematic roles.

| Male star | Movie | Male star | Movie |
|---|---|---|---|
| Ben Affleck | *Hollywoodland* | Morgan Freeman | *Nurse Betty* |
| Nicholas Cage | *Bangkok Dangerous* | Mel Gibson | *Lethal Weapon* |
| Bruce Dern | *Tracy the Outlaw* | Michael Keaton | *Birdman* |
| Robert De Niro (assisted by cop) | *The Fan* | Jack Nicholson | *Flight to Fury* |
| Michael Douglas (assisted by cop) | *Falling Down* | Sean Penn | *Assassination of Richard Nixon* |
| Clint Eastwood (assisted by gang) | *Grand Torino* | Brad Pitt (assisted by outlaw) | *Assassination of Jesse James* |

*Hammersmith Is Out* (1972). Hammersmith (Richard Burton, a major star of his times) provides a firearm for the suicide of crippled Billy Breedlove (Beau Bridges). Mr. Breedlove fears being framed for felonies and being sent back to prison. Essentially all cinematic-assisted suicides involving firearms involve male suicides. Hence a cultural script is provided in film linking this form of assisted suicide to definitions of masculinity. J Cornelius Crean Films. Director: Peter Ustinov.

**Table 2.2.** The effect of gender on the portrayal of firearm suicide in films, 1900–2013 (*N* = 1,145).

| Method | Females | Males |
|---|---|---|
| Firearm suicides | 15.5% | 42.3% |
| Non-firearm suicides | 84.5% | 57.7% |
| | 100% | 100% |
| Chi square = 85.58, *p*<0.000 | | |

**Table 2.3.** The association between gender and firearm suicide controlling for time, 1900–2013.

| Variable | Logistic regression coefficient | Standard error | Odds ratio |
|---|---|---|---|
| Male suicide victim (1), female = 0 | 1.36* | 0.16 | 3.90 |
| Time (year) | 0.0036* | 0.0021 | 1.0036 |
| Constant | −8.80* | 4.13 | − |
| *p* < 0.05 | | | |
| Nagelkerke *r*-squared | 0.105 | | |
| −2 log likelihood | 1373.17* | | |
| Cases correctly predicted | 66.29% | | |

Table 2.2 provides the results of the percentage of suicides that are done with firearms for females and males, respectively. Only 15.5 percent of female cinematic suicides are carried out with firearms. In contrast, nearly three times that percentage of male suicides is with guns (42.3 percent). This difference is statistically significant according to a standard chi square test. The cinematic suicides of males are more apt than those of females to be portrayed as firearm suicides.

Table 2.3 presents the results of the logistic regression analysis. Controlling for time (in years), male suicide victims are more apt than female suicide victims to use guns in their suicides. The logistic regression coefficient for gender is 8.5 times its standard error, indicating a high level of significance. From the odds ratio, males are 3.9 times more likely than females to suicide with firearms in the cinema.

Year or time is also predictive of firearm suicide. From the odds ratio, for each one unit change in year, the chances of a gun suicide increase

*Sin City (2005).* The depiction of cinematic firearm suicides departs substantially from media guidelines, which discourage providing the details of a suicide method. This graphic portrayal is animated to perhaps lessen its brutality. Bruce Willis plays a detective with a young female to protect. However, the leader of the mob is infuriated with him for Willis's castration of his son, a former rapist. The gangster is trying to punish Willis by attempting to murder the woman. He perceives that the mob will only leave her alone if he is dead. He opts for an altruistic suicide, a suicide for the benefit of another. While women are sometimes portrayed as using firearms, we could not find a single case where the depiction included such graphic detail. Dimensions Films. Directors: Frank Miller and Robert Rodriguez.

0.36 percent. Over 100 years this would amount to a 36 percent increase in film gun suicides.

The model provides a reasonably good fit to the data. For example, the Nagelkerke $r$-squared indicates that 10.5 percent of the variance in firearm versus non-firearm suicide is explained. A total of 66.29 percent of the cases are correctly predicted as firearm or non-firearm suicides.

In results not fully reported here, the analysis was restricted to movies made after 1950. A logistic regression model similar to the one in table 2.3 was estimated for the 1951–2013 period. The strength of the association between the independent variables and firearm suicides appeared stronger in this more recent period. Males, for example, were 4.28 times more apt than females to use firearms in their suicides. Each year of time was associated with a 1.16 percent increase in the chances of a firearm suicide.

In additional results not fully reported here, females dominated the cinematic depictions of suicides by poisons, a relatively less lethal form of method of attempting suicide. Well-known female stars from recent decades that suicide by poison include Kathy Bates in *The Family that Preys* and Meryl Streep in *Sophie's Choice*. We did not find a single major male star that used poison as a method of suicide.

## Conclusions

A central issue in the etiology of suicide is the gender paradox (Canetto & Sakinofsky, 1998; Stack, 2000). While females have an equal or greater incidence of mental disorders compared to males, their rate of suicide is much lower (Canetto & Sakinofsky, 1998; Lester, 2000; Mergl et al., 2015; Stack, 2000; Wasserman & Stack, 2009). Currently, the female rate is one quarter that of the male rate (Murphy et al., 2013).

While there continues to be much debate over what cultural and other factors account for the gender paradox (e.g., Canetto & Sakinof-sky, 1998; Denning et al., 2000; Lester, 2000; Mergl et al., 2015; Stack, 2000; Wasserman & Stack, 2009), a leading explanation is the gender differential in suicide methods. Men are far more likely than women to choose firearms in their efforts to kill themselves. This amounts to a nearly ten to one ratio between the percentages of male attempts with guns divided by the percentage of female attempts with guns (Shenassa et al., 2003). Women are far less likely than men to choose firearms for their suicides. Instead women choose less lethal methods such as poison. The cinema is thought to play a role through social learning in the gendering of suicide methods (e.g., Schmidtke & Hafner, 1988; Stack, 2009; Stack & Bowman, 2012).

The present investigation's core finding is that the gender differential in suicide in society corresponds to the gender differential in firearm suicide in the movies. Reflecting and reinforcing suicides in the real world, males are over three times more apt than females to be portrayed in cinematic firearm suicides. Through social learning mechanisms such as role modeling and differential identification with suicidal protagonists and antagonists (Schmidtke & Hafner, 1988; Stack, 2009), it is speculated that the suicidal members of the audience may imitate cinematic suicides, including method of suicide.

Recent qualitative work has buttressed the social learning perspective on how persons select suicide methods. Three-quarters of suicide attempters reported that movies in theaters and television influenced their selection of suicide methods (Biddle et al., 2012). Males, in particular, may follow the lead on the screen and take firearms as the right way for men to accomplish their suicides.

This study did not aspire to solve the debate over which factors are most important in explaining the large gender gap in suicide (e.g., Canetto & Sakinofsky, 1998; Denning et al., 2000; Lester, 2000; Mergl et al., 2015; Stack 2000; Wasserman & Stack, 2009). Instead, it advances a new explanation based on the cinema. Future research will be needed to come closer to a consensus on which factors may be most critical to understanding why males complete suicide more than females. This study simply suggests that the media plays a part in the cultural definition of what means should be used by men when they opt to kill themselves.

Caution needs to be applied to the interpretation of the relationship between gender and firearm suicide in the movies. The direction of causality is an open question. We assume that the relationship is bidirectional, that is, films suggest a script that males should use firearms in their suicides, but given that males in society at any given time already use guns more than females in suicides, the movies also reflect what is already there. The movies can simultaneously promote as well as reflect this cultural script.

Future work is needed on the link between suicide method in the movies and suicide method in society in other nations. For example, while males select more lethal methods (e.g., firearms) than females in both society and the cinema in the United States, is this same pattern found elsewhere? A recent study of four European nations determined that males were, on average, 2.03 times more likely than females to choose highly lethal methods (Mergl, Koburger, Heinrichs et al., 2015). Future investigations are needed to see if this gender differential is reflected in European cinematic depictions of suicide methods.

Work seeking to test for Werther or copycat effects of method of suicide may search for appropriate interaction effects with film genre. For example, Till et al. (2014) recently found that a preference for the film noir genre predicted suicide ideation. Possibly films depicting lethal suicide methods in this context might have the greatest imitative impacts.

# References

Abate, K. H. (2013). Gender disparity in prevalence of depression among patient population: A systematic review. *Ethiopian Journal of Health Science, 23,* 283–288.

Biddle, L., Gunnell, D., Owen-Smith, A., Potokar, J., Longson, D., Hawton, K . . . Donovan, J (2012). Information sources used by the suicidal to inform choice of method. *Journal of Affective Disorders, 136,* 702–709.

Canetto, S., & Sakinofsky, I. (1998). The gender paradox in suicide. *Suicide & Life Threatening Behavior, 28,* 1–23.

Denning, D. G., Conwell, Y., King, D., & Cox, C. (2000). Method choice, intent, and gender in completed suicide. *Suicide and Life Threatening Behavior, 30,* 282–288

Lester, D. (2000). *Why people kill themselves.* Springfield, IL: Charles Thomas.

Lester, D., & Stack, S., (Eds.). (2015). *Suicide as a dramatic performance.* New Brunswick, NJ: Transaction Books.

Mergl, R., Koburger, N., Heinrichs, K., Székely, A., Tóth, M. D. . . . Hegerl, U. (2015). What are the reasons for the large gender differences in the lethality of suicidal acts? An epidemiological analysis of four European countries. *Plos One, July 6,* 1–18.

Moller-Leimkuhler, A. M. (2013). Barriers to help seeking by men: A review of sociocultural and clinical literature with particular reference to depression. *Journal of Affective Disorders, 71,* 1–9.

Murphy, S., Xu, J., & Kochanek, K. D. (2013). *Deaths: Final data for 2010, national vital statistics reports, 61,* May 8.

Pampel, F. (2000). *Logistic regression.* Thousand Oaks, CA: Sage.

Proquest. (2014). *Proquest statistical abstract of the United States 2015.* Bethesda, MD: Proquest.

Schmidtke, A., & Hafner, H. (1988). The Werther effect after television films: New evidence for an old hypothesis. *Psychological Medicine, 18,* 665–676.

Schnabel, L. (2015). How religious are American women and men? Gender differences and similarities. *Journal for the Scientific Study of Religion, 54,* 616–622.

Shenassa, E. D., Catlin, S. N., & Buka, S. L. (2003). Lethality of firearms relative to other suicide methods: A population based study. *J. of Epidemiology & Community Health, 57,* 120–124.

Stack, S. (2000). Suicide: A 15-year review of the sociological literature: Part I: Cultural & economic factors. *Suicide & Life Threatening Behavior, 30,* 145–162.

Stack, S. (2009). Copycat effects of fictional suicide: A meta analysis. In S. Stack & D. Lester (Eds.), *Suicide in the creative arts* (pp. 231–245). New York: Nova Science.

Stack, S., & Bowman, B. (2012). *Suicide movies: Social patterns, 1900–2009.* Cambridge, MA: Hogrefe.

Till, B., Tran, U. S., Voracek, M., Sonneck, G., & Niederkrotenthaler, T. (2014). Associations between film preferences and risk factors for suicide: An online survey. *Plos One, 9, 7,* 1–8.

US Department of Commerce. (1913). *Mortality statistics.* Washington, DC: Government Printing Office.

Wasserman, I., & Stack, S. (2009). Gender and wound site in firearm suicides. *Suicide & Life Threatening Behavior, 39,* 13–20.

# 3

# Suicide Stories in the US Media: Rare and Focused on the Young

*Silvia Sara Canetto, Phillip T. Tatum, and Michael D. Slater*

The media play a powerful role in informing the public about health and social issues. What do the US media teach the public about suicide? If one were to rely on US media for information about suicide in the United States, what conclusion might one reach about how common suicide is, relative, for example, to homicide, or about who is most likely to die of suicide?

In this chapter we focus on the quantity and content of suicide stories in US media. Specifically, we describe the findings of our research on the reporting of suicide and homicide in US media, relative to their actual occurrence. We also document the characteristics of the suicides typically featured in US media stories, relative to the typical features of suicide cases in the population. Finally, we discuss the implications of this study and related study's findings for future suicide research and for suicide prevention.

## Is US Media Reporting of Suicide Cases Consistent with Suicide Trends in the Country?

Research on the quantity and content of suicide stories in US media is very limited. Only two studies (Genovesi, Donaldson, Morrison, & Olson, 2010; Jamieson, Jamieson, & Romer, 2003) have explored these questions.

The first study focused on suicide stories in *The New York Times* (Jamieson et al., 2003). With regard to quantity of suicide reporting, this study found an increase in the number and in the prominence of suicide stories placement over the three years targeted for analysis

(1990, 1995, and 1999). This study also documented an abundance of homicide-suicide stories (one-third of the suicide stories were about homicide-suicide), relative to the actual occurrence of homicide-suicide. The authors concluded that *The New York Times* provided considerable opportunities for "exposure to information about individual cases of suicide" (p. 1646). Jamieson and colleagues' study also examined the frequency and placement of suicide stories in the ten top-circulation newspapers in the United States, over the course of one year (1998) and found that the number of suicide stories varied widely across newspapers (from 35 in *USA Today*, to 90 in *The New York Times*, to 181 in *The Dallas Morning News*). About 60 percent of the suicide stories appeared in the first nine pages of any section, with more than 50 percent of the headlines emphasizing suicide as the topic of the story. Jamieson and colleagues concluded that suicide stories were appropriately common and prominently featured in major US newspapers. Finally, with regard to the content of suicide stories in *The New York Times*, Jamieson and colleagues' study documented a disproportionate focus on acute suicide antecedents (e.g., negative life events) relative to long-standing potential suicide precursors (e.g., depression). Jamieson and colleagues interpreted their overall findings as indicating appropriate quantity of suicide stories coverage, but inadequate and distorted information, in these stories, about suicide precipitants. A limitation of Jamieson and colleagues' study is that it mostly focused on a single, though influential, newspaper, *The New York Times*.

The second, more recent study (Genovesi et al., 2010) compared suicide, homicide, and homicide-suicide stories in Utah newspapers with medical examiners' reports about the same suicide, homicide, and homicide-suicide events (collectively called violent deaths), as documented in the National Violent Death Reporting System (NVDRS) for the year 2005. Its main finding was that, in 2005, suicide represented 11 percent of Utah's violent deaths in newspapers stories, though suicide accounted for more than three quarters (83 percent) of Utah's violent deaths in the same year. By contrast, 79 percent of violent deaths reported in newspapers were homicides, though homicide represented only 13 percent of Utah's violent deaths. Another finding of this study was that in newspapers, suicide was typically associated with a recent crisis, while in the NVDRS record, mental health problems were commonly listed as suicide antecedents. A limitation of the Utah's study is that it used data from a single state, and representing a single year.

## Is Media Reporting of Suicide Cases in Countries Other than the United States Consistent with Suicide Trends in Those Countries?

Internationally, many studies have investigated the amount and content of suicide reporting in the media. Across countries (i.e., Australia, Austria, Switzerland), suicide was found to be underreported, relative to its occurrence (Eisenwort, Hinterbuchinger, & Niederkrotenthaler, 2014; Frey, Michel, & Valach, 1995; Machlin, Pirkis, & Spittal, 2012; Niederkrotenthaler et al., 2009; Pirkis, Burgess, Blood, & Francis, 2007). There was however variability by country, and within country, over time, regarding which suicides were the most and least reported. In Switzerland, there was also variability by paper type, suicide reporting being rare in the majority of newspapers, but common in the main tabloid paper (Frey et al., 1995). In all countries (i.e., Australia, Austria, China, Hong Kong, Switzerland, Taiwan) where media studies were conducted, suicide among the young was overreported (Au, Yip, Chan, & Law, 2004; Chen, Yip, Tsai, & Fan, 2012; Fu, Chan, & Yip, 2011; Machlin, Pirkis, & Spittal, 2012; Michel, Frey, Schlaepfer, & Valach, 1995; Niederkrotenthaler et al., 2009)—the exception being Australia for the year 2000–2001, when suicide among persons over 64 was overreported (Pirkis et al., 2007). Suicide by certain methods also appeared to draw media attention, across countries. This usually included suicide by locally uncommon methods. For example, in Taiwan, charcoal-burning suicides were overreported, especially when they involved women. Suicides by firearms were overreported in Australia, Austria, and Taiwan—countries where firearms are a rare method. By contrast, suicides by locally common methods, such as suicides by hanging in Austria and Australia, were underreported in those countries (Chen et al., 2012; Machlin, Pirkis, & Spittal, 2012; Niederkrotenthaler et al., 2009; Pirkis, Burgess, Blood, & Francis, 2007). In addition, there was variability by country on the quantity of media coverage of women's and men's suicides. For example, in Israel, male suicide was overreported in newspapers (Weimann & Fishman, 1995). Similarly, in Guangzhou, China, and in Taiwan (but not in Hong Kong), female suicide was underreported in newspapers (Fu, Chan, & Yip, 2011). Finally, it was found the reported suicide precursors often varied depending on the sex of the deceased and based on gender stereotypes rather than evidence (Cheng & Yip, 2012; Cheng, Yip, Tsai, & Fan, 2012; Eisenwort et al., 2014; Weimann & Fishman, 1995). For example, in Hong Kong's newspapers, men's suicides were typically explained as a response to unemployment and unmanageable debt, though Hong Kong's psychological autopsy data did not support such an account (Cheng & Yip, 2012). Similarly, in Austria's print media, women's suicides were more likely to be attributed to a mental disorder and also more often stigmatized via pejorative language (e.g., crazy) than men's suicides (Eisenwort et al., 2014), consistent with dominant scripts of gender and suicide (Canetto, 1992–1993; Canetto, 1997; Canetto & Sakinofsky, 1998).

## This Study's Focus and Rationale

This study examined the quantity of individual suicide and homicide stories in a nationally representative sample of US newspaper and TV sources, relative to the occurrence of suicide and homicide in the country, over the course of two years. This study also documented the characteristics (i.e., age, sex) of persons who died of suicide, as well as other features (i.e., suicide method and antecedents) of suicide cases in the media, relative to the characteristics and features of actual US suicide cases, during the same time period. Research on the reporting of suicide in the media is critical because the media can influence public perceptions of suicide, as well as policies about suicide prevention. There has been growth in research on this topic internationally but not nationally. Only two studies were conducted in the United States on media reporting about suicide. One study focused on a single, though high-circulation newspaper, and the other used regional data. Therefore, a study of suicide reporting using US national data is overdue.

## Method

### Sample

The suicide and homicide stories examined in this study came from local and national newspaper and TV sources. Two hundred and ten Designated Marketing Areas (DMA®) capturing the geographic distribution of television and newspaper outlets (Nielsen Media Research, 2005) were grouped into six strata each representing approximately one-sixth of all US households. Fifty-six sample dates were then chosen from the years 2002 and 2003 to balance the sample with respect to day of the week and season of the year. For each sample date, one DMA® was randomly selected for each of the six strata (see Long, Slater, Boiarsky, Stapel, & Keefe, 2005, for additional method details). In this way, a sampling frame was created that reasonably represented the news media to which the general US population was exposed to in those years.

*Newspaper Sample.* Three daily regional newspapers were chosen per sample date and based on circulation, from each randomly selected DMA°. One was the newspaper with the highest circulation in that DMA°. The rest of the newspapers in that DMA° were then divided into a higher circulation group and a lower circulation group, using a median split, and one newspaper was randomly selected from each of these groups. In addition, one issue of *USA Today* was examined for each sampling date.

*Television Sample.* One local TV broadcast (balancing for network affiliation) was selected from each randomly selected DMA° for each sample date, in addition to a national broadcast randomly sampled from NBC, ABC, CBS, or CNN.

*Total Sample.* Approximately 1,000 daily newspapers were examined, as well as approximately 560 TV news broadcasts from both local and national news programs.

### Suicide and Homicide Stories Selection

For the newspaper sample, a suicide or homicide story was defined as a story that contained mention of suicide and/or homicide in the headline, teaser, or lead (first two paragraphs). For the TV sample, mention of homicide/suicide in the teaser or lead (first fifteen seconds of story) qualified the story for the study. Stories of suicide and homicide were drawn from a previously constructed sample of "violent death" stories. Due to the extensive amount of time involved in selecting suicide and homicide stories from the much larger sample of violent death stories, inter-rater reliability for story selection was assessed using Cohen's kappa at four points in time (using a random selection of newspapers and TV newscasts): at the beginning, and then after 25 percent, 50 percent, and 75 percent of the sample had been coded. Suicide and homicide stories' selection kappas ranged from 0.70 to 0.88.

### Suicide Stories Coding

Descriptive information about the 2002 and 2003 suicide stories, including the demographic characteristics of the suicidal person, the suicide method, as well as mention that the suicidal person experienced mental disorders, and mention of events presumed to have precipitated the suicide, were independently recorded by two coders. Inter-rater agreement for suicide-story features was assessed using

Krippendorff's alpha (Hayes, 2005; Krippendorff, 2004), and ranged from 0.67 to 1.0.

*Suicide and Homicide Statistics*

Center for Disease Control and Prevention suicide and homicide mortality statistics for the years 2002 and 2003 were used as referents for media suicide and homicide stories information (CDC, n.d. a). When CDC statistics were not available, research findings were used as a referent.

## Results

*Suicide and Homicide in US Media Stories versus US Official Mortality Records*

One-hundred thirty-seven suicide stories and 2,391 homicide stories were found in our sample of US newspapers for the years 2002 and 2003. According to CDC (n.d. a) mortality statistics, there were 63,139 suicides and 35,370 homicides in 2002 and 2003 in the United States. The proportion of suicides (5 percent) to homicides (95 percent) stories in newspapers was considerably different than the proportion of suicides (64 percent) to homicides (36 percent) in US official mortality records.

In our sample of TV news broadcasts for the same time period, there were 24 suicide stories and 432 homicide stories. In the TV news, the proportion of suicide (5 percent) to homicide (95 percent) stories was considerably different than the proportion of suicides (64 percent) to homicides (36 percent) in CDC (n.d. a) mortality statistics for the same period.

Of the 167 newspaper suicide stories, 49 (29 percent) were about homicide-suicide. Of the twenty-four TV suicide stories, 15 (63 percent) involved homicide-suicide. These proportions are substantially different than the estimate, provided by Nock and Mazurk (1999), that homicide-suicides represent 1.5 percent of the suicides in the United States. According to CDC National Violent Death Reporting System data for five states (CDC, n.d. b), the rate of homicide followed by suicide in 2003 was 0.17 per 100,000.

*Demographic Profile and Suicide Method of Suicide Cases Featured in Newspapers Stories versus US Official Mortality Records*

*Sex of the Deceased by Suicide.* Of the 137 persons deceased by suicide featured in newspaper stories, 116 were male and 20 female. In one case, there was no mention of the sex of the deceased by suicide. In 2002 and 2003, there were 50,612 male suicides and 12,527 female suicides in the United States (CDC, n. d. a). The proportion of male to female suicides in newspaper suicide stories (85 percent and 15 percent, respectively) was similar to the proportion of male to female suicides (80 percent and 20 percent, respectively) in US mortality statistics during the same years.

*Age of the Deceased by Suicide.* Information about the age of the deceased by suicide was provided in 85 (62 percent) newspaper stories in our sample. The proportion of suicides in the 15–24 age category, compared to all other ages, was considerably higher in newspapers stories (39 percent) than the proportion of suicides in the 15–24 age category, compared to suicides in all other age group (13 percent0), in CDC (n.d. a) mortality statistics for the same time period. The proportion of suicides by person 65 and older, as compared to suicides in all other ages, was somewhat higher (27 percent) in newspaper stories than in CDC (n.d. a) mortality statistics (17 percent).

*Suicide Method.* Information about suicide method was reported in 106 individual suicide newspaper stories in our sample. Most suicide cases involved firearms (57 deaths), followed by other means (31), suffocation (14), and poison (4). In the United States in 2002 and 2003, there were 34,015 suicides by firearms, 13,097 suicides by suffocation, 10,948 by poison, and 5,079 by other means. The proportions of suicide by firearms in newspaper stories and in CDC national suicide records for 2002 and 2003 were the same (54 percent). By contrast, the proportions of suicide by other means (29 percent) and by poisoning (4 percent) in newspaper stories were different than proportions of suicide by other means (8 percent) and by poison (17 percent) recorded in CDC (n.d. a) mortality statistics.

*Suicide Antecedents.* The proportion of deceased by suicide described, in newspaper stories, as having experienced a mental disorder (7 percent) was considerably smaller than the 90 percent estimate often cited in the suicidology literature—however inflated that estimate may be (American Foundation for Suicide Prevention, n.d.). Also, in newspaper stories considerably more individuals who died of suicide were described as having experienced a precipitating negative life event (59 percent) than a mental disorder (7 percent).

## Discussion

This study documented, at the national level, that suicide is rarely reported in the US media, relative to its occurrence, and compared to homicide. During our two-year observation period, there were fourteen and eighteen times *fewer* suicide stories than homicide stories in our newspaper and TV samples, respectively, despite the fact that almost twice as many people died from suicide than from homicide in the United States during that time period. Also, a rare form of suicide, homicide-suicide, was overreported in newspapers and TV media, relative to its occurrence.

Our study found that newspaper stories featured suicide among the young (i.e., among individuals aged 15–24) three times more frequently than its occurrence in this age group. At the same time, newspaper stories covered suicides by women and men in proportion to their occurrence in the population. Newspaper stories on suicide by firearms were also at rates proportionate to the actual occurrence of firearm suicide. By contrast, newspapers less frequently covered suicide by poisoning, relative to its frequency, while they overreported suicide by unusual methods, relative to its occurrence. Finally, the potential role of long-standing suicide precursors was underrepresented in the media, relative to the potential role of acute precipitants. Therefore, if one were to rely on US media for information about suicide in the United States, one would likely come to believe that suicide is less common than homicide or homicide-suicide, and also that the young are the most vulnerable to suicide, because of acute problems, and via methods other than firearms or poisoning.

Our study confirms, at the national level and for a two-year observation period (2002–2003), the findings of a US regional-level study covering one year (2005) (Genovesi et al., 2010) that the US media underreport suicide cases and overreport homicide and homicide-suicide cases, respectively. Our national-level findings for 2002 and 2003 about amount of suicide reporting are in contrast to the findings by Romer and colleagues (2003). Romer and colleagues found that suicide reporting was "common and prominently placed" in major US newspapers in 1998 (2003, p. 1647). Finally, our study's findings on the rarity of suicide stories in the US media, except for homicide-suicide stories, are consistent with the findings of international studies of suicide reporting. For example, only about 1 percent of Australian suicides were reported in the Australian media over the selected one-year study periods (2006–2007 in Machlin et al.'s 2012 study; 2000–2001 in Pirkis et al.'s 2007 study). Similarly, only 3.9 percent of Austrian 2005 suicides were reported in the Austrian print media during that time period, with suicides involving homicide or homicide attempt being overrepresented (Niederkrotenthaler et al., 2009).

This study's findings on which suicides are typically featured in the US media are similar to the findings of similar studies from other countries. For example, in our US newspaper sample, we found an overrepresentation of stories of suicide by younger individuals. Disproportionate coverage of suicide among younger persons was also documented, for example, in an Australian print and broadcast media study (Machlin et al., 2012), in an Austrian print-media study (Niederkrotenthaler et al., 2009), and in a Hong Kong's newspaper study (Fu et al., 2011). The media's focus on suicide among younger persons may be due to suicide being less common among younger than among older adults (Fu et al., 2011; Niederkrotenthaler et al., 2009). After all, newsworthiness of an event is typically defined on the basis of the event being out of the ordinary, deviant, dramatic, or sensational (Gekoski, Gray, & Adler, 2012; Jamieson et al., 2003). The focus on suicide among the young may also be an indication of an ageist bias, as documented by evidence, in the United States, of the relative acceptability of older adult suicide (Stice & Canetto, 2008; Winterrowd, Canetto, & Benoit, 2016). The paradox of overreporting of suicide by younger persons is that media coverage may actually increase suicidal behavior in this age group, as younger persons appear more likely to engage in imitation suicide than older individuals (Hawton & Williams, 2005).

In our current US study as well as in the Austrian (Niederkrotenthaler et al., 2009), Australian (Pirkis et al., 2007), and Taiwan studies, locally rare-method suicide cases (e.g., suicides by firearms in Australia, Austria, and Taiwan) were more likely to be reported than locally-common-method cases (i.e., suicides by poisoning in the United States; and suicide by hanging in Austria and Australia). It has been speculated that these suicide methods may be more newsworthy because of their peculiarity. Unfortunately, these methods are also typically ones that have high fatality rates. This is of concern given the evidence that those who engage in suicidal behavior following media reports of suicide also imitate the method described (Machlin et al., 2013).

Before proceeding with the discussion of our findings, we wish to acknowledge the strengths and limitations of this study. A strength is that it examined media coverage of suicide cases at the national level, and including both newspapers and TV sources, thereby significantly expanding the scope of prior US studies. A limitation is it focused on newspaper and TV suicide stories from 2002 and 2003. At the time, television and newspapers were the most common sources of news (Saad, 2007). Other media have since become important as source of information. Therefore, future studies should examine suicide stories in other media, including the Internet. We also wish to clarify that although our study indirectly focused on the quality of reporting via measures of amount and content of individual suicide stories in the media, as related suicide trends in the population, we did not evaluate the quality of suicide media coverage, for example, in relation to the media guidelines for the reporting of suicide. Such focus has been the attention of other media studies (e.g., Tatum, Canetto, & Slater, 2010).

What do our study's findings, together with the findings of related studies, mean? Why is suicide underreported in the news media? What explains the overreporting of certain suicides? And what may be the consequences of selective reporting? The views of US reporters about the newsworthiness of suicide were explored in a study by Jamieson and colleagues (2003). The fifty-seven US reporters interviewed for their study for the most part believed that suicide is a personal and private event. According to them, suicide becomes newsworthy only when it involves a public person or when it occurs in a public place (and therefore it is widely witnessed or disruptive). The reporters also said that suicide is always newsworthy when it is preceded by homicide. Homicide-suicide involves the killing of another person as well as multiple deaths—elements which these reporters believed contributed to newsworthiness. In the case of homicide-suicide the fact that it often occurs in a private context actually increases its public relevance and newsworthiness, according to the reporters. The family tragedy element of many homicide-suicides also adds to readers' interest in and identification with the story, they said.

The limited interest in suicide stories by reporters and the consequent under-coverage of suicide cases in the media may be an asset with regard to suicide prevention. Low interest in suicide cases, on the part of reporters, may reduce the likelihood of inappropriate coverage and, with that, the risk of suicide imitation and suicide clusters. There is evidence that suicide modeling is most likely when suicide reporting is extensive, prominent, dramatic, or romanticizing, features a celebrity, or includes details of the suicide method (Gould, 2001;

Gould, Kleinman, Lake, Forman, & Midle, 2014; Sisask & Värnik, 2012; Stack, 2005).

At the same time, the underreporting of suicide, relative to its occurrence, together with the overreporting of certain kinds of suicide, may have negative implications for suicide prevention. The relative invisibility, in the news media, of suicide, relative to homicide, may be a factor in the public perception that suicide is less of a problem than homicide, potentially contributing to low interest in investing public resources in suicide prevention. Similarly, the media focus on suicide among young persons may not only contribute to underestimating the suicide vulnerability of middle-aged and older adults, but also reduce the drive for research and suicide prevention initiatives focusing on these most-affected age groups.

The findings of this study, together with those of related studies, call for greater collaboration between social scientists and media professionals about the reporting of suicides. This collaboration might start with communications regarding common discrepancies between suicide characteristics in the media versus in the population and the implications of such discrepancies for public information, and for suicide prevention. Media reporting of suicide involves a balance between reducing public exposure to information that may lead to imitation and protecting the public's right to know, including about those who die by suicide. Suicide experts disagree on what that balance looks like. We agree with those who say that it is most important to ensure that "we are doing no harm in reporting individuals' deaths," but also that the media should contribute to providing the public with an accurate picture about suicide, who is most vulnerable, and what is known about prevention (Machlin et al., 2013, p. 312). Suicide media coverage that makes it possible for public to grasp the seriousness of the suicide problem, and whom suicide typically affects, may not only improve suicide prevention at the community level, in terms of collective resource allocation for suicide prevention. It may also promote the kind of individual-level sensibility that can make a difference in terms of suicide clues detection and suicide prevention at the private-relationship level.

## References

American Foundation for Suicide Prevention. (n.d.). *About suicide. Treatment.* Retrieved from http://afsp.org/about-suicide/preventing-suicide/

Canetto, S. S. (1992–1993). She died for love and he for glory: Gender myths of suicidal behavior. *Omega–Journal of Death and Dying, 26,* 1–17.

Canetto, S. S. (1997). Gender and suicidal behavior: Theories and evidence. In R. W. Maris, M. M. Silverman, & S. S. Canetto (Eds.), *Review of suicidology* (pp. 138–167). New York: Guilford.

Canetto, S. S., & Sakinofsky, I. (1998). The gender paradox in suicide. *Suicide and Life-Threatening Behavior, 28,* 1–23.

Center for Disease Control and Prevention (CDC). (n.d. a). *Web Based Injury Statistics Query And Reporting System – Leading Causes of Death Reports.* Retrieved from http://www.cdc.gov/ncipc/wisqars/default.htm

Center for Disease Control and Prevention (CDC). (n.d. b). *Web Based Injury Statistics Query and Reporting System, National Violent Death Reporting System for Number of Deaths, Bureau of Census for Population Estimates.* Retrieved from https://wisqars.cdc.gov:8443/nvdrs/nvdrsController.jsp

Cheng, Q., & Yip, P. S. F. (2012). Suicide news reporting accuracy and stereotyping in Hong Kong. *Journal of Affective Disorders, 141,* 270–275.

Eisenwort, B., Till, B., Hinterbuchinger, B., & Niederkrotenthaler, T. (2014). Sociable, mentally disturbed women and angry, rejected men: Cultural scripts for the suicidal behavior of women and men in the Austrian print media. *Sex Roles, 71,* 246–260.

Frey, M. F., Michel, K., & Valach, L. (1997). Suicide reporting in Swiss print media: Responsible or irresponsible? *European Journal of Public Health, 7,* 15–19.

Fu, K. W., Chan, Y. Y., & Yip, P. S. F. (2011). Newspaper reporting of suicides in Hong Kong, Taiwan and Guangzhou: Compliance with WHO media guidelines and epidemiological comparisons. *Journal of Epidemiology and Community Health, 65,* 928–933.

Gekoski, A., Gray, J. M., & Adler, J. R. (2012). What makes a homicide newsworthy? UK national tabloid newspaper journalists tell all. *British Journal of Criminology, 52,* 1212–1232.

Genovesi, S. L., Donalson, A. E., Morrison, B. L., & Olson, L. M. (2010). Different perspectives: A comparison of newspaper articles to medical examiner data in the reporting of violent deaths. *Accident Analysis and Prevention, 42,* 445–451.

Gould, M. (2001). Suicide and the media. In H. Hendin & J. Mann (Eds.), *The clinical science of suicide prevention. Annals of the New York Academy of Sciences* (pp. 200–224). New York: New York Academy of Sciences.

Gould, M. S., Kleinman, M. H., Lake, A. M., Forman, J., & Midle, J. B (2014). Newspaper coverage of suicide and initiation of suicide clusters in teenagers in the USA, 1988–96: A retrospective, population-based, case control study. *Lancet Psychiatry, 1,* 34–43.

Hawton, K., & Williams, K. (2005). Media influences on suicidal behavior: Evidence and prevention. In K. Hawton (Ed.), *Prevention and treatment of suicidal behavior: From science to practice* (pp. 293–306). Oxford: Oxford University Press.

Hayes, A. F. (2005). *A SPSS procedure for computing Krippendorff's alpha* [Computer software]. Retrieved from http://www.comm.ohio-state.edu/ahayes/macros.htm

Jamieson, P., Jamieson, K. H., & Romer, D. (2003). The responsible reporting of suicide in print journalism. *American Behavioral Scientist, 46,* 1643–1660.

Krippendorff, K. (2004). *Content analysis: An introduction to its methodology.* Thousand Oaks, CA: Sage.

Long, M., Slater, M. D., Boiarsky, G., Stapel, L., & Keefe, T. (2005). Obtaining nationally representative samples of local news media outlets. *Mass Communication and Society, 8*(4), 299–322.

Machlin, A., Pirkis, J., & Spittal, M. J. (2013). Which suicides are reported in the media – And what makes them "newsworthy"? *Crisis, 34*, 305–313.

Michel, K., Frey, M. F., Schlaepfer, T. E., & Valach, L. (1995). Suicide reporting in Swiss print media: Frequency, form and content of articles. *European Journal of Public Health, 5*, 199–203.

Niederkrotenthaler, T., Till, B., Herberth, A., Voracek, M., Kapusta, N. D., Etzersdorfer, E. . . . Sonneck, G. (2009). The gap between suicide characteristics in the print media and in the population. *European Journal of Public Health, 19*, 361–364.

Nielsen Media Research. (2005). *Nielsen media research local universe estimates.* Retrieved from http://www.nielsenmedia.com/DMAs.html

Nock, M. K., & Marzuk, P. M. (1999). Murder-suicide. In D. G. Jacobs (Ed.), *The Harvard Medical School guide to suicide assessment and intervention* (pp. 188–209). San Francisco, CA: Jossey-Bass.

Pirkis, J. E., Burgess, P. M., Blood, R. W., & Francis, C. (2007). The newsworthiness of suicide. *Suicide and Life-Threatening Behavior, 37*, 278–283.

Saad, L. (2007, January). *Local TV is No.1 source of news for Americans.* Retrieved from http://www.gallup.com/poll/26053/local-no-source-news-americans.aspx#!mn-business

Sisask, M., & Värnik, A. (2012). Media roles in suicide prevention: A systematic review. *International Journal of Environmental Research and Public Health, 9*, 123–138.

Stack, S. (2005). Suicide in the media: A quantitative review of studies based on nonfictional stories. *Suicide and Life-Threatening Behavior, 35*, 121–133.

Stice, B. D., & Canetto, S. S. (2008). Older adult suicide: Perceived precipitants and protective factors. *Clinical Gerontologist: The Journal of Aging and Mental Health, 31*(4), 1–25.

Tatum, P. T., Canetto, S. S., & Slater, M. (2010). Suicide coverage in U.S. newspapers following the publication of the media guidelines. *Suicide and Life-Threatening Behavior, 40*, 524–534.

Weimann, G., & Fishman, G. (1995). Reconstructing suicide: Reporting suicide in the Israeli press. *Journalism & Mass Communication Quarterly, 72*(3), 551–558.

Winterrowd, E., Canetto, S. S., & Benoit, K. (2016). Permissive beliefs and attitudes about older adult suicide: A suicide enabling script? *Aging & Mental Health, 23*, 1–9.

# 4

# Mass Shootings and Murder-Suicide: Review of the Empirical Evidence for Contagion

*Madelyn S. Gould and Michael Olivares*

## Mass Shootings

The phenomenon of mass shootings has loomed larger in the public consciousness recently as such incidents occur with disturbing regularity. In the last six months of 2015, for instance, there were four mass shootings, cumulatively killing and wounding dozens of individuals. Despite a ubiquitous sense that such events are increasing, estimates vary as to their frequency, and whether it has accelerated, due to the conflicting and overlapping constructs used to classify and measure multiple-victim shootings.

### Terminology

A myriad of terms and constructs have been used to describe public, mass acts of violence, the most common of which include mass shooting, school shooting, active shooting, mass killing, and mass murder. The types of events delimited by the various terms and constructs are differentiated primarily by setting (e.g., public, school-based), the number of victims injured or killed (e.g., three or more individuals killed), and the motivations of the perpetrators (e.g., anger/revenge, gang-/drug-related). Further obfuscating the matter, the same constructs are sometimes differentially termed (e.g., shootings targeting at least three individuals have been referred to as both "rampage shootings" and "mass shootings"), and, conversely, the same terms are often applied to distinct constructs (e.g., "mass shooting" has been used to refer both to shootings producing a certain number of fatalities and to those simply targeting a certain number of people). Throughout this chapter, the term "mass shooting" will be used to refer to the various constructs discussed above.

*Frequency of Mass Shootings*

The resultant taxonomic morass with which the field is currently burdened has created a pronounced lack of consensus as to which types of events are increasing, if any, and to what degree (see Schultz et al., 2014; and Fox and Levin, 2015). Nevertheless, studies employing constructs (however termed) that specifically measure public, indiscriminate mass shootings—as opposed to those utilizing overly broad constructs (e.g., multiple-victim shootings in all contexts; see Fox and Levin, 2015)—consistently demonstrate that those events have been increasing in frequency. For example, an FBI report on 160 active shootings—defined as shootings in which an individual is actively engaged in killing or attempting to kill people in a populated area—in the United States since 2000 found that their annual incidence had increased from an average of 6.4 shootings between 2000 and 2006 to an average of 16.4 between 2007 and 2013 (Blair and Schweit, 2014). Similarly, Cohen et al. (2014), analyzed the series of time intervals between mass shootings—defined as public shootings resulting in four or more deaths in which the shooter and victims were generally strangers—in the past few decades and found that the frequency of mass shootings significantly increased after September 2011; between that month and the end of 2013 mass shootings occurred every sixty-four days on average, compared to the prior twenty-nine-year period in which they occurred every two hundred days on average. Cohen et al. (2014) also applied the same methodology to the FBI's above-referenced data set and likewise found that active shootings had significantly increased in frequency. Furthermore, in examining only the forty-four active shooting incidents that also met the criteria for mass shootings (as defined above) they found that such incidents had become more frequent between 2011 and 2012.

Additionally, research focused specifically on multiple-victim shootings at schools has yielded consistent findings, with occasional exceptions (e.g., Schultz et al., 2013). For instance, Agnich (2015) found that school-based mass homicides (both attempted and completed, with and without firearms) have increased in the past few decades, with attempted mass shootings having risen especially sharply.

Correspondingly, Drysdale et al. (2010) examined the incidence of targeted violence at schools—potentially lethal acts directed at individuals in a school setting—and discovered that, of a total of 272 incidents since 1900, 162 have occurred since 1990 and 83 since 2000.

### Suggested Relation to Suicide

In addition to recent evidence that public multiple-victim shootings are increasing, research has reliably found that a substantial portion of perpetrators end their own lives, suggesting that such events could be motivated by suicidal desire (e.g., Auxemery, 2015; Marzuk et al., 1992; Preti, 2008; Stack 1989). For example, of the 160 active shooting incidents examined in the previously cited FBI report, 40 percent ended with the shooter's suicide (Blair & Schweit, 2014). Additionally, Agnich (2015) found that shooters died by suicide in about 31 percent of all the school-based mass shootings between 1900 and 2010 (see also Vossekuil et al., 2002; Drysdale et al., 2010). While the commission of public multiple-victim shootings may frequently have a suicidal component—some have suggested using the term "suicide preceded by mass murder" in these cases (Bell & McBride, 2010)—such shootings have a wide array of possible motivations and are evidently not exclusively accompanied by suicidal behavior (Petee et al., 1997). Nevertheless, the understanding and prevention of suicidal behavior could inform the prevention of a substantial proportion of public, multiple-victim shootings.

## Murder-Suicide

The fact that perpetrators of mass shootings are frequently suicidal raises the question as to whether these acts are related to the phenomenon of murder-suicide. Though the term "murder-suicide" may indeed technically apply to many instances of mass shootings—within which, as aforementioned, murder and suicide sometimes coincide—the prototypical murder-suicide is distinct from mass shootings. A murder suicide is typically a form of intimate partner violence perpetrated with a firearm by a man against an estranged or soon-to-be estranged female companion (i.e., femicide-suicide), in a domestic setting, often within the context of a history of domestic violence (Marzuk et al., 1992; Harper and Voigt, 2007; Eliason, 2009; Large, 2009; Bell & McBride, 2010). Smaller proportions of murder-suicides also include elderly spousal murder-suicides (perpetrated primarily by elderly men, often unilaterally, against their ailing spouses), filicide-suicides (perpetrated by either male or female parents), among other even less frequent types of familicide-suicide (e.g., Cohen, 2000; Eliason, 2009; Marzuk et al., 1992; Harper & Voigt, 2007). Additionally, murder-suicides occur more frequently than mass shootings, occurring at a fairly consistent, annual rate between 0.20 and 0.32 per 100,000 individuals—about 600 to 1,000 incidents per year—in the United States (e.g., Coid, 1983; Eliason, 2009; Felthous & Hempel, 1995; Large et al., 2009; Marzuk et al., 1992). Thus, while many mass shootings are also murder-suicides, most murder-suicides are not mass shootings.

Incidentally, in light of legal distinctions, there is contention as to whether to use the term "homicide-suicide" in place of "murder-suicide" (e.g., Marzuk et al., 1992). Following the example of Marzuk et al. (1992) and the practice of studies examined by this review, the term "murder-suicide" will be used throughout the chapter.

## Media and Contagion

Most individuals experience and learn about mass shootings and murder-suicides only indirectly, through coverage provided by the media—and that coverage is immense, disproportionate to the relative frequency of such events, and intentionally framed to increase the events' salience and elicit the public's attention (e.g., Jamieson, 2003; Machlin et al., 2013; Schultz et al., 2014; Sitzer et al., 2013). Mass shootings and murder-suicides are in actuality a relatively rare form of violence; the vast majority of firearm deaths are composed of single-victim suicides and single-victim-targeted homicides. For example, fatalities from all forms of school shootings only comprised 0.12 percent and 0.05 percent of total firearm homicides and deaths between 1990 and 2011 (Schultz et al., 2013).

However, the media's disproportionate levels of attention devoted to these events has created a social landscape in which perpetrators are afforded a national audience for the display of their violent acts—acts which often posthumously earn the perpetrators celebrity and publicize their desired message (e.g., Kellner, 2008; Preti, 2008). Thus, it seems reasonable to worry that the heavily "mediatized" nature of these events will inspire others to engage in similar behaviors and incite further incidents (e.g., Muschert, 2013).

Legitimating this concern, there already exists ample evidence that media reports on myriad types of violence can lead to imitative acts (e.g., Huessman & Taylor, 2006). Most relevantly, given the nature of murder-suicides and the frequent suicidal intentions of mass shooters, reporting on suicide has been shown to increase the probability of subsequent suicides. Seminal work by Phillips (1974) first established the phenomenon empirically, and thereafter an ever-growing body of work has corroborated and extended those findings (see Gould et al., 2003; Pirkis & Blood, 2001; Niederkroten-thaler et al., 2012, for reviews).

While there is a substantive body of research on the incidence and etiology of mass violence and murder-suicide, there is a relative dearth of published articles on its contagion. However, the number of such studies appears to be growing given recent attention to the issue. A preliminary search revealed only three relevant reviews to date, none of which were systematic or considered contagion with respect to both mass violence and murder-suicide.

Self-professed to be the first review of its kind, Kinkel and Josef (1991) reviewed research on the relationship between multiple forms of mass media (e.g., fictionalized television media, television and newspaper reporting) and violent imitative behavior, finding substantial evidence that nonfictional events portrayed in the media can trigger increased violence. However, the authors only examined one study regarding murder-suicide (Phillips, 1980) and none regarding mass shootings. Similarly, Huessman and Taylor (2006) reviewed "key empirical studies" investigating the connection between violence in different avenues of media (e.g., television, film, video games) and violent behavior and determined that violence reported in the media can incite further aggression and violence. Yet, their review only considered one study on mass shootings (Berkowitz & Macaulay, 1971) and none on murder-suicides. Lastly, a more recent review by Sitzer (2013) specifically focused on the impact of various media on the incidence of school shootings. More comprehensive in its analysis and depth, despite its narrow scope, the review determined that while studies on the media's role in the contagion of school shootings are limited, there appears to be evidence of a possible contagion effect.

Given the pronounced increase in attention devoted to mass shootings and murder-suicides in the past couple of years and the suggestive yet limited findings of the prior reviews, there is a clear need for an updated review of the literature on the contagion of such violence that is comprehensive and systematic in its analysis, and thus informative for policy decisions.

## Review of Empirical Research

A search was conducted in two major online databases, PsycINFO and PubMed, to identify articles of any publication date pertaining to the contagion of mass shootings and murder-suicide. The following search terms were used: ((murder AND suicid*) OR (homicid* AND suicid*) OR murder-suicide OR homicide-suicide OR (amok AND suicid*) OR "school violence" OR "mass shoot*" OR "active shoot*" OR shooter OR "mass murder" OR "mass killing" OR "school shoot*" OR "mass homicid*") AND (contagio* OR copycat OR imitat* OR modeling). An asterisk was added to certain terms in order to capture all derivations of the root term.

First, the titles and abstracts of all articles returned by the search were reviewed by one author (MO) against the following broad inclusion criteria: (1) the article was published in English in a peer-reviewed journal; and (2) the article examined the contagion of either multiple-victim homicides—however defined by the author(s)—or murder-suicides. Contagion was comprehensively defined to include any phenomena describing a situation in which one event would potentially impact or incite another. (Explicit reference to the media as a generator or intermediary of contagion was not a criterion, as any examination of contagion necessarily implicates the media and bears on its role in the reporting and framing of such events.) Dissertations, abstracts, and reviews were excluded.

Second, articles that met the initial two criteria were selected for a thorough full-text review by two authors (MG and MO), who measured articles against an additional criterion: that the article be empirical (i.e., employ a methodological, data-driven analysis). Articles that upon the more substantive review were discovered to not meet the initial inclusion criteria were excluded thereafter. Third, a hand search of the references of both the prior reviews and the articles subjected to a full-text review was conducted in order to identify additional relevant articles. Lastly, upon determining the final set of articles meeting the full inclusion criteria, two authors (MO and MG) extracted and summarized their data, particularly focusing on the nature and extent of their evidence for contagion.

## Results

The database searches resulted in a total of 194 articles: 106 from PsycINFO and 88 from PubMed. After the removal of 24 duplicates, the titles and abstracts of 170 articles were reviewed against the initial

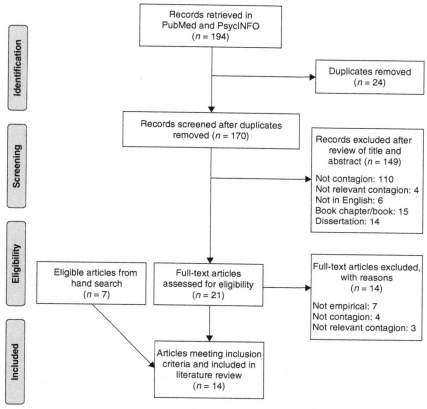

**Figure 4.1.** Flow diagram of the search methodology and process.

inclusion criteria. The twenty-one remaining articles were subjected to a full-text review, yielding seven eligible articles. A hand search yielded an additional seven eligible articles. See figure 4.1 for a PRISMA flow diagram of our search history. The resulting fourteen articles were included in the final review.

*Study Characteristics*

Of the fourteen studies reviewed, nine exclusively examined the contagion of multiple-victim shootings (table 4.1), four exclusively concerned the contagion of murder-suicides (table 4.2), and one investigated both phenomena (listed in both tables). The specific terms and inclusion criteria used to classify and measure multiple-victim shootings varied across the studies and included mass shooting, active shooting, school

**Table 4.1.** Empirical studies on the contagion of mass shootings.

| Citation | Period, exposure stimulus, and population studied | Methodology | Comparison group/period | Findings | Support of imitation (on outcome) |
|---|---|---|---|---|---|
| Berkowitz and Macaulay (1971) | Homicides and other forms of violent crime (supplied by FBI reports) between 1960 and 1966 in 40 cities in the United States, in relation to the JFK Assassination (November 1963) and the Speck and Whitman mass shootings (July and August 1966) in Chicago and Texas, respectively. | Examined the impact of the JFK Assassination and Speck and Whitman shootings on subsequent violent crime rates (only the effects of the Speck/Whitman shootings are relevant for the current review). | Time series analyses compared the expected rate of violent crime based on the determined trend with the actual rate of violent crime after the incidents. | Found a significant increase in the incidence of total violent crime in four of the five months following the Speck/Whitman mass shootings. Also found significant increases in rates of aggravated assault in the five months following the shootings, and significant increases in rates of robbery in four of the five months following the shootings. Did not find a significant increase in rates of homicide, rape, or manslaughter following the shootings. | Yes (on total violent crime, aggravated assault, robbery)/No (on homicide, rape, manslaughter) |
| Cantor, Sheehan, Alpers, and Mullen (1999) | Seven mass shootings in Australia, New Zealand, and the United Kingdom between 1987 and 1996. | Examined time linkage and similarities between shootings and compared statements made by perpetrators as reported by expert informants (coroners, criminologists, forensic psychiatrists, police officer, sentencing judge, public inquiry). | N/A, assessed likelihood of linkage based upon review of spatial-temporal proximity between events. Qualitatively examined, with consultation of involved experts, statements of perpetrators to determine whether they were influenced by previous shootings in the studied series. | Found that three of the seven incidents demonstrate a probable time linkage. In two of the incidents, statements made by the perpetrators indicated identification with other perpetrators within the studied series of shootings. | Yes (on mass shootings) |

| Carcach, Mouzos, and Grabosky (2002) | All homicides occurring between 7/1/1989 and 6/30/1999 in Australia, in relation to the Port Arthur Massacre (4/27/1996). Data source was the National Homicide Monitoring Program at the Australian Institute of Criminology. | Examined the difference in characteristics of homicides before and after the Port Arthur incident (disaggregation analysis); also examined whether the Port Arthur incident resulted in a significant change to the time series of daily homicides (intervention analysis). | In disaggregation analysis compared characteristics of homicides among three time periods: 7/1/1989 to 4/27/1996 (date of incident), 4/29/1996 to 5/4/1996, and 5/5/1996 to 6/30/1999 (during which new gun laws were implemented). In intervention analysis (with incident treated as instantaneous, impulse, and continuing interventions) compared the time series of daily homicides before and after the incident. | Found in the intervention analysis that the Port Arthur incident had a significant sudden (instantaneous) effect (increase) on the temporal behavior of total firearm homicide during the five days following the incident but not on the rate thereafter. But the disaggregation analysis found that there was a low proportion of incidents involving strangers and none involving multiple victims following the incident. In response to the Port Arthur Massacre, the Australian government instituted "one of the most dramatic changes in Australian public policy" to implement firearm control reforms. | Yes (on firearm homicides, short-term)/No (on firearm homicides, long-term) |

*(Continued)*

**Table 4.1.** (Continued)

| Citation | Period, exposure stimulus, and population studied | Methodology | Comparison group/period | Findings | Support of imitation(on outcome) |
|---|---|---|---|---|---|
| Kissner (2015) | 148 active shooting incidents in the United States between 2000 and 2012. Active shooter defined as "an individual actively engaged in killing or attempting to kill people in a confined and populated area . . ."; used the NYPD compendium of active shooter incidents from 1966 to 2012 and excluded incidents that were foiled, in which no one was killed or wounded, that did not take place in the United States, and that occurred before 2000. | Fit a series hazard model (extension of the Cox proportional hazard model) to the series of active shooting incidents to determine whether incidents were temporally contagious. | Examined with a series hazard model the series of 148 incidents (without any assumption about event distribution) to determine the likelihood of active shooting incidents occurring (i.e., the temporal gap in days from one incident until the next) as a function of four independent variables (the number of days since the immediately preceding incident, number of incidents in the previous week, in the previous two weeks, and in the previous month). | Found that the number of active shootings in the preceding two weeks had a significant effect on the temporal gap until another incident occurred, i.e., gap times between one incident to the next diminished significantly as a function of the number of incidents in the preceding two weeks. An addition of one incident in the preceding two weeks had a corresponding 27% increase in the probability of a subsequent incident. (The other independent variables were not significant in the models.) Incidental finding: approximately 39% of active shooters died by suicide. | Yes (on active shootings) |

| Kostinksy, Bixler, and Kettl (2001) | All threats of school violence reported to the Pennsylvania Emergency Management Agency from 4/22/1999 to 6/9/1999, the 50 days following the massacre at Columbine High School in Littleton, CO (4/20/1999). | Examined the incidence of threats of school violence in the 50-day period following the Columbine incident and analyzed the relationship between county and school district variables and threat frequency. | Examined the frequency of threats of school violence as a function of the number of days following the Columbine incident. (Noted the difference between the frequency of threats post-incident and the estimated frequency pre-incident.) Conducted a Poisson regression analysis to determine county and school district characteristics that predict incidence of threats. | Found that the frequency of threats (of all school violence and of only bomb threats following the Columbine incident) demonstrated a crescendo-decrescendo pattern—similar to that found with imitative suicides—with 56% of the threats occurring before day 10, after which the number of threats decreased exponentially. (Noted the stark increase in threats following the incident compared with the estimated 1 or 2 threats per year pre-incident.) | Yes (on threats of school violence) |

(Continued)

**Table 4.1.** (Continued)

| Citation | Period, exposure stimulus, and population studied | Methodology | Comparison group/ period | Findings | Support of imitation (on outcome) |
|---|---|---|---|---|---|
| Larkin (2009) | Compiled list of 55 "rampage" shootings from August 1966 through November 2007. Incidences were derived from lists generated by academic researchers, various media outlets, and Internet sites. Rampage shooter defined as a student or former student bringing to and discharging a gun at school with the intention of shooting someone and attempting to shoot and injuring more than one person, at least one of whom was not specifically targeted. | Descriptive analysis of rampage shootings post-Columbine High School Massacre on 4/20/1999, in and outside the United States. | N/A, descriptively assessed whether rampage shooters directly referred to the Columbine shooting and whether they appeared to be imitative by virtue of perpetrators copying aspects of the Columbine shooting. | Found that of the 12 documented school rampage shootings in the United States between Columbine and the end of 2007, 8 (66.7%) of the rampage shooters directly referred to Columbine and 5 (41.7%) imitated aspects of the shooting. Of the 11 rampage shootings outside the United States, 6 had direct references to Columbine and 5 (45%) imitated aspects of the shooting. | Yes (on school "rampage" shootings) |
| Schmidtke, Schaller, and Muller (2002) | 132 reports of "amok" events in two German newspapers between 1/1/1993 and 6/30/2000. | Examined the temporal distribution of and similarities between amok events; also tested whether amok events ending in suicide were likely to be followed by similar cases. | Compared observed and expected temporal distribution by dividing the time period studied into four 10-day time intervals and conducting a chi-square test of the distribution. | Found a significant difference between the temporal distribution of amok events and a random distribution. 44% of all events followed in the first 10 days after an amok event. Additionally, qualitatively, a high similarity between some of the amok events. | Yes (on mass "amok" violence) |

| Simon (2007) | School shootings, bomb threats against schools, and media coverage of school violence in three locales were examined in relation to the Columbine Massacre in Littleton, CO. Yearly number of school shootings in California, the San Antonio school district in Texas, and Colorado; data for each were obtained from the Secret Service and the National School Safety Center. Bomb threats against schools: California (Internet, 1998–99); San Antonio, TX (directly from the school district, monthly from 1998 to 2000); and Colorado (Bureau of Investigation and National Crime Information Center, daily from 1998 to 1999). Magazine and newspaper articles from 1998 to 1999, from the Reader's Guide to Periodical Literature and the Wall Street Journal, San Antonio Express News, and New York Times, respectively. | Examined the post-Columbine incidence of school shootings, bomb threats, and media coverage on school violence to determine whether there was a subsequent increase in school violence and media coverage thereof. | Method and period of comparison varied by locale and subject. San Antonio school district: compared the monthly and daily frequencies of bomb threats in 1999 to those on the same months and days, respectively, in 1998 and 2000. Colorado: compared the monthly frequency of bomb threats between 1998 and 1999. California: conducted descriptive comparison of bomb threats between the 1998 and 1999 school years based on an Internet BBC report. Media coverage: compared the number of magazine articles on school violence from April to December 1998 with the number from May to December 1999; and qualitatively compared the number of newspaper articles on the Columbine shooting to that on the Jonesboro shooting the year prior (comprising altogether a temporal period from 3/23/1998 to 5/8/1999). | Found no significant increase in school homicides by teenagers after the Columbine incident. However, found a significant increase in the daily (but not monthly) number of bomb threats against schools following the incident in the San Antonio school district (but not in Colorado). (Authors note that California had 236 bomb threats in the 1997–98 school year, and 548 in the subsequent year, of which 80% occurred after Columbine.) Found a significant increase in magazine articles on school violence during May to December 1999 compared with similar months in the prior year. | Yes (on bomb threats)/ No (mass shootings) |

(*Continued*)

**Table 4.1.** (Continued)

| Citation | Period, exposure stimulus, and population studied | Methodology | Comparison group/ period | Findings | Support of imitation (on outcome) |
|---|---|---|---|---|---|
| Stack (1989)* | Monthly suicide and homicide rates in the United States between August 1968 and 1980 (obtained from the National Center for Health Statistics) in relation to televised news stories on mass murder (that made two or more network news programs on ABC, NBC, and CBS) between 1975 and 1980 (obtained from the Vanderbilt Television News Archive). | Examined the relationship between publicized stories of mass murder and the monthly rates of suicide and homicide. | Regression analyses (OLS regression with Cochrane–Orcutt procedure to correct for autocorrelation) employed to examine the impact of publicized news stories regarding mass murder on monthly suicide and mass murder on monthly suicide and homicide rates. | Found that months with publicized gangland (but not other types, together or alone, of) mass murders had a significantly higher likelihood of suicide (but not homicide). | Yes (on suicides)/No (on homicides) |
| Towers, Gomez-Lievano, Khan, Mubayi, and Castillo-Chavez (2015) | Data on mass killings (four or more people murdered, by any means) in the United States between 2006 and 2013 compiled by USA Today study (of FBI Supplemental Homicide Reports, media reports, and police documents), data on school shootings from 1998 to 2013 inclusive from the Brady Campaign to Prevent Gun Violence, and data on mass shootings (at least three people shot, not necessarily killed) from February 2005 to January 2013 from the Brady Campaign. | Fit a "self-excitation" contagion model to the series of mass killings, mass shootings, and school shootings to determine whether the incidents were temporally contagious. | Examined with a "self-excitation" contagion model the data on mass killings, mass shootings, and school shootings to determine the probability of another event's occurring as a function of the preceding event's occurrence (controlling, when necessary, for day-of-the-week and seasonal effects, with a baseline of non-contagion-related events). | Found that the probabilities of mass killings (with and without firearms) and school shootings are significantly increased by similar incidents in the immediate past; each incident incites 0.30 and 0.22 new incidents, respectively. The increase in probability for each lasts about 13 days. Found no significant effect for mass shootings.Incidental findings: 46% and 8% of the mass killings with and without firearms, respectively, ended in suicide (76% of mass killings involved firearms), 18% of the school shooters died by suicide, and 17% of mass shooters died by suicide. | Yes (on mass killings and school shootings)/No (on mass shootings) |

*As this paper studied both mass murders and murder-suicides, it is listed in both tables.

**Table 4.2.** Empirical studies on the contagion of murder-suicide.

| Citation | Period, exposure stimulus, and population studied | Methodology | Comparison group/ period | Findings | Support of imitation (on outcome) |
|---|---|---|---|---|---|
| Phillips (1978) | Noncommercial airplane accidents during the same period (data obtained from the National Transportation Safety Board) in relation to all news stories (appearing on the front page of the NYT or LAT or appearing on CBS, NBC, or ABC evening news) regarding murder-suicides (involving at least two victims) in the United States between 8/5/1968 and 1973; data were obtained from the Vanderbilt Television News Archive. | Examined the frequency and temporal distribution of noncommercial airplane accidents in the 7 days preceding and following publicized stories on murder-suicide to identify distributions suggesting contagion. | Compared observed and expected frequencies of airplane fatalities and accidents in the 7 days before and following publicized stories regarding murder-suicide (used binomial distribution). | Found a significant day-3 peak in noncommercial airplane accidents with multiple fatalities after publicized stories regarding murder-suicide. Additionally found a dose–response effect, such that the amount of newspaper publicity devoted to a murder-suicide story was significantly correlated with the number of accidents with multiple fatalities following the story. (Did not find an effect for television publicity.) Found that these accidents occurred disproportionately in the region where the murder-suicide stories were publicized. | Yes (on airplane crashes, presumed to be murder-suicides) |
| Phillips (1979) | Daily motor vehicle fatalities in Los Angeles and San Francisco (obtained from the California Highway Patrol's Annual Report of Fatal and Injury Motor Vehicle Traffic Accidents) in relation to front-page stories on suicide and murder-suicide in the LA Times and San Francisco Chronicle (obtained from the papers' reference libraries), from 1969 to 1973. | Examined the incidence and characteristics of motor vehicle fatalities on the third day following publicized stories on suicide and murder-suicide (with the seventh day before and after the third day constituting the control period). Did not specifically examine the probability of accidents increasing after murder-suicide stories. | Compared characteristics of motor vehicle fatalities following suicide stories and those following murder-suicide stories. | Found that fatalities from motor vehicle accidents after publicized stores on murder-suicide are significantly different from those following stories on suicide. Multiple-vehicle accidents, as opposed to single-vehicle ones, tend to be more frequent after murder-suicide stories (and vice versa). | Yes (on multiple-vehicle accidents, presumed to be murder-suicides) |

(Continued)

**Table 4.2.** (Continued)

| Citation | Period, exposure stimulus, and population studied | Methodology | Comparison group/period | Findings | Support of imitation (on outcome) |
|---|---|---|---|---|---|
| Phillips (1980) | Commercial airplane accidents* in relation to all news stories (appearing on the front page of the NYT or LAT, or appearing on CBS, NBC, or ABC evening news) regarding murder-suicides in the United States between 1950 and 1973. | Examined the frequency and temporal distribution of commercial airplane accidents in the 1–8 days preceding and 0–7 days following publicized stories on murder-suicide. | Compared observed and expected frequencies of airplane accidents in the 1–8 days before and the 7 days following publicized murder-suicide stories to test the prediction that the number of accidents would be greater after the stories (used binomial distribution). | Found that there were significantly more commercial airplane accidents in the 7 days after publicized stories on murder-suicide than in the 1–8 days before. Found that such accidents were significantly more lethal (i.e., resulted in more deaths) as well. Additionally found a dose–response effect, such that the amount of newspaper publicity devoted to a murder-suicide story was significantly correlated with the number of commercial airplane accident fatalities following the story. Fatalities after a publicized murder-suicide story appear to peak on the third or fourth subsequent day and rise again the seventh or eighth day. | Yes (on airplane crashes, presumed to be murder-suicides) |

| Study | Data | Aim | Method/Outcome | Findings | Suicide/Homicide |
|---|---|---|---|---|---|
| Pirkis, Burgess, Francis, Blood, and Jolley (2006a) | National data on completed suicides (Australian Bureau of Statistics) in relation to 4,635 suicide-related items appearing in newspapers and news shows on TV and radio between 3/1/2000 and 2/28/2001 (Media Monitoring Project). | Examined the likelihood of there being an increase in suicides after suicide-related media items to determine which characteristics (including quality), if any, were predictive of an increase in suicides. | The outcome variable in the regression analyses was the difference between the number of suicides in the 7 days after the given media item (i.e., on days 0–6) and the number of days 1–8 before. This was conceptualized as a binary variable: increase vs. no increase. | Overall, found that items regarding murder-suicides were significantly less likely than items without such content to be followed by an increase in male or female suicides. In the subset of data rated for quality, found no significant relationship between murder-suicide-related content and subsequent increases in suicide. | No (on suicides) |
| Stack (1989)** | Monthly suicide and homicide rates in the United States between August 1968 and 1980 (obtained from the National Center for Health Statistics) in relation to televised news stories on murder-suicide (that made two or more network news programs on ABC, NBC, and CBS) between 1968 and 1981 (obtained from the Vanderbilt Television News Archive). | Examined the relationship between publicized stories of murder-suicide and the monthly rates of suicide and homicide. | Regression analyses (OLS regression with Cochrane–Orcutt procedure to correct for autocorrelation) employed to examine the impact of publicized news stories regarding mass murder-suicide and mass murder on monthly suicide and homicide rates. | Found that months with publicized murder-suicide stories have a significantly higher likelihood of suicides (but not homicides). Found that months with publicized gangland (but not other types, together or alone, of) mass murders had a significantly higher likelihood of suicide (but not homicide). | Yes (on suicides)/No (on homicides) |

* The findings on non-commercial airplane accidents reported in this study were also reported in Phillips, 1978; therefore, they are not included here.
** As this paper studied both mass murders and murder-suicides, it's listed in both categories.

shooting, rampage shooting, mass murder, and "amok." Murder-suicides were uniformly referred to as such.

Seven of the ten mass shooting studies were conducted from the United States, two from Australia, and one from Germany. All examined data from their respective countries, excepting two—of which one examined global data (Larkin, 2009) and the other, an Australian study (Cantor et al., 2009), additionally examined data from the United Kingdom and New Zealand. The oldest study was published in 1971 (Berkowitz and Macaulay) and the most recent was published in 2015 (Towers et al.). Of the five murder-suicide studies, four were conducted from the United States and one from Australia. All of the studies examined data from their countries of origin with the exception of the above-mentioned study that assessed global data.

The studies varied with respect to the exposure stimuli in relation to which they measured contagion. Those investigating the contagion of mass shootings tended to examine either the effect of one such event (e.g., the massively publicized shooting at Columbine High School) on subsequent violent acts or the temporal linkage between different, serial events. In contrast, all of the studies concerned with the contagion of murder-suicide identified a population of published news stories on murder-suicide (either in print media or on television) within a designated time period and examined their subsequent impact.

Furthermore, the studies utilized a diversity of outcome measures to determine the extent of contagion, which will be presented in the subsequent sections on mass shootings and murder-suicide. Diverse methodologies were employed across the studies, ranging from model-fitting to descriptive analyses of spatial-temporal linkage.

*Mass Shooting Findings*

All ten studies found some evidence of contagion (see table 4.1). The incidence of multiple constructs of multiple-victim shootings—including mass shooting, active shooting, school shooting, rampage shooting, mass murder, and amok—was found to facilitate subsequent imitative violent acts. These subsequent acts included mass shootings, mass killings, school shootings, amok events, firearm homicide, suicide, threats of school violence, bomb threats, aggravated assault, robbery, and total violent crime. A wide range of methodologies was employed, including descriptive analyses, Poisson regression analyses, time linkage analyses, and other model-fitting analyses.

Five studies utilized a specific mass shooting as the exposure stimulus in relation to which the incidence of imitative acts was examined. Of these, three used the Columbine shooting (at Columbine High School in Littleton, CO, on April 20, 1999) (Kostinsky et al., 2001; Larkin, 2009; Simon, 2007), one used the Port Arthur shooting (in Australia on April 27, 1996) (Carcach et al., 2002), and one used the Speck and Whitman shootings (in Chicago and Texas, respectively, in the summer of 1966) (Berkowitz & Macaulay, 1971). Two studies assessed the incidence of imitative acts in relation to media reports (Schmidtke et al., 2002; Stack, 1989). The remaining three studies examined a particular series of mass shootings within an arbitrarily defined time period.

A notable brief period of heightened incidence of imitative acts following mass shootings was found in several studies. The increased likelihood of subsequent acts appears temporally limited to a one- to two-week period. Towers and colleagues (2015) found a thirteen-day increase in probability for mass killings and school shootings; Kostinsky et al. (2001) found that 56 percent of threats occurred within the ten days following the Columbine shooting; Carcach et al. (2002) found an effect on the firearm homicide rate for the five days following the Port Arthur shooting but not thereafter; and Kissner (2015) found a two-week effect on the time between events, "suggesting that active shootings arrive in contagious 'micro-bursts.'"

*Murder Suicide Findings*

Four of the five studies found evidence of contagion (see table 4.2). The empirical support for contagion varied according to the outcome measure utilized. The subsequent incidence of commercial and noncommercial airplane crashes presumed to be murder-suicides, significantly increased after murder-suicide stories (Phillips, 1978, 1980). Multiple-vehicle accidents resulting in fatalities, also presumed to be murder-suicides, were disproportionately frequent after murder-suicide stories in contrast to pure suicide stories (Phillips, 1979). There was no evidence of subsequent homicides after murder-suicide news reports (Stack, 1989), and findings on suicides subsequent to murder-suicide stories were inconsistent (Pirkis et al., 2006; Stack, 1989). Stack (1989) found that months with murder-suicide stories had a higher likelihood of suicides and Pirkis et al. (2006) found that murder-suicide-related news items, compared to those without, had no impact on the subsequent incident of murder-suicide.

Similar to the findings of studies on mass shootings, subsequent imitative acts were more likely to occur within a relatively short period of time following the murder-suicide stories. Phillips (1978, 1980) found a peak in airplane accidents on the third or fourth day subsequent to a publicized murder-suicide story, with an additional peak on the seventh or eighth day (Phillips, 1980).

## Discussion

The goal of this review was to determine the extent to which the empirical literature on the contagion of mass shootings and murder-suicides provides evidence that processes of imitation may be contributing to the further incidence of such phenomena. Although the literature on this subject is relatively sparse, strong evidence of such contagion exists. Studies have consistently demonstrated that the occurrence of mass shootings increases the likelihood of similar instances of violence. Likewise, though they were fewer in number, studies on murder-suicide found that the reporting of murder-suicides can increase the likelihood of subsequent incidents. Additional research is necessary to substantiate and replicate these findings, assess possible moderating factors, and ascertain the precise mechanisms by which the incidence and reporting of these events impacts the likelihood of individuals engaging in imitative acts. Furthermore, the field would benefit from the establishment of a common taxonomy of mass shootings, the lack of which impedes the integration of disparate streams of research and confuses the public.

While media reports were not always explicitly examined as the exposure stimuli from which contagion may originate, reporting on mass shootings and murder-suicides is, as discussed above, typically the only means by which the public experiences and learns about such events. Clearly, therefore, the media's reporting of these events is a necessary precondition to the operation of contagion. While further research is needed to elucidate exactly how media reports may induce a greater likelihood of imitative violence, until these processes are better understood, the media should tread carefully with respect to how it reports and socially constructs these events to the public.

For example, concerns have been raised that the dramatic framing and disproportionate coverage of mass shootings and murder-suicides might inadvertently legitimize and perpetuate cultural norms and scripts that encourage angry and marginalized individuals to externalize their discontent through such acts (e.g., Kellner, 2008; Preti, 2008;

Sitzer, 2013). Men, who almost exclusively comprise the perpetrators of mass shootings, may, when faced with circumstances felt to be emasculating (e.g., bullying by higher status men fitting the hegemonic conception of masculinity), consider highly public mass shootings as a compensatory means for attaining masculinity through domination and violent celebrity. Furthermore, aside from disseminating potentially pernicious cultural scripts, media reports on mass shootings and murder-suicide can produce other harmful consequences. For example, in simplistically and disproportionately focusing on mental illness as a causal factor, media reports can increase the stigmatization of mental illness (Schultz et al., 2014).

Altogether, this review's findings and the aforementioned concerns necessitate the development of recommendations for the reporting of mass shootings and murder-suicides. Similarly, the validation of suicide contagion as a phenomenon led to an effort to develop media recommendations with an aim to change how the media reports on suicide (see Pirkis et al., 2006a; reportingonsuicide.org). A similar effort needs to be undertaken to help the media determine how to report on mass shootings and murder-suicide while mitigating the possibility of contagion. Some possible recommendations suggested by the current review, previous studies on mass shootings and murder-suicide (Kostinksy, 2001; Neuner, 2009; Preti, 2008; Richards, 2014), and suicide-reporting recommendations (e.g., reportingonsuicide.org) include

1. Perpetrators of mass shootings and murder-suicides should not be glorified, demonized, or simplified. This may include not providing their personal information, such as their names.
2. The exact details of the act (e.g., methods of killing or acquiring arms) should not be included.
3. The frequency of mass shootings and murder-suicide should not be exaggerated.
4. When there is evidence of mental illness in the perpetrator, it could be mentioned, providing that straightforward, non-stigmatizing descriptions of symptoms are used, for example, depression/anxiety as opposed to madman.
5. Contextualize mass shootings and murder-suicides appropriately so that their underlying motivations are differentiated. For example, the majority of mass shootings appear not to involve suicide, and murder-suicides are typically a form of intimate partner violence.
6. Information regarding seeking help for mental health issues should be provided (e.g., telephone numbers, web sites, suggestions regarding contacting school counselors).
7. Avoid prolonged coverage of mass shooting and murder-suicides.

These recommendations do not propose censorship; rather, they encourage the media to balance their institutional role of keeping the public informed with the societal need to prevent, to the extent possible, further episodes of mass violence. The onus is also on psychologists, social scientists, and public health professionals to work with the media to ensure that findings on the contagion of mass-shootings and murder-suicide are translated into policies that protect the public (Perrin, 2016).

## References

Agnich, L. E. (2014). A comparative analysis of attempted and completed school-based mass murder attacks. *American Journal of Criminal Justice, 40*(1), 1–22. http://doi.org/10.1007/s12103-014-9239-5

Auxemery, Y. (2015). The mass murderer history: Modern classifications, socio-demographic and psychopathological characteristics, suicidal dimensions, and media contagion of mass murders. *Comprehensive Psychiatry, 56*, 149–154. http://doi.org/10.1016/j.comppsych.2014.09.003

Bell, C. C., & McBride, D. F. (2010). Commentary: Homicide-suicide in older adults—Cultural and contextual perspectives. *Journal of the American Academy of Psychiatry and the Law Online, 38*(3), 312–317.

Berkowitz, L., & Macaulay, J. (1971). The contagion of criminal violence. *Sociometry, 34*(2), 238–260. http://doi.org/10.2307/2786414

Blair, J. P., & Schweit, K. W. (2013). A study of active shooter incidents, 2000–2013. Texas State University and Federal Bureau of Investigation, U.S. Department of Justice, Washington, DC, 2014.

Burns, R., & Crawford, C. (1999). School shootings, the media, and public fear: Ingredients for a moral panic. *Crime, Law and Social Change, 32*(2), 147–168. http://doi.org/10.1023/A:1008338323953

Cantor, C. H., Sheehan, P., Alpers, P., & Mullen, P. (1999). Media and mass homicides. *Archives of Suicide Research, 5*(4), 283–290. http://doi.org/10.1080/13811119908258339

Carcach, C., Mouzos, J., & Grabosky, P. (2002). Carcach et al. (2002) – The mass murder as quasi-experiment. *Homicide Studies, 6*(2), 109–127.

Cohen, A. P., Azrael, D., & Miller, M. (2014). Rate of mass shootings has tripled since 2011, new research from Harvard shows. Retrieved February 16, 2016, from http://www.motherjones.com/politics/2014/10/mass-shootings-increasing-harvard-research

Cohen, D. (2000). Homicide-suicide in older people. *Psychiatric Times, 17*(1), 49–52.

Coid, J. (1983). The epidemiology of abnormal homicide and murder followed by suicide. *Psychological Medicine, 13*(4), 855–860.

Drysdale, D., Modzeleski, W., & Simons, A. (2010). *Campus attacks: Targeted violence affecting institutions of higher education.* U.S. Secret Service, U.S. Department of Homeland Security, Office of Safe and Drug-Free Schools, U.S. Department of Education, and Federal Bureau of Investigation, U.S. Department of Justice. Washington, DC, 2010.

Eliason, S. (2009). Murder-suicide: a review of the recent literature. *The Journal of the American Academy of Psychiatry and the Law, 37*(3), 371–376.

Felthous, A. R., & Hempel, A. (1995). Combined homicide-suicides: a review. *Journal of Forensic Sciences, 40*(5), 846–857.

Fox, J. A., & Levin, J. (2015). Mass confusion concerning mass murder. *The Criminologist, 40*(1), 8–11.

Gould, M. S., Greenberg, T., Velting, D. M., & Shaffer, D. (2003). Youth suicide risk and preventive interventions: a review of the past 10 years. *Journal of the American Academy of Child and Adolescent Psychiatry, 42*(4), 386–405. http://doi.org/10.1097/01.CHI.0000046821.95464.CF

Harper, D. W., & Voigt, L. (2007). Homicide followed by suicide: An integrated theoretical perspective. *Homicide Studies, 11*(4), 295–318. http://doi.org/10.1177/1088767907306993

Huesmann, L. R., & Taylor, L. D. (2006). The role of media violence in violent behavior. *Annual Review of Public Health, 27*(1), 393–415. http://doi.org/10.1146/annurev.publhealth.26.021304.144640

James, M., & Shultz, A. M. C. (2013). Fatal school shootings and the epidemiological context of firearm mortality in the United States. *Disaster Health, 1*(2), 1–18. http://doi.org/10.4161/dish.26897

Jamieson, P., Jamieson, K. H., & Romer, D. (2003). The responsible reporting of suicide in print journalism. *American Behavioral Scientist, 46*(12), 1643–1660. http://doi.org/10.1177/0002764203254620

Kellner, D. (2013). School shootings, crises of masculinities, and the reconstruction of education: Some critical perspectives. In N. Böckler, T. Seeger, P. Sitzer, & W. Heitmeyer (Eds.), *School shootings* (pp. 497–518). New York: Springer.

Kinkel, R. J., & Josef, N. C. (2010). The mass media and violent imitative behavior: A review of research. In G. Albrecht & H. Otto (Eds.), *Social prevention and the social sciences: Theoretical controversies, research problems, and evaluation strategies* (pp. 499–522). Meuchen, DEU: Walter de Gruyter.

Kissner, J. (2015). Are active shootings temporally contagious? An empirical assessment. *Journal of Police and Criminal Psychology,* 1–11. http://doi.org/10.1007/s11896-015-9163-8

Kostinsky, S., Bixler, E. O., & Kettl, P. A. (2001). Threats of school violence in Pennsylvania after media coverage of the columbine high school massacre: Examining the role of imitation. *Archives of Pediatrics & Adolescent Medicine, 155*(9), 994–1001. http://doi.org/10.1001/archpedi.155.9.994

Large, M., Smith, G., & Nielssen, O. (2009). The epidemiology of homicide followed by suicide: A systematic and quantitative review. *Suicide and Life-Threatening Behavior, 39*(3), 294–306. http://doi.org/10.1521/suli.2009.39.3.294

Larkin, R. W. (2009). The columbine legacy rampage shootings as political acts. *American Behavioral Scientist, 52*(9), 1309–1326. http://doi.org/10.1177/0002764209332548

Machlin, A., Pirkis, J., & Spittal, M. J. (2013a). Which suicides are reported in the media – And what makes them "newsworthy"? *Crisis, 34*(5), 305–313. http://doi.org/10.1027/0227-5910/a000177

Machlin, A., Pirkis, J., & Spittal, M. J. (2013b). Which suicides are reported in the media – And what makes them "newsworthy"? *Crisis, 34*(5), 305–313. http://doi.org/10.1027/0227-5910/a000177

Marzuk, P. M., Tardiff, K., & Hirsch, C. S. (1992). The epidemiology of murder-suicide. *JAMA, 267*(23), 3179–3183. http://doi.org/10.1001/jama.1992.03480230071031

Muschert, G. W. (2007). Research in school shootings. *Sociology Compass, 1*(1), 60–80. http://doi.org/10.1111/j.1751-9020.2007.00008.x

Muschert, G. W. (2013). School shootings as mediatized violence. In N. Böckler, T. Seeger, P. Sitzer, & W. Heitmeyer (Eds.), *School shootings* (pp. 265–281). New York: Springer.

Neuner, T., Hubner-Liebermann, B., Hajak, G., & Hausner, H. (2009). Media running amok after school shooting in Winnenden, Germany! *Journal of Public Health, 19*(6), 578–579. http://doi.org/10.1093/eurpub/ckp144

Niederkrotenthaler, T., Fu, K., Yip, P. S. F., Fong, D. Y. T., Stack, S., Cheng, Q., & Pirkis, J. (2012). Changes in suicide rates following media reports on celebrity suicide: A meta-analysis. *Journal of Epidemiology and Community Health*, jech–2011–200707. http://doi.org/10.1136/jech-2011-200707

Perrin, P. B. (2016). Translating psychological science: Highlighting the media's contribution to contagion in mass shootings: Comment on Kaslow (2015). *The American Psychologist, 71*(1), 71–72. http://doi.org/10.1037/a0039994

Petee, T. A., Padgett, K. G., & York, T. S. (1997). Debunking the stereotype: An examination of mass murder in public places. *Homicide Studies, 1*(4), 317–337. http://doi.org/10.1177/1088767997001004002

Phillips, D. P. (1974). The influence of suggestion on suicide: Substantive and theoretical implications of the werther effect. *American Sociological Review, 39*(3), 340–354. http://doi.org/10.2307/2094294

Phillips, D. P. (1978). Airplane accident fatalities increase just after newspaper stories about murder and suicide. *Science, 201*, 748–750.

Phillips, D. P. (1979). Suicide, motor vehicle fatalities, and the mass media: Evidence toward a theory of suggestion. *American Journal of Sociology, 84*(5), 1150–1174.

Phillips, D. P. (1980). Airplane accidents, murder, and the mass media: Towards a theory of imitation and suggestion. *Social Forces, 58*(4), 1001–1024.

Pirkis, J., & Blood, R. W. (2001). Suicide and the media. Part II: Portrayal in fictional media. *Crisis, 22*(4), 155–162. http://doi.org/10.1027//0227-5910.22.4.155

Pirkis, J., Blood, R. W., Beautrais, A., Burgess, P., & Skehans, J. (2006a). Media guidelines on the reporting of suicide. *Crisis, 27*(2), 82–87. http://doi.org/10.1027/0227-5910.27.2.82

Pirkis, J. E., Burgess, P. M., Francis, C., Blood, R. W., & Jolley, D. J. (2006b). The relationship between media reporting of suicide and actual suicide in Australia. *Social Science & Medicine, 62*(11), 2874–2886. http://doi.org/10.1016/j.socscimed.2005.11.033

Preti, A. (2008). School shooting as a culturally enforced way of expressing suicidal hostile intentions. *Journal of the American Academy of Psychiatry and the Law Online, 36*(4), 544–550.

Richards, T. N., Gillespie, L. K., & Givens, E. M. (2014). Reporting femicide-suicide in the news: The current utilization of suicide reporting guidelines and recommendations for the future. *Journal of Family Violence, 29*(4), 453–463. http://doi.org/10.1007/s10896-014-9590-9

Schmidtke, A., Schaller, S., & Muller, I. (2002). Imation [sic] of amok and amok-suicide. *Kriz Dergisi, 10*(2), 49–60.

Shultz, J. M., Thoresen, S., Flynn, B. W., Muschert, G. W., Shaw, J. A., Espinel, Z., . . . Cohen, A. M. (2014). Multiple vantage points on the mental health effects of mass shootings. *Current Psychiatry Reports, 16*(9), 469. http://doi.org/10.1007/s11920-014-0469-5

Simon, A. (2007). Application of fad theory to copycat crimes: quantitative data following the columbine massacre. *Psychological Reports, 100*(3c), 1233–1244. http://doi.org/10.2466/pr0.100.4.1233-1244

Sitzer, P. (2013). The role of media content in the genesis of school shootings: The contemporary discussion. In N. Böckler, T. Seeger, P. Sitzer, & W. Heitmeyer (Eds.), *School shootings* (pp. 283–307). New York: Springer.

Stack, S. (1989). The effect of publicized mass murders and murder-suicides on lethal violence, 1968–1980. A research note. *Social Psychiatry and Psychiatric Epidemiology, 24*(4), 202–208.

Towers, S., Gomez-Lievano, A., Khan, M., Mubayi, A., & Castillo-Chavez, C. (2015). Contagion in mass killings and school shootings. *PLoS One, 10*(7), e0117259. http://doi.org/10.1371/journal.pone.0117259

Vossekuil, B. (2002). *The final report and findings of the safe school initiative: Implications for the prevention of school attacks in the United States.* Washington, DC: U.S. Department of Education, Office of Elementary and Secondary Education, Safe and Drug-Free Schools Program and U.S. Secret Service, National Threat Assessment Center.

# 5

# Internet Bullying Distinguishes Suicide Attempters from Ideators

*Steven Stack*

Bullying has been defined as intentional harm done by one person or group toward a victim. There is substantial evidence that traditional, offline, bullying, such as face-to-face encounters in schools, increases the risk of suicide ideation and suicide attempts (for reviews see Bauman et al., 2013; Hinduja & Patchin, 2010). However, a relatively new venue for bullying has emerged and gained momentum: the Internet. Cyber bullying is generally defined as "willful and repeated harm inflicted through the use of computers, cell phones and other electronic devices." An estimated 15–30 percent of students report cyber bullying (see review in Hinduja & Patchin, 2010). Nevertheless there is little research regarding the impact of Internet bullying on suicide.

Rapid advances in information and communication technologies have provided bullies with a range of new tools for aggression. Cyber bullying can involve such behaviors as harassing or threatening messages (e.g., via text message or e-mail), posting derogatory comments and pictures about someone on a website or social networking site (e.g., Facebook or Myspace), and physically threatening or intimidating someone in a variety of online settings.

That the Internet may be more effective in hurting peoples' reputations can be illustrated by spreading of false hurtful rumors. Communications on the Internet can reach far more people and do so much faster than rumor-mongering by use of telephones and face-to-face communication. Use of these older communication venues can take considerably more time and reach a more limited audience than employment of Internet-based communications.

While cyber bullying has received considerable media attention, there has not been much rigorous research on its relationship to suicide. A systematic review of work on cyber bullying found only two studies on cyber bullying and suicide ideation (SI) or suicide attempts (SA) (Daine et al., 2013). Hay and Meldrum (2010), in a study of 426 rural youth in Florida, determined that cyber bullying was the second most important predictor of SI. They controlled for a six-item negative emotions index, but no measure of many other risk factors including depression per se or violence involvement. Hinduja and Patchin (2010), in a study of 1,963 high school students in Florida, determined that cyber bullying victimization predicted both SI and SA. However, the list of control variables was short: age, gender, and race. Bauman et al. (2013) studied 1,491 high school students in the state of Arizona. Here cyber bullying victimization did not predict SA independent of depression. The findings on the possible linkage between Internet bullying and suicidality are inconclusive. The mixed nature of the findings may be related to such methodological considerations as differences in samples of youth (e.g., different regions of the nation) and model specification.

This study addresses several limitations of previous investigations. First, unlike all previous investigations, it focuses on a salient but neglected issue. It explores whether or not cyber bullying (CB) can distinguish SI from SA. None of the previous investigations raised the question: can CB differentiate suicide ideators from suicide attempters? For example, may the social humiliation of cyber bullying victimization drive some already suicidal youth over the edge toward suicide attempts? Second, this study addresses sampling issues. Previous work has been based on local, sometimes rural, samples. This study is the first investigation to assess the role of cyber bullying on SI and SA for the United States as a whole. Third, this study also controls for depression, a factor rendering cyber bullying nonsignificant in the previous work on Arizona. Further, depressed persons may be more apt to be targeted as victims by exploitative bullies. Is it the bullying or the preexisting depression that drives the suicidality? Fourth, this study controls for other psychiatric symptoms and socio-demographic constructs often left out of the models in past work (e.g., eating disorders, violence involvement, and ethnicity). With a wider host of controlled constructs, the results from this study are more suited to fully documenting any independent influence of Internet bullying on suicide. Finally, this study is able to weight the influence of a media factor, Internet bullying, against the importance of a host of traditional non-media constructs. That is, how important is bullying on the Internet relative to traditional psychiatric predictors of suicidality such as eating disorders, depression, and substance abuse? A key concern is: does Internet bullying have an impact on suicidality once traditional predictors of suicidality are controlled?

## Methodology: Measurement of Variables

All data are taken from the Youth Risk Behavior Survey (YRBS) of 2013. The YRBS is based on a representative sample of 13,583 students enrolled in 143 high schools and selected through a multi-stage cluster sampling procedure. The student response rate was 88 percent. For a further description of the YRBS, see CDC (2014) *2013 YRBS Data Users Guide* at http://www.cdc.gov/yrbs.

*Suicidality*

Suicidality is measured along two dimensions; both are based on twelve- month prevalence. Suicide attempt is measured as a positive (one or more times) response to the question "During the last 12 months how many times did you actually attempt suicide?" Suicide ideation is measured as a positive response to the item "During the last 12 months did you ever seriously consider attempting suicide?" For the main analysis the sample is restricted to only those students reporting a suicide attempt ($N = 1,007$) or suicide ideation ($N = 1,339$). The dependent variable for the main analysis differentiates attempters from ideators, where 1= suicide attempter and 0=suicide ideator. Since the dependent variable is a dichotomy, logistic regression techniques are appropriate (Menard, 2002).

*Cyber Bullying*

The central independent variable is cyber bullying. Cyber bullying is measured by the one available item in the YRBS: "During the past 12 months, have you ever been electronically bullied?" where 1=yes and 0=no.

In a quest for approximating a fully specified model, within the confines of available data, a series of fifteen control variables are included. The first three are related to Joiner's (2005) construct, the acquired capability for suicide, and tap violence involvement (Stack, 2014).

*Violence Involvement*

(1) Fighting: "During the past 12 months how many times were you in a physical fight in which you were injured and had to be treated by a doctor or nurse?" where 1 = one or more times and 0 = never; (2) Dating violence: "During the past 12 months did your boyfriend or girlfriend ever hit, slap,

or physically hurt you on purpose?" where 1= yes and 0=no; (3) Violence preparedness/weapons: "During the last 30 days, on how many days did you carry a weapon such as a gun, knife, or club?" Responses ranged from 0 to 6 or more days. Carrying a weapon signals an anticipation of violence either as a victim or perpetrator and is a marker of membership in the subculture of violence (Stack, 2012; Wolfgang, 1958).

*Psychiatric factors*

(1) Depression: "During the past 12 months did you ever feel so sad or hopeless almost every day for 2 weeks or more in a row that you stopped doing some usual activities?" Yes=1, no=0; (2) Eating disorder: "During the past 30 days did you vomit or take laxatives to lose weight or keep from gaining weight?" Yes=1, no=0; (3) Substance abuse: (a) "During the last 30 days how many times did you use marijuana?" 1= 3 or more, 0=all others; (b) "During the last 30 days how many times did you use any form of cocaine, including powder, crack, or freebase?" 1= 3 or more, 0=all others; (c ) "During the last 30 days how many times did you have five or more drinks of alcohol in a row, that is, within a couple of hours?" 1=2 or more days, 0=all others; (4) Suicide plan: "During the past 12 months did you make a plan about how you would attempt suicide?" 1=yes, 0=no.

*Risky Sexual Behavior and Social Integration*

Finally, controls are incorporated for two additional constructs taken from the literature on bullying and youth risk behavior (e.g., Stack, 2014). First, risky sexual behavior is measured in terms of two items: (1) number of sexual partners in the last thirty days, responses: 0 through 6 or more, and (2) unsafe sex: not using a condom during last sexual intercourse (=1), all others=0. Second, school integration is indexed by the one available measure in the YRBS: (1) sports team member (0=no, 1=yes).

*Demographics*

The model is rounded out by demographic controls: (1) Gender: male=1, female=0; (2) ethnicity is taken into account by a series of binary variables: African American (0,1), Hispanic (0,1), Asian (0,1), Caucasian (0,1), Native American (0,1), and Asian (0,1), with the reference category=other. Age is measured in years.

## Results

Table 5.1 presents the findings for the entire sample of 13,583 high school youth. Cyber bullying victimization is over three times more

**Table 5.1.** Prevalence of cyber bullying victimization, Youth Risk Behavior Survey: (A) full sample, (B) suicide ideators, and (C) suicide attempters, 2013.

| Status | Percentage victims of cyber bullying |
|---|---|
| (A) Total sample | 14.8 |
| (B) Suicide ideators only | 47.8 |
| (C) Suicide attempters only | 52.2 |

prevalent among suicide ideators (47.8 percent) and attempters (52.2 percent) than for the general population of high school students (14.8 percent). Table 5.2 presents the results of the multivariate logistic regression analysis.

*Cyber Bullying*

Controlling for the other variables, cyber bullying significantly differentiated the attempters from the ideators. The odds ratio for cyber bullying was 1.51, meaning that victims of electronic bullying were 1.51 times more likely than non-victims to have attempted suicide.

*Violence Involvement*

The three violence involvement measures significantly differentiated between the ideators and the attempters: fighting (odds ratio=1.91), dating violence (OR=1.37), and weapons (OR=1.12).

*Psychiatric Controls*

All six psychiatric controls differentiated SA from SI. Major depression increased the odds of an attempt by 33 percent (OR=1.33). Additional odds ratios were eating disorder (1.83), marijuana use (OR=1.41), cocaine use (OR=1.54), binge drinker (SA 33 percent less apt, OR=0.67), and suicide plan (OR=3.35).

*Risky Sexual Behaviors and School Integration*

None of these variables were significant. They are omitted from the table.

*Demographics*

Males were 28 percent less apt (1–0.72) to be attempters than females (OR=0.72). Older students were also less apt to be attempters (OR=0.88). Each additional year of age lowered the odds of an attempt by 12 percent. With respect to ethnicity, two types predicted attempts

**Table 5.2.** Constructs differentiating between suicide ideators (=0) and suicide attempters (=1): multiple logistic regression analysis ($N$ = 2,136 ideators and suicide attempters only). Youth Rick Behavior Survey, 2013.

| | Logistic regression coefficient | Odds ratio |
|---|---|---|
| Internet bullying victim | 0.41* | 1.51 |
| Violence exposure | | |
| Fighting with injuries requiring medical attention | 0.64* | 1.91 |
| Dating violence | 0.31* | 1.37 |
| Days carried a weapon | 0.11* | 1.12 |
| Psychiatric controls | | |
| Major depression | 0.28* | 1.33 |
| Eating disorder | 0.60* | 1.83 |
| Marijuana use | 0.34* | 1.41 |
| Cocaine use | 0.42* | 1.54 |
| Binge drinker | −0.39* | 0.67 |
| Suicide plan | 1.21* | 3.35 |
| Risky sexual behavior, school integration (not shown, not significant) | | |
| Demographics | | |
| Male | −0.32* | 0.72 |
| Age | −0.12* | 0.88 |
| Ethnicity | | |
| African American | 0.46* | 1.59 |
| Hispanic | 0.48* | 1.61 |
| Constant term | −0.13 | – |
| Model chi square: 371.37* | | |

*$p$ < 0.05

Nagelkerke $r$-squared: 0.216

Cases correctly classified: 68%

over SI. Both the ethnic status of African American (OR=1.59) and Hispanic (OR=1.61) differentiated attempters from ideators. Both groups were more apt to attempt.

The model provides a good fit to the data according to the significant model chi square. The model explains 21.6 percent of the variance in the dependent variable (Nagelkerke $r$-squared=0.216). The model also correctly predicts 68 percent of the cases as either attempters or ideators.

## Conclusions

Previous studies on cyber bullying and suicidality did not explore the question of whether or not cyber bullying could differentiate suicide ideators from attempters (Bauman et al., 2013; Hay & Medlrum, 2010; Hinduja & Patchin, 2010). Cyber bullying may be a factor that pushes some ideators over the edge, fostering a transition from ideation to attempting suicide. This study is the first investigation that shows that cyber bullying does indeed differentiate the ideators from the attempters. Among students who were suicidal, victims of cyber bullying were 51 percent more apt than non-victims to be attempters. This result is robust in the sense that it holds after controls are incorporated for a host of psychiatric and other predictors of suicidality. The controls include violence involvement, depression, eating disorders, and substance abuse.

This study has several limitations. First, the study design is cross-sectional. We cannot infer cause and effect. While suicidality is associated with bullying, it may come before the bullying has occurred. It is plausible, for example, that suicidal individuals are more apt than non-suicidal individuals to be singled out or targeted for bullying. Suicide attempts may precede bullying victimization. Future work is needed to control for depression and suicidality at baseline and then measure the impact of subsequent bullying on suicidality at follow-up. Another shortcoming of this study is that it could not assess the association between bullying *perpetration* and suicidality. There are no YRBS measures of perpetration. In addition, there are no measures of the subtypes of Internet bullying victimization (e.g., email, Facebook posts).

Future work is also needed to determine if cyber bullying differentiates suicide attempts from actual completed suicides. While suicide attempts are a risk factor for deaths from suicide, it is also true that most persons who killed themselves have no history of suicide attempts (e.g., Stack, 2014). It is plausible that cyber bullying, while differentiating ideators from attempters, may not differentiate completers from attempters.

Finally, research is needed for other age groups. The results based on youth in the YRBS may not generalize to adults. To the extent that youth make more use of the Internet (e.g., Facebook, Twitter) than adults, cyber bullying may cause more harm to the young than the old.

# References

Bauman, S., Toomey, R. B., & Walker, J. L. (2013). Associations among bullying, cyber bullying and suicide in high school students. *Journal of Adolescence, 36,* 341–350.

Centers for Disease Control. (2014) *2013 YRBS Data Users Guide.* http://www.cdc.gov/yrbs.

Daine, K., Hawton, K., Singaravelu, V., Stewart, A., Simkin, S., & Montgomery, P. (2013). The power of the web: A systematic review of studies of the Influence of the internet on self harm and suicide among young people. *Plos One, 8,* e77555.

Hay, C., & Meldrum, R. (2010). Bullying victimization & adolescent self harm: Hypotheses from general strain theory. *Journal of Youth & Adolescence, 39,* 446–459.

Hinduja, S., & Patchin, J. W. (2010). Bullying, cyber bullying and suicide. *Archives of Suicide Research, 14,* 206–221.

Joiner, T. (2005). *Why people die by suicide.* Cambridge, MA: Harvard University Press.

Menard, S. (2002). *Applied logistic regression analysis.* Thousand Oaks, CA: Sage.

Stack, S. (2012). The culture of violence & suicidality. In G. R. Hayes & M. H. Bryant (Eds.), *Psychology of culture* (pp. 201–212). New York: Nova Science.

Stack, S. (2014). Differentiating suicide ideators from attempters: Violence. *Suicide & Life Threatening Behavior, 44,* 46–57.

Wolfgang, M. (1958). *Patterns in criminal homicide.* Philadelphia: University of Pennsylvania Press.

# 6

# The Use of Social Media in the Aftermath of a Suicide: Findings from a Qualitative Study in England

*Jo Bell and Louis Bailey*

## Introduction

The research draws on the experiences of bereaved individuals who utilize Facebook to memorialize loved ones who have died by suicide. Aspects of the research have been published elsewhere. In Bailey et al. (2014), we explore how the use of social media in the aftermath of a suicide contributes to the continuing social presence of the deceased and how this, in turn, facilitates continuing bonds between the deceased and the bereaved. In Bell et al. (2015), we expand on this to explore the impact of continuing bonds on the grieving process. We show how the online identity of the deceased evolves and, simultaneously, how the online activity of mourners shifts over time. In this chapter, we highlight the benefits and constraints of Facebook use in the aftermath of a suicide. While we have touched on this in previous articles (Bailey et al., 2014 and Bell et al., 2015), this topic has yet to be explored in detail.

## Methods

After securing ethical approval, a call for participants was issued via two leading UK charities—PAPYRUS Prevention of Young Suicide and Survivors of Bereavement by Suicide (SOBS). The subsequent interviews were conducted with those who had created or maintained online memorial sites (such as stand-alone websites or social networking pages) dedicated to the memory of a loved one who had died by suicide. Eleven people were interviewed in total—nine of whom utilized Facebook, two of whom created stand-alone websites. Participants included those who had lost a child, a sibling, or a friend. For the purposes of this chapter, only those who utilized social media (Facebook) are included.

Interviews followed a semi-structured narrative style (Cooper, 1999) and emphasis was placed on encouraging participants to "tell the story" in the way they chose (Owens et al., 2008). Participants were asked about what motivated them to create their online sites, how they used the sites, their experiences (good and bad) of interacting online, and the impact of this on their experiences of bereavement and grief. Interviews were recorded and transcribed. A coding frame was then constructed and emerging themes identified. Data were then analyzed through a qualitative interpretive approach, which combined constant comparison with thematic analysis (Glaser & Strauss, 1967; Green & Thorogood, 2004; Chapple & Ziebland, 2011). Pseudonyms have been used in order to protect the identities of participants. For a more detailed description of the study methodology, please see Bailey et al. (2014) and Bell et al. (2015).

Of the participants interviewed in our study who utilized Facebook for the purposes of memorialization, some maintained the existing (in-life) Facebook profile page of the deceased while others had chosen to convert the profile into a memorial page. Some set up a new "memorial page" and continued to visit the "live" profile page of the deceased. At the time of writing, in the United Kingdom when a "live" page becomes a "memorial" page the page is left intact, as it had been left by the deceased when they were still alive. This means that no one can log into the account, and therefore the status update and private messaging functions are disabled. Depending on the privacy settings of the account, friends can still post onto the page timeline but static content—such as the profile picture or "about" section—cannot be changed. Content previously posted by the deceased (such as links and status updates) remains intact.

In terms of activity, some participants sent private messages to the deceased; some posted content onto the page timeline so that it could be viewed by others (depending on the settings). Participants used the sites to publicly express their grief, to communicate with the deceased, and to communicate with other mourners.

## Positive Impact on the Mental Health of the Suicide Bereaved

*Bringing People Together*

Respondents described how Facebook came into its own during the immediate aftermath of the death as a means of informing people outside of the family's immediate social circle about news of the death and subsequent funeral arrangements. Facebook therefore became a more convenient mechanism for relaying the news to a larger group of people and, in the process, alleviated some of the stress and trauma associated with the need to make repeated telephone calls.

One mother, who had lost her son some months previously, described how using Facebook was preferable to phoning distant relatives and friends because she did not want to get into the details of the series of events, which she found upsetting. It also avoided having to repeat the news to each contact. She went on to describe how people who she was not otherwise in contact with found out about the funeral and traveled long distances in order to attend, all because of Facebook.

Another respondent remarked on the speed by which news of her son's death had spread around Facebook. For this participant and others we interviewed, the instantaneous nature of Facebook helped them to manage their grief, especially during the early stages when their pain and suffering felt particularly acute. It enabled the bereaved the chance to say their final farewells to the deceased in the hopes of starting to come to terms with the death and ensuing loss. In the following example, she describes the ways in which Facebook assisted in the bringing together of family members to share memories, which was particularly important during the early days of the bereavement:

> people found out by the next morning that he'd died . . . it all got round by Facebook and people were writing on it straightaway . . . and we would all read them and get upset, or read them and laugh . . . we did ask people to put photos on and . . . their memories of Mark and . . . the funny stories really comforted us . . . Facebook page . . . enabled us to get together and laugh and . . . actually share some nice memories

Facebook enabled participants to connect with others affected by the suicide in order to both seek and provide emotional support. It served as a key mechanism for bringing people together for the purpose of remembrance and to initiate the grieving process: they were able to talk with family members and friends of the deceased online—either via private messaging or by interacting with one another and the deceased by posting comments, photographs, and links onto the deceased's "wall." Participants described feeling comforted as they shared happy memories online—often triggered by the posting of favorite songs and other items which helped them to remember the deceased.

In terms of expressing grief and managing the trauma of suicide bereavement, Facebook provides a place where the bereaved can express their grief instantly, anonymously, and publicly without ever physically interacting with another person. For some, it provides a safe and accessible place for individuals to express their grief and gain acceptance and support from others:

> I've got sixty-seven people in his life who I can share my grief with . . . and they all understand where I'm coming from.

For this participant, Facebook became the vehicle that allowed him to connect with others who were grieving for his son and make sense of his death.

### Reaching Out

Participants in our study talked about how the use of the sites continued beyond the immediate aftermath of the death and how the functions and nature of activity evolved. Users continued to share memories and messages long after the death had occurred; they began to use the pages for sharing information, signposting support, and raising awareness. Some had initiated support forums and incorporated links to suicide prevention or suicide bereavement charity pages and fundraising events.

### Communicating with the Deceased

The most common motivating factor among our respondents for initiating, sustaining, and maintaining website and Facebook pages was the need to stay connected to the deceased and to keep the deceased alive: many described how they used the sites to communicate with lost loved ones and their friends both in the immediate aftermath and long after the death. Accounts of others communicating with the deceased via Facebook were common:

> People go up there and put mementoes on and they'll say on Facebook, been to see you today Mark . . . yesterday I went up and I just chatted to him . . . now more three and a half years on . . . they write and say really miss you Mark or I'm doing this and it reminded me of you . . . he's still being included in what his friends are doing.

Communicating with the deceased online via private messaging was helpful in the grief process for some of our participants: they were able to tell the deceased they were loved and important which had the effect of erasing regret. This is significant for those who are bereaved by suicide because of the associated guilt and responsibility often experienced (Bell, Stanley, Mallon, & Manthorpe, 2012; Jordan & McIntosh, 2011; Ratnarajah & Maple, 2011). The sharing of new and existing memories (i.e., anniversaries in real time as well as things like "do you remember when") highlights how Facebook facilitates continually evolving bonds with the deceased.

## Negative Impact on the Mental Health of the Bereaved

### Tensions: Private/Public Expressions of Grief

One of the important findings in our study was that family members sometimes differed in the ways in which they chose to use and contribute to the sites. Some actively chose not to use the site altogether. Lucinda described how her son refused to look at his deceased brother's Facebook page ("I think he's trying to forget about him"). Those who wish to disengage may be motivated by a desire for private grief and the fact that forgetting can allow wounds to heal. This process is thwarted by constant reminders on Facebook which may be too confronting as in Lucinda's son's case: ". . . it's like a pain . . . a painful memory."

One respondent described the Facebook page as his "lifeline," but others in the family had never looked at it; one family member had chosen to stop going on altogether after being actively involved in the maintenance of the site. Another younger member of the family had asked to join it but had been prevented by others in the family. These findings highlight a sense of uneasiness created between some who want those online connections and others who wish to disengage with the possibilities that Facebook offers.

Walter (2015) suggests that potential for conflict can arise as different ways of mourning become more apparent to others, but not necessarily more understood: Facebook provides constant reminders of the loss, potentially making things much more difficult for aspects of the loss which have not yet been neutralized or redefined (Rosenblatt, 1983). This is especially true of suicide deaths where the process of making sense of the death is more complex (Bell et al., 2012; Jordan, 2001) and therefore more difficult to "neutralize" and "redefine."

Another participant described how the page was initially public but that they changed the settings to private because of outpourings of grief on the site which they felt were not genuine. They also feared it would provoke copycat suicides—a point we return to later. Linked to this, another participant described family tension around adding friends to the Facebook page. For example, a parent who was managing his deceased son's Facebook page was receiving "friends requests" more than two years after his death. Some members of the family were troubled as to why someone would do that. In another case, a parent described similar experiences and her reluctance to accept requests from individuals not known to family members or immediate friends:

> I've had a few people asking to join the page and I haven't let them because I haven't known who they are . . . and I've done a bit of like asking around . . . and nobody's known who they are, and I can't see any connection with anyone . . .

DeGroot (2012) referred to the presence of those posting who did not appear to have a close relationship with the deceased as "Emotional Rubberneckers." Because many Facebook walls are accessible to all Facebook users, strangers have the opportunity to gawk at others' reactions to losing a loved one. In the case of suicide death, the fallout of this on the intimate bereaved could be particularly difficult and could heighten the sensationalism of the death which, in turn, could contribute to suicide contagion (explained later).

*Double Loss*

Some Facebook sites were still very active years after the death. This provided mourners with a positive legacy and longevity for the memory of a loved one being kept alive via these activities as the sites evolved. Others, however, were much more short lived which raises the question of what happens when interest and activity on the page starts to wane? In the case of Samantha (who set up a memorial page on Facebook for her friend who took her own life), witnessing the disappearance of visitors to the site was distressing. The site experienced a massive surge of activity in the beginning (it peaked at approximately five hundred people in the first month). During this time it kept her busy and served as a distraction from grief, reducing her own solitude and isolation. Five months on and the activity had almost stopped. This online silence was interpreted by Samantha as a sign that others had "forgotten" about the deceased and had moved on with their lives (. . . *have people forgotten? Don't people care? . . . now . . . it . . . doesn't seem to have a function for anyone . . .*).

Her distress reiterates the importance of remembrance and keeping the deceased alive for some people in managing their grief. Here, grief is intensified by watching others withdraw from public to more private expressions of grief (or else "move on" with their lives). The dangers of becoming overly attached to sites were highlighted further by one respondent who described her experience of "double loss" when the Facebook page she created for her son disappeared unexpectedly. In both instances, the retreat from a public sharing of grief served to isolate these participants, further compounding their grief experience.

*Contagion*

> ... since Mike died, two of his friends have attempted suicide ... and so often I'll put inspirational things on there ...

A number of respondents in our study described how other young people in the friendship group of the deceased had subsequently made attempts to take their own lives in the aftermath of the suicide. Some had communicated their suicidal feelings via the Facebook sites, either in private messages or on the public pages. In all cases, respondents felt the need to act or intervene in some way, feeling some level of responsibility for averting further tragedy or alleviating distress. In some cases this prompted the turn to the promotion of suicide prevention, support, and awareness raising on Facebook sites discussed previously.

Catherine and her family observed how activity on Jacob's Facebook site evolved. In the immediate aftermath of his death, visitors used his Facebook site to express how they felt about losing him (posting messages, memories, photographs, and comments about how he would be missed). Over time they began to see changes in the content and frequency of the postings from friends. They noticed in particular the gradual idealization of Jacob and aspiration to death in some of the comments. In particular, they observed that some of the comments began to take on a "hopelessness" type quality and that others would read these comments and return to say similar things, which were darker or a bit more disturbing. For example, posts characterizing natural outpourings of grief such as *"rest in peace"* and celebratory memories or amusing anecdotes were replaced with *"you're in a much better place, I'll see you soon"* and *"I can't function without you . . . I understand why you did what you did . . ."*

It was via the Facebook site that Catherine and others were able, in turn, to reach out and engage with particular individuals who were leaving these posts. They also observed others responding directly or commenting on the site with offers of support and encouragement to seek further help.

These examples demonstrate how Facebook can be instrumental in both increasing the likelihood of suicide contagion and alleviating it in the aftermath of a suicide. What matters most is how sites are managed and moderated, the importance of which, when seen in this light, cannot be overstated.

## Discussion

A death by suicide forces those surrounding it to face huge and terrifying questions about what life means, how to connect with others, how to stop pain from overwhelming us, and other questions that go to the very center of the human condition (Hollander, 2001). Those who are bereaved by suicide are likely to experience additional challenges that do not feature in other types of death, including shock, stigma, blame, guilt, and anger (Bell, Stanley, Mallon, & Manthorpe, 2012; Jordan & McIntosh, 2011; Ratnarajah & Maple, 2011), and can be therefore forced to endure complicated or traumatic grief (Jacobs & Prigerson, 2000) or disenfranchised grief (Maple, Edwards, Minichiello, & Plummer, 2013).

It is crucial therefore that survivors find a place to share their feelings and experiences.

This is where the Internet comes into its own, as a place which enables conversation about otherwise sensitive and "taboo" topics. The relative anonymity of the online world serves to free up inhibition (Suler, 2004) and profits from a number of benefits: people in online environments are likely to self-disclose personal intimate information more rapidly than in offline environments, increasing connection between "strangers" and establishing a veil of trust and intimacy much more readily than in offline relationships. The net effect of this enables suicide survivors to post things which might otherwise be met with silence or chastisement. The bereaved can then connect with others who are going through a similar situation, people who may live hundreds or thousands of miles away.

As such, social networking platforms such as Facebook offer opportunities for those bereaved by suicide to share their experiences and explore their grief with others in a similar position (who they might not otherwise meet) and enable a form of uncensored self-expression not comparable with face-to-face conversations. This is important in relation to grief from suicide, which can be stigmatizing and disenfranchising (Doka, 1999, 2002) and especially complicated and difficult to grieve (Bell et al., 2012; Ellenbogen & Gratton, 2001; Jordan, 2001, 2008). In encouraging the building of online relationships, Facebook can be said to provide a mechanism for overcoming stigma and alleviating disenfranchised grief (Hensley, 2012) as in Philip's case (*I've got sixty-seven people in his life who I can share my grief with . . . and they all understand where I'm coming from*).

All this highlights the positive impact of the use of Facebook on the mental health of those who are bereaved by suicide. For all of our participants it fulfilled a range of functions which spanned across social, emotional, and practical realms. It served as a memorial to their loved one and as a means of staying connected to the deceased, bringing people together, gaining support, reaching out to others, and keeping the deceased "alive." Reaching out to others offers the opportunity to connect and enables the bereaved to feel proactive in that they are helping others who are isolated, in distress, or otherwise in need of support (potentially saving someone who is at risk); educating; raising awareness; and becoming a force for change.

However, while some participants found solace in this, others were wary of it. Differences in perceptions of the use of Facebook in this context and in ways of grieving were shown to cause tension within some families: it can ease grief for some but have the opposite effect for others. As our study revealed, suicide survivors have to negotiate the following pitfalls when engaging with online memorials: tailing off interest due to time lapse, feeling responsible for the thoughts and actions of others, censorship, unwanted interest from strangers, changes to the site without their consent, and removal of the page without their consent. Thus Facebook in this context has the potential for compounding grief or creating disenfranchised grief especially if users become overly attached to the sites, when activity on the site starts to wane, or when the site disappears.

Finally, while Facebook ensures that the deceased are remembered by a wide penumbra of friends, it also brings suicide much closer to everyone. And as the number of people exposed to the suicide death via Facebook increases along with the number of contributors, so does the potential for alternative narratives, conflict, and suicide contagion.

## Directions for Future Research and Implications for Postvention

The term suicide "contagion" refers to the process by which one suicide facilitates the occurrence of another (Gould, Wallenstein, & Davidson 1989) and is often used in relation to media reporting (e.g., the Werther effect; Philips, 1974). We have suggested that Facebook brings suicide closer to everyone and that exposure to suicide via Facebook could increase the potential for suicide contagion. Cerel et al. (2014) discussed how the conceptualization of "survivorship" (those who are bereaved by suicide) has broadened over recent years to account for the complexity of relationships with others who are connected to the deceased but not related. Their analysis takes into account those who are bereaved in the long and short term, those who are affected, and those who are exposed and calls for closer investigation of these categories in future studies. They argue that from a public health perspective we need to know how many people are exposed to suicide, who is impacted, and what the outcomes of this impact are. Our study suggests that further research into the use of Facebook in the aftermath of a suicide could provide clues to these questions. Social networks on the Facebook sites of those who have died by suicide (like the ones described in our study) bring together individuals from each of these categories in one place. This has two important implications: first, it may be possible through analysis of these networks online to identify who they are and, importantly, the outcomes of the impact. An example might be with the use of an online survey across Facebook populations to explore this.

Cerel et al. (2014) also argue that future research should investigate what interventions are most likely to work and how best to target these to the people who most need them. Again it is possible that Facebook could be instrumental in providing some of this information. Future research could examine ways in which Facebook can be harnessed to reach those in need of intervention (as was seen in some cases in our study) and what interventions will work.

The question of how long online identities can survive the deaths of those they represent (Brubaker et al., 2013) and whether (or why) users prefer to visit the "in-life" Facebook pages of the deceased rather than dedicated memorial sites needs more research. We have explored questions about the negative consequences of people starting to "forget" and what happens when they become overly attached to the sites, but more research in this area is needed along with implications for safe-guarding privacy and enfranchising and disenfranchising grief.

This is a new and burgeoning area where there is still much to learn. While the benefits of the use of Facebook in the aftermath of a suicide cannot be doubted, it nevertheless presents a number of problems which need addressing, particularly in the area of postvention (e.g., the ways in which Facebook may serve to delay, disrupt, distract from, and potentially exacerbate the grieving process). It is crucial that both bereavement workers and the bereaved are informed about the potential risks of utilizing Facebook for the purposes of aiding grief and memorialization and how to responsibly manage the continuing Facebook presence of those who have died by suicide.

## Acknowledgments

The authors would like to thank the Wellcome Trust and the University of Hull (UK) for supporting this research, as well as PAPYRUS Prevention of Young Suicide (a national UK charity working to prevent suicide in young people) and Survivors of Bereavement by Suicide (a self-help organization for suicide survivors in the United Kingdom) for promoting the research by listing a call for participants via their website and networks. Lastly, the authors would like to thank the participants themselves, without whom this research would not have been possible.

## Funding

This work was supported by the Wellcome Trust under grant number 102615/Z/13/Z.

## References

Bailey, L., Bell, J., & Kennedy, D. (2014). Continuing social presence of the dead: Exploring suicide bereavement through online memorialisation. *New Review of Hypermedia and Multimedia, 21*(1–2), 72–86. doi:10.1080/13614568.2014.983554

Bell, J., Bailey, L., & Kennedy, D. (2015). 'We do it to keep him alive': Bereaved individuals' experiences of online suicide memorials and continuing bonds. *Mortality, 20*(4), 375–389. Doi: doi:10.1080/13576275.2015.1083693

Bell, J., Stanley, N., Mallon, S., & Manthorpe, J. (2012). Life will never be the same again: Examining grief in survivors bereaved by young suicide. *Illness, Crisis, and Loss, 20*(1), 49–68. doi:10.2190/IL.20.1.e

Brubaker, J. R., Hayes, G. R., & Dourish, P. (2013). Beyond the grave: Facebook as a site for the expansion of death and mourning. *The Information Society, 29*, 152–163.

Cerel, J., McIntosh, J. L., Neimeyer, R. A., Maple, M., & Marshall, D. (2014). The continuum of "survivorship": Definitional issues in the aftermath of suicide. *Suicide and Life-Threatening Behavior, 44*(6), 591–600.

Chapple, A., & Ziebland, S. (2011). How the internet is changing the experience of bereavement by suicide: A qualitative study in the UK. *Health, 15*(2), 173–187.

Cooper, J. (1999). Ethical issues and their practical application in a psychological autopsy study of suicide. *Journal of Clinical Nursing, 8*(4), 467–475. doi:10.1046/j.1365-2702.1999.00276.x

Doka, K. (Ed.). (2002). *Disenfranchised grief: New directions, challenges, and strategies for practice.* Champaign, IL: Research Press.

Degroot, J. M. (2012). Maintaining relational continuity with the deceased on Facebook. *Omega, 65*, 195–212.

Ellenbogen, S., & Gratton, F. (2001). Do they suffer more? Reflections on research comparing suicide survivors to other survivors. *Suicide and Life-threatening Behavior, 31*, 83–90.

Glaser, B., & Strauss, A. (1967). *The discovery of grounded theory.* New York: Aldine.

Gould, M. S., Wallenstein, S., & Davidson, L. (1989). Suicide clusters: A critical review. *Suicide and Life-threatening Behavior, 19*, 17–29.

Green, J., & Thorogood, N. (2004). *Qualitative methods for health research.* London: Sage.

Hensley, L. D. (2012). Bereavement in online communities: Sources of and support for disenfranchised grief. In C. Sofka & I. N. Cupit (Eds.), *Dying, death, and grief in an online universe: For counselors and educators* (pp. 119–134). New York: Springer Publishing Company LLC.

Hollander, E. M. (2001). Cyber community in the valley of the shadow of death. *Journal of Loss and Trauma, 6*(2), 135–146. doi:10.1080/108114401753198007

Jacobs, S., & Prigerson, H. (2000). Psychotherapy of traumatic grief: A review of evidence for psychotherapeutic treatments. *Death Studies, 24*(6), 479–495. doi:10.1080/07481180050121462

Jordan, J. R. (2001). Is suicide bereavement different? A reassessment of the literature. *Suicide and Life-Threatening Behavior, 31*(1), 91–102. doi:10.1521/suli.31.1.91.21310

Jordan, J. R. (2008). Bereavement after suicide. *Psychiatric Annals, 38*, 679–685.

Jordan, J., & McIntosh, J. (Eds.). (2011). *Grief after suicide: Understanding the consequences and caring for the survivors.* New York: Routledge.

Maple, M., Edwards, H. E. Minichiello, V., & Plummer, D. (2013). Still part of the family: The importance of physical, emotional and spiritual memorial places and spaces for parents bereaved through the suicide death of their son or daughter. *Mortality, 18*(1), 54–71. doi:10.1080/13576275.2012.755158

Owens, C., Lambert, H., Lloyd, K., & Donovan, J. (2008). Tales of biographical disintegration: How parents make sense of their sons' suicides. *Sociology of Health and Illness, 30*(2), 237–254. doi:10.1111/j.1467–9566.2007.01034.x

Phillips, D. (1974). The influence of suggestion on suicide: Substantive and theoretical implications of the Werther effect. *American Sociological Review, 39*(3), 340–354.

Ratnarajah, D., & Maple, M. (2011). Learning from the bereaved by suicide in the face of stigma. In K. McKay & J. Schlimme (Eds.), *Making sense of suicide.* Oxfordshire: Interdisciplinary Press.

Rosenblatt, P. C. (1983). *Bitter, bitter tears: Nineteenth century diarists and twentieth century grief theories.* Minneapolis: University of Minnesota Press.

Suler, J. (2004). The online disinhibition effect. *Cyber Psychology and Behavior, 7*(3), 321–326. doi:10.1089/1094931041291295

Walter, T. (2015). Old mourners, new mourners: Online memorial culture as a chapter in the history of mourning. *New Review of Hypermedia and Multimedia, 21*, 10–24. doi:10.1080/13614568.2104.983555

# 7

# Suicide and Newer Media: The Good, the Bad, and the Googly

*Jane Pirkis, Katherine Mok, and Jo Robinson*

Views about suicide and the Internet are quite polarized. Some people are very positive about the Internet's potential as a medium for suicide prevention ("the good"). Others are adamant that the Internet can cause harm, particularly for already-vulnerable individuals who are searching for information about suicide methods ("the bad"). Our own view is that the influence of the Internet is much more nuanced than this; it is a volatile medium that presents a plethora of both positive and negative content to at-risk individuals who are often ambivalent about suicide and interpret these messages in a variety of ways ('the Googly'[1]). This chapter presents the evidence for these different points of view. Several other reviews have also been written in this area (Christensen, Batterham, & O'Dea, 2014; Daine et al., 2013; Jacob, Scourfield, & Evans, 2014; Mok, Jorm, & Pirkis, 2015; Robinson, Cox et al., 2015).

## The Good

Newer forms of media have great potential as conduits for suicide prevention, not least because of their visibility, accessibility, and reach. A multitude of suicide prevention apps and websites exist, varying in terms of what they provide and how they offer it. Aguirre, McCoy, and Roan (2013) recently searched iTunes and the Google Play Store for suicide prevention apps for Apple and Android devices and found twenty-seven. Recupero, Harms, and Noble (2008) took the top "hits" identified by inputting various suicide-related terms into a range of search engines in 2007 and found 373 unique web pages, 29 percent of which were coded as having an "anti-suicide" or suicide prevention slant. Biddle and colleagues used a similar search strategy in 2007 and 2014, returning 480 hits in each year (Biddle et al., 2016; Biddle, Donovan, Hawton, Kapur, & Gunnell, 2008). Sites relating to suicide prevention and/or offering support and sites that actively discouraged suicide accounted for 25 percent of all hits in the former year and 17 percent in the latter.

As noted, the content of these Internet-based suicide prevention platforms varies considerably (Robinson, Rodrigues, Fisher, & Herrman, 2014). One way of thinking about this is that they sit on two sets of dimensions: passive to active/interactive; and informative/educational to interventionist, although obviously some apps and websites feature characteristics of more than one dimension. Figure 7.1 shows the kind of content that relates to these dimensions.

The passive–informative/educational websites and apps (upper left quadrant, figure 7.1) provide users with a range of information and

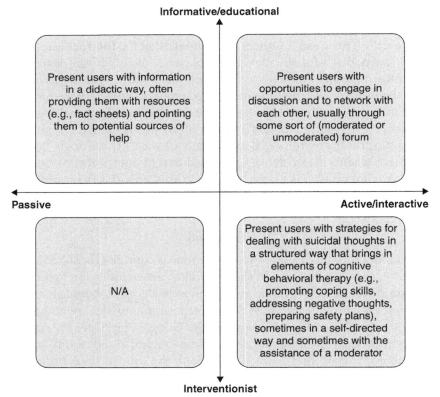

**Figure 7.1.** A dimensional perspective of suicide prevention apps and websites based on their content.

resources designed to educate users about suicide and its prevention (e.g., presenting facts and figures, dispel myths, providing advice about warning signs, and directing users to help services); this information is presented in a didactic way, with no opportunities for interaction. The active/interactive–informative/educational platforms (upper right quadrant, figure 7.1) are also designed to further users' understanding of suicide, but they are much more interactive in nature and encourage discussion and networking between users via chat rooms, discussion boards, and other forums, some of which are moderated by professionals. The active/interactive–interventionist websites and apps (lower right quadrant, figure 7.1) have been designed to have a more therapeutic focus, taking users through a structured series of steps—usually based on the principles of cognitive behavioral therapy (CBT)—that are designed to teach them strategies for dealing with suicidal thinking. Passive–interventionist websites and apps (lower left quadrant, figure 7.1) do not really exist; for platforms to be interventionist they must, by definition, also be active/interactive.

Of the three types of websites and apps listed above, only two have been subject to any evaluation, but there is increasing evidence of their positive impacts. The benefits of active/interactive–informative/educational platforms have been explored in a number of studies, most of which have focused on forum use, with researchers either analyzing the discussion that takes place or interviewing or surveying forum users (Baker & Fortune, 2008; Barak & Dolev-Cohen, 2006; Eichenberg, 2008; Jones et al., 2011; Smithson et al., 2011; Whitlock, Powers, & Eckenrode, 2006). These studies suggest that forums allow suicidal individuals to make connections with others facing similar situations and that users find this support useful as a coping mechanism and as a means of reducing their levels of distress. Forum users do not always seek advice, but the interactions that take place on forums can reinforce positive behaviors, particularly when members of the online community congratulate each other for not engaging in suicidal behaviors and encourage each other to seek professional help.

The active/interactive–interventionist websites and apps are also beginning to show promise as an effective and efficient means of combating suicide. As noted above, they usually draw on therapeutic approaches like CBT that have a well-established evidence base in face-to-face settings. Delivery via the Internet has advantages over delivery in more traditional settings that include accessibility and acceptability (Robinson et al., 2016; Robinson, Hetrick et al., 2015), and randomized controlled trials are beginning to emerge in this area. van Spijker and colleagues conducted one such trial in Holland which showed that a modularized, unguided, and CBT-informed web-based intervention designed to reduce suicidal thinking in adults was not only effective in doing so, but also cost-effective (van Spijker, Majo, Smit, van Straten, & Kerkhof, 2012; van Spijker, van Straten, & Kerkhof, 2014). Other trials are currently underway that test different modalities (e.g., apps vs. websites) and different types of intervention (e.g., moderated vs. unmoderated) designed for different target groups (e.g., adolescents and indigenous people vs. adults)—see, for example, Robinson, Hetrick et al. (2014) and Shand, Ridani, Tighe, and Christensen (2013).

## The Bad

A number of authors have warned that the unregulated nature of the Internet means that it may unduly influence individuals to engage in suicidal behavior, especially if they are already vulnerable. In particular, these authors have expressed concerns about "pro-suicide" websites (that explicitly endorse suicide by providing information about how to obtain and/or use particular suicide methods or by promoting discussion that encourages suicide), noting that the potential risks associated with these may outweigh any benefits from the positive websites and apps (Aitken, 2009; Luxton, June, & Fairall, 2012; Thompson, 1999; Westerlund, 2011). "Pro-suicide" websites are certainly relatively easy to find. In the studies described above, Recupero et al. (2008) found that 11 percent of all the sites they identified in 2007 were "pro-suicide" sites, and Biddle and colleagues reported similar proportions (9 percent) in both 2007 and 2016 (Biddle et al., 2008, 2016).

We know that explicit descriptions of suicide in newspaper and television reports can influence those who read or watch these media (Pirkis & Blood, 2010), so it makes sense that pernicious representations of suicide on "pro-suicide" websites would also have an impact. This impact may even be amplified because of the Internet's reach. There is a growing body of literature to support this contention.

Various cross-sectional studies have been conducted in this area, some at an ecological level and some at an individual level. The ecological studies have typically looked at the numbers of online suicide-related terms and suicide rates—sometimes in general and sometimes with respect to particular suicide methods—and found them to be correlated (Gunn & Lester, 2013; Hagihara, Miyazaki, & Abe, 2012; McCarthy, 2010). The individual-level studies have tended to involve community-based surveys and have usually found that those who engage in suicide-related Internet use report higher levels of suicidal ideation than those who don't (Aiba, Matsui, Kikkawa, Matsumoto, & Tachimori, 2011; Harris, McLean, & Sheffield, 2009; Katsumata, Matsumoto, Kitani, & Takeshima, 2008; Mok, Jorm, & Pirkis, in press-b).

The cross-sectional nature of these studies makes it difficult to determine whether the observed associations are causal, so evidence has been sought using other study designs. At the most basic level, these take the form of case studies linking an individual's suicidal act to his or her exposure to a particular "pro-suicide" website. In some instances, computers of individuals who have died have been searched and websites giving advice about their suicide method of choice have been found "bookmarked" (Athanaselis, Stefanidou, Karakoukis, & Koutselinis, 2002). On other occasions, individuals have presented to health services—often in a critical state following self-poisoning or self-injury—and reported to staff that they purchased the means of harm or sourced information about it from a particular website (Beatson, Hosty, & Smith, 2000). Cases of suicide pacts that have been facilitated by particular websites have also been documented (Mishara & Weisstub, 2007).

Several authors have tried to go beyond the case study approach and seek evidence for Internet involvement in the suicides of larger groups of individuals. A key example is a large-scale audit done by Gunnell et al. (2012). These authors took suicide inquest reports from twelve British coronial jurisdictions over a three-year period in the mid-2000s and examined them for evidence that the person who had died was influenced by material he or she had found on the Internet. They found definitive evidence for this influence in 1.5 percent of suicides, but noted that this was likely to be an underestimate because it relied on explicit enquiries about the Internet having been made during the coronial process.

The use of forums for "pro-suicide" purposes has received considerable attention in the literature, usually being examined by studies that have elicited responses from forum users or analyzed their posts (Barak & Dolev-Cohen, 2006; Dunlop, More, & Romer, 2011; Eichenberg, 2008; Smithson et al., 2011; Whitlock et al., 2006). These studies have identified a number of undesirable outcomes for young people going online for suicidal purposes. These include individuals being encouraged to view suicide as a normal and/or acceptable course of action, advised to hide their suicidal thoughts and intentions from others rather than find help, guided toward using particular suicide methods, and invited to form suicide pacts.

## The Googly

As we foreshadowed at the beginning of this chapter, our own view is that thinking about the influence of the Internet on suicidal individuals as all good or all bad is too blunt an approach. The Internet is a complex medium, and suicidal individuals—as creators and recipients of content on that medium—are also complex. This more nuanced view of the area may help to advance suicide prevention efforts in this area.

The searches conducted by Recupero et al. (2008), Biddle et al. (2008), and Biddle et al. (2016) outlined above identified both suicide prevention websites and "pro-suicide" websites. There is an argument that classifying whole sites in this way misses some of the complexity of suicidal content on the Internet. For this reason, we conducted a study of our own in 2014 to examine the content that someone searching the Internet for information might find (Mok, Jorm, & Pirkis, Submitted). We modified the method used by Biddle et al. (2008) and entered a range of suicide-related terms into four search engines, retrieving the top ten hits from each search. We rolled the hits up into websites, and then examined the content of the top ten10 websites. We considered the whole website if it was created by a single author, and individual pages if they were created by different authors. Where websites were interactive and included comments from users, we limited our analysis to the first fifty comments. Our findings were complex. For example, most sites provided information on suicide methods and acted as a springboard for discussions about particular methods among users, some of which was positive (e.g., steering individuals away from using a given method) and some of which was not (e.g., suggesting which methods might be more likely to be fatal). Similarly, although explicit encouragement of suicide was rare and there were many comments that were supportive and life-affirming, there were also often instances where dismissive or hostile responses to individuals' situations were posted.

Thinking about the Internet in terms of individual websites may also be limiting. In recognition of this, Kemp and Collings (2011) conducted a study which examined the connections between websites with suicidal content. They identified a "seed" set of websites via a Google search, using various suicide-related terms. They then "crawled" these sites to create a "connectivity" database for each search term, retaining those seed sites that were linked to or from at least two discrete sites. They then used a modified version of the classification developed by Biddle et al. (2008) to categorize the retained seed sites and used a set of algorithms to quantify the linkages between them. They found that pro-suicide sites were uncommon and tended to be isolated in network terms (i.e., not linked to other sites). By contrast, they found that sites with more preventive or factual content were relatively well connected.

The above finding is relevant in the context of the behavior of individuals who go online to search for information about suicide. Several studies have shown that such individuals traverse a number of websites in the process. For example, Harris et al. (2009) conducted an online survey of suicidal individuals who used the Internet for suicide-related purposes and found that they typically visited both websites that could be classified as having a suicide prevention focus and websites that were regarded as "pro-suicide." This perhaps reflects the ambivalence associated with suicidal thinking that has been described elsewhere in the literature (O'Connor et al., 2012).

Individuals obviously interpret and respond to information in different ways. This, combined with the fact that they may be exposed to a mix of positive and negative information during any Internet session (both within and across websites), means that it is not surprising that people report different impacts from viewing suicide-related content online. We recently conducted a study in which we surveyed 102 young Australian 18–24-year-olds who had gone online for suicide-related reasons in the past twelve months (Mok, Jorm, & Pirkis, in press-a). Overall, respondents reported that their online experiences were associated with a decrease in suicidal thoughts and behaviors, but the orientation of the websites they visited had no bearing on this. They described positive and negative experiences, even for similar forms of Internet use (e.g., some found that reading detailed information about a particular suicide method deterred them from using it, whereas others found that doing this gave them confidence that if they chose to use it in the future, it would be lethal).

## Implications for Practice

The complexity of the influence of the Internet has implications for practice. Various ways of promoting good and minimizing harm have been suggested, all of which require careful thought. For example, some authors have suggested that guidelines should be developed for those who create web content (Maloney et al., 2014), based on those that have been developed for journalists and editors working in the traditional media (Pirkis, Blood, Beautrais, Burgess, & Skehan, 2006).

Various guidelines have already been rolled out, such as those of the Entertainment Industries Council (2014) in the United States. There is certainly a role for these guidelines, but they are unlikely to be viewed by the majority of "average" users who are, for example, taking part in discussions on forums, and they are likely to be ignored by those who post "pro-suicide" content online with malicious intent.

Another solution that has been proposed is legislation that bans "pro-suicide" material in an online environment. This has generally been regarded as too difficult (Mehlum, 2000; Mishara & Weisstub, 2007), for reasons that include the borderless nature of the Internet. Australia is unique in having introduced legislation of this kind, making it a punishable offence to disseminate material designed to counsel or incite suicide. There are suggestions that the legislation has led to the removal of entire websites that might be regarded as "pro-suicide" (Pirkis, Neal, Dare, Blood, & Studdert, 2009), but our recent study has shown that there is still potentially harmful material being posted online that is accessible to Australian Internet users, often in the context of mixed discussions on forums (Mok et al., submitted).

Search engine optimization strategies have also been proposed as an approach. These strategies are designed to increase the chances that someone searching for suicidal information online will find preventive or supportive information, rather than "pro-suicide" material. The fact that sites with a preventive orientation are well linked (Kemp & Collings, 2011) and the fact that those who seek suicide-related information online often display ambivalent searching behavior (Harris et al., 2009) suggests that there may be mileage in this approach. Again, however, it will be imperfect because of the fact that positive and negative content is simultaneously available on the same sites (Mok et al., submitted).

Suicide prevention organizations have a responsibility for ensuring that their own online activities have their desired effect, and their monitoring of this represents another strategy. There are certainly some excellent examples of suicide prevention organizations using the Internet to positive effect. For example, some have developed a high profile on social media (Luxton et al., 2012) and put in place rapid response strategies when individuals post content that indicates they may be at imminent risk (Ogburn, Messias, & Buckley, 2011; Ruder, Hatch, Ampanozi, Thali, & Fischer, 2015). There are also examples of paradoxical effects, however, such as that observed by Smithson et al. (2011) when they set up a forum in which self-harming young people could communicate with their peers and a range of health professionals.

They found that many of the online interactions between young people "normalized" self-harm, treating it as a routine and acceptable response to stressful life events.

The above strategies all involve influencing the kind of content that suicidal individuals might be exposed to. A final solution that has been proposed approaches the issue from the other end and involves educating Internet users about safe ways to talk about suicide online. To the best of our knowledge there are no published studies that have examined the impact of this approach. However, we are currently conducting a small study along these lines that comprises two components (Robinson, Bailey et al., 2015). The first involves providing education to participants about safe and potentially unsafe ways of talking about suicide online and the second involves working in direct partnership with the participants to develop safe and acceptable suicide prevention messaging that can be delivered via social media platforms. The project is still in its infancy but early evaluation data indicate that participants do feel better able to talk safely about suicide online and better able to help others to do the same.

## Conclusions

The Internet is far-reaching and very influential, and the information available on it changes rapidly. Individuals who search for suicide-related content online may interpret and be influenced by the information they find in different ways, depending on a range of factors, including their current mood state. Something that they skip over at one point may be extremely salient for them at another. This complexity is amplified by the fact that suicidal users of the Internet are also the creators of content on it. The suicide prevention sector and the online media sector must work together to maximize the preventive capacity of the Internet and minimize any harms that it might cause.

## Note

1. We have used the term "the Googly" to describe this more complex and less predictable influence that can be exerted by the Internet. The term has obvious meaning in relation to searching the Internet, but is also used in cricket to refer to a particular type of delivery used by a spin bowler, in which the ball moves in a different direction to that expected by the batsman, introducing an element of surprise.

## References

Aguirre, R., McCoy, M., & Roan, M. (2013). Development of guidelines from a study of suicide prevention mobile applications (apps). *Journal of Technology in Human Services, 31*(3), 269–293.

Aiba, M., Matsui, Y., Kikkawa, T., Matsumoto, T., & Tachimori, H. (2011). Factors influencing suicidal ideation among Japanese adults: From the national survey by the Cabinet Office. *Psychiatry and Clinical Neurosciences, 65*(5), 468–475.

Aitken, A. (2009). Suicide and the internet. *Bereavement Care, 28*(2), 40–41.

Athanaselis, S., Stefanidou, M., Karakoukis, N., & Koutselinis, A. (2002). Asphyxial death by ether inhalation and plastic-bag suffocation instructed by the press and the Internet. *Journal of Medical Internet Research, 4*(3), e18.

Baker, D., & Fortune, S. (2008). Understanding self-harm and suicide websites: A qualitative interview study of young adult website users. *Crisis, 29*(3), 118–122.

Barak, A., & Dolev-Cohen, M. (2006). Does activity level in online support groups for distressed adolescents determine emotional relief. *Counselling and Psychotherapy Research, 6*(3), 186–190.

Beatson, S., Hosty, G., & Smith, S. (2000). Suicide and the internet. *Psychiatric Bulletin, 24*(11), 434–434.

Biddle, L., Derges, J., Mars, B., Heron, J., Donovan, J., Potokar, J. . . . Gunnell, D. (2016). Suicide and the Internet: Changes in the accessibility of suicide-related information between 2007 and 2014. *Journal of Affective Disorders, 190*, 370–375.

Biddle, L., Donovan, J., Hawton, K., Kapur, N., & Gunnell, D. (2008). Suicide and the Internet. *British Medical Journal, 336*, 800–802.

Christensen, H., Batterham, P., & O'Dea, B. (2014). E-health interventions for suicide prevention. *International Journal of Environmental Research and Public Health, 11*(8), 8193–8212.

Daine, K., Hawton, K., Singaravelu, V., Stewart, A., Simkin, S., & Montgomery, P. (2013). The power of the web: A systematic review of studies of the influence of the internet on self-harm and suicide in young people. *PLOS One, 8*(10), e77555.

Dunlop, S. M., More, E., & Romer, D. (2011). Where do youth learn about suicides on the Internet, and what influence does this have on suicidal ideation. *Journal of Child Psychology and Psychiatry, 52*(10), 1073–1080.

Eichenberg, C. (2008). Internet message boards for suicidal people: A typology of users. *Cyberpsychology and Behavior, 11*(1), 107–113.

Entertainment Industries Council. (2014). Social Media Guidelines for Mental Health Promotion and Suicide Prevention. Retrieved from http://www.eiconline.org/teamup/wp-content/files/teamup-mental-health-social-media-guidelines.pdf

Gunn, J., & Lester, D. (2013). Using google searches on the internet to monitor suicidal behavior. *Journal of Affective Disorders, 148*(2), 411–412.

Gunnell, D., Bennewith, O., Kapur, N., Simkin, S., Cooper, J., & Hawton, K. (2012). The use of the Internet by people who die by suicide in England: A cross sectional study. *Journal of Affective Disorders, 141*(2–3), 480–483.

Hagihara, A., Miyazaki, S., & Abe, T. (2012). Internet suicide searches and the incidence of suicide in young people in Japan. *European Archives of Psychiatry and Clinical Neuroscience, 262*(1), 39–46.

Harris, K. M., McLean, J. P., & Sheffield, J. (2009). Examining suicide-risk individuals who go online for suicide-related purposes. *Archives of Suicide Research, 13*, 264–276.

Jacob, N., Scourfield, J., & Evans, R. (2014). Suicide prevention via the Internet: A descriptive review. *Crisis, 35*(4), 261–267.

Jones, J., Sharkey, S., Ford, T., Emmens, T., Hewis, E., Smithson, J. . . . Owens, C. (2011). Online discussion forums for young people who self-harm: User views. *The Psychiatrist, 35*, 364–368.

Katsumata, Y., Matsumoto, T., Kitani, M., & Takeshima, T. (2008). Electronic media use and suicidal ideation in Japanese adolescents. *Psychiatry and Clinical Neurosciences, 62*(6), 744–746.

Kemp, C., & Collings, S. (2011). Hyperlinked suicide: Assessing the prominence and accessibility of suicide websites. *Crisis, 32*(3), 143–151.

Luxton, D., June, J., & Fairall, J. (2012). Social media and suicide: A public health perspective. *American Journal of Public Health, 102*(2), s195–s200.

Maloney, J., Pfuhlmann, B., Arensman, E., Coffey, C., Gusmao, R., Postuvan, V. . . . Schmidtke, A. (2014). How to adjust media recommendations on reporting suicidal behaviour to new media developments. *Archives of Suicide Research, 18*(2), 156–169.

McCarthy, M. J. (2010). Internet monitoring of suicide risk in the population. *Journal of Affective Disorders, 122*(3), 277–279.

Mehlum, L. (2000). The Internet, suicide, and suicide prevention. *Crisis, 21*(4), 186–188.

Mishara, B., & Weisstub, D. (2007). Ethical, legal, and practical issues in the control and regulation of suicide promotion and assistance over the internet. *Suicide and Life Threatening Behavior, 37*(1), 58–66.

Mok, K., Jorm, A., & Pirkis, J. (2015). Suicide-related Internet use: A review. *Australian and New Zealand Journal of Psychiatry, 49*(8), 697–705.

Mok, K., Jorm, A., & Pirkis, J. (In press-a). The perceived impact of suicide-related internet use: A survey of young Australians who have gone online for suicide-related reasons. *Digital Health.*

Mok, K., Jorm, A., & Pirkis, J. (In press-b). Who goes online for suicide-related reasons? A comparison of suicidal people who use the Internet for suicide-related reasons and those who do not. *Crisis.*

Mok, K., Jorm, A., & Pirkis, J. (Submitted). Availability of information on suicide methods online: A search engine web analysis.

O'Connor, S., Jobes, D., Yeargin, M., FitzGerald, M., Rodríguez, V., Conrad, A., & Lineberry, T. (2012). A cross-sectional investigation of the suicidal spectrum: Typologies of suicidality based on ambivalence about living and dying. *Comprehensive Psychiatry, 53*, 461–467.

Ogburn, K., Messias, E., & Buckley, P. (2011). New-age patient communications through social networks. *General Hospital Psychiatry, 33*(200), e1–3.

Pirkis, J., & Blood, R. W. (2010). *Suicide and the news and information media.* Retrieved from Canberra http://www.mindframe-media.info/__data/assets/pdf_file/0016/5164/Pirkis-and-Blood-2010,-Suicide-and-the-news-and-information-media.pdf

Pirkis, J., Blood, R. W., Beautrais, A., Burgess, P., & Skehan, J. (2006). Media guidelines on the reporting of suicide. *Crisis, 27*, 82–87.

Pirkis, J., Neal, L., Dare, A., Blood, R. W., & Studdert, D. (2009). Legal bans on pro-suicide web sites: an early retrospective from Australia. *Suicide & Life Threat Behavior, 39*(2), 190–193. doi:10.1521/suli.2009.39.2.190

Recupero, P. R., Harms, S. E., & Noble, J. M. (2008). Googling suicide: Surfing for suicide information on the Internet. *Journal of Clinical Psychiatry, 69*(6), 878–888.

Robinson, J., Bailey, E., S., H., Cox, G., Pirkis, J., Ftanou, M. . . . Skehan, J. (2015). *Suicide and social media.* Paper presented at the 28th World Congress of the International Association for Suicide Prevention, Montreal.

Robinson, J., Cox, G., Bailey, E., Hetrick, S., Rodrigues, M., Fisher, S., & Herrman, H. (2015). Social media and suicide prevention: A systematic review. *Early Intervention in Psychiatry, 10*(2), 103–121.

Robinson, J., Hetrick, S., Cox, G., Bendall, S., Yuen, H.-P., Yung, A., & Pirkis, J. (2016). Can an Internet-based intervention reduce suicidal ideation, depression and hopelessness among secondary school students: results from a pilot study. *Early Intervention in Psychiatry, 10*(1), 28–35.

Robinson, J., Hetrick, S., Cox, G., Bendall, S., Yung, A., & Pirkis, J. (2015). The safety and acceptability of delivering an online intervention to secondary students at risk of suicide: Findings from a pilot study. *Early Intervention in Psychiatry, 9*(12), 498–506.

Robinson, J., Hetrick, S., Cox, G., Bendall, S., Yung, A., Templer, K. . . . Yuen, H. -P. (2014). Study protocol: The development of a randomised controlled trial testing the effects of an online intervention among school students at risk of suicide. *BMC Psychiatry, 14,* 155.

Robinson, J., Rodrigues, M., Fisher, S., & Herrman, H. (2014). *Suicide and social media.* Melbourne: Young and Well Cooperative Research Center.

Ruder, T. D., Hatch, G. M., Ampanozi, G., Thali, M. J., & Fischer, N. (2015). Suicide announcement on Facebook. *Crisis, 32*(5). 280–282.

Shand, F., Ridani, R., Tighe, J., & Christensen, H. (2013). The effectiveness of a suicide prevention app for indigenous Australian youths: Study protocol for a randomized controlled trial. *Trials, 14,* 396.

Smithson, J., Sharkey, S., Hewis, E., Jones, R., Emmens, T., Ford, T., & Owens, C. (2011). Problem presentation and responses on an online forum for young people who self-harm. *Discourse Studies, 13*(4), 487–501.

Thompson, S. (1999). The Internet and its potential influence on suicide. *Psychiatric Bulletin, 23*(8), 449–451.

van Spijker, B., Majo, M., Smit, F., van Straten, A., & Kerkhof, A. (2012). Reducing suicidal ideation: Cost-effectiveness analysis of a randomized controlled trial of unguided web-based self-help. *Journal of Medical Internet Research, 14*(5), e141.

van Spijker, B., van Straten, A., & Kerkhof, A. (2014). Effectiveness of online self-help for suicidal thoughts: Results of a randomised controlled trial. *Plos One, 9*(2), e90118.

Westerlund, M. (2011). The production of pro-suicide content on the internet: A counter-discourse activity. *New Media and Society, 14*(5), 764–780.

Whitlock, J., Powers, J., & Eckenrode, J. (2006). The virtual cutting edge: The Internet and adolescent self-injury. *Developmental Psychology, 42*(3), 407.

# 8

# The Heroic and the Criminal, the Beautiful and the Ugly: Suicide Reflected in the Mirror of the Arts

*Karolina Krysinska and Karl Andriessen*

In his comprehensive review of the iconography of suicide, Cutter (1983) identified six self-injury themes prevalent in the Western art after Renaissance (i.e., after 1350): heroic themes, suicide as a stigmatized act, irrational themes, depressive themes, ambivalent themes, and suicide as "a cry for help." Cutter based his classification on three criteria: the motivation of the suicide, the morality of suicide, and feelings induced in the viewer.

The *heroic theme* (1484–1844) presented suicide as a rational and reasonable solution to contemporary dilemmas and as a good behavior, affirmative of virtue. The viewers' reaction was admiration for the hero or the heroine, and they were encouraged to follow the virtuous example. This theme was based on historical or mythological accounts of suicide in the context of patriotism (e.g., Hasdrubal's wife), the aftermath of a military failure (e.g., Ajax), sacrifice for a greater cause (e.g., Samson), devotion to ethics (e.g., Socrates, Cato), expiation of dishonor (e.g., Lucretia), preservation of dignity (e.g., Sophonisba, Cleopatra, Dido), and loss of a lover (e.g., Pyramus and Thisbe, Hero and Leander).

The theme of *suicide as a stigmatized act* (1660–1854) seems to be opposite to the heroic theme, but both coexisted quite comfortably for almost two centuries. The stigmatized suicide was conceptualized (in line with the Church's view of suicide as a mortal sin) as an evil end befitting an evil life motivated by a rational pursuit of immoral goals. The intended reaction of viewers was rejection and contempt. The advent of the *irrational theme* (1827–1880) followed the Industrial Revolution and the changing conceptualization of mental illness, especially consideration of social and psychological factors in its etiology and in the treatment of psychiatric patients. Such changes resulted in adopting a more neutral and relative moral position toward suicide, reducing the stigma, and putting an emphasis on the irrationality of the act, now viewed as unreasonable means to a desired end. The viewers' reaction was sympathy or pity toward the suicide rather than condemnation.

Some of the nineteenth-century suicide art themes continued into the next century but, "(. . .) in the 20th Century, representation of suicide became truly problematic. In the godless remains of Europe after World War I, suicide's meanings were primarily linked with depression; subsequently suicidal representation took on certain ambivalence, as if life itself were deemed pointless. It was in Germany, and above all in the anxious images of Expressionism, that the extreme motif of suicide was most prevalent in the first part of the twentieth century" (Brown, 2001, p. 201). In Cutter's classification, images of suicide created in the twentieth century (at least until the 1960s which was the last decade discussed in his book) can be grouped into three major, partly overlapping themes: depressive (1887–1927), ambivalent (1930–61), and suicide as a "cry for help" (1938–67). The *depressive theme* presented suicide in a morally neutral manner and considered apathy as the main motivation behind the act. The viewers' reaction was a feeling of regret, sadness, and pity. The other two themes, *ambivalence* and *suicide as a "cry for help"* present suicide in a morally neutral manner and see the motivation behind the death either as explicable (ambivalent theme) or obscure ("cry for help"). The ambivalent theme stressed the shock value of the art, evoking mixed reactions in viewers and drawing their attention to the painful sense of unhappiness experienced by suicides and their ambivalent wish to live mixed with the desire to die.

Still, the twentieth- and twenty-first-century iconography suicide escaped the neat and relatively clear-cut categories prevalent in earlier centuries. Modern suicide imagery has escaped the confines of high culture and has merged into a kaleidoscope of popular mass media such as film, television, newspapers, magazines, photography, music, and Internet art. Suicide as tragic and comical, realistic and metaphorical, in stories of real-life tragedies and commercialized pornography of violence became a part of the everyday landscape of popular culture. One of the icons of the twentieth-century art is Andy Warhol's *Marilyn Diptych* (1962), voted as the third most influential painting in the history of art after Marcel Duchamp's *Fountain* and Pablo Picasso's *Les Demoiselles d'Avignon* (Higgins, 2004). The series of color and black-and-white silkscreen paintings of Marilyn Monroe were made soon after her death in August 1962 and were based on a publicity photograph from the movie *Niagara* shot in 1953. According to the art critics, "Warhol found in Monroe a fusion of two of his consistent themes: death and the cult of celebrity. By repeating the image, he evokes her ubiquitous presence in the media. The contrast of vivid color with black and white, and the effect of fading in the right panel are suggestive of the star's mortality" (TATE Online, 2004).

It is clear that the meanings and visual representations of suicide have been changing over centuries reflecting the evolving cultural and philosophical understanding of the behavior and attitudes toward it, with frequently coexisting contradictory meanings and representations. To better understand the links between suicide, the arts, and the broader sociocultural context, this chapter will focus on three (partly overlapping) issues: the semantics of suicide, the gender of suicide, and the esthetics of suicide, and it will conclude by presenting some thoughts regarding possible ways in which these three might have an impact on suicidal behavior of an individual.

## The Semantics of Suicide

Looking at the major themes in the representation of suicide in Western art from antiquity to the modern times and their evolution and revivals, one can hardly fail to notice that both literally and metaphorically "suicide has been pictured as beautiful, heroic, bold, as well as ugly, criminal, cowardly" (Brown, 2001, p. 10). The very word "suicide" was coined only in mid-seventeenth century and before that terms such as "self-killing" were used. Changing words affects the meanings of the behavior (Edwards & Osborne, 2005; van Hooff, 1990). This cultural relativity of suicide has also been stressed by Shneidman in his definition of suicide—"Currently in the Western world, suicide is a conscious act of self-induced annihilation, best understood as a multidimensional malaise in a needful individual who defines an issue for which the suicide is perceived as the best solution" (Shneidman, 1985, p. 203). By using the word "currently" Shneidman stresses its "contextual endeavor," the importance of the times in which a particular suicide occurs and in which it is studied. Consequently, it is difficult (and often simply inappropriate) to cluster together or compare actions of ancient Romans such as Cato or Seneca, biblical kings such as Saul and Samson, semi-mythical heroines from antiquity represented by Lucretia, and "fallen Victorian women" drowning themselves in the River Thames.

Indeed, an analysis of iconography of suicide calls for consideration of a wider sociocultural and historical context embedded in the wider art-historical problem of textual reading, and "the issue of representation assumes the coexistence of a variety of texts, visual, verbal, semiotic, philosophic and political, and demands a diversity of approaches" (Brown, 2001, p. 11). Edwards and Osborne (2005) write about the "scenography of suicide" and its "moral and semantic framing," "Suicides can be staged in many different ways: as theatre, as gesture, as refusal, as affirmation, and as pedagogy. In this sense suicide is not just an 'act' but at its limit can be a kind of 'ethical work,' a moment of truth that is the culmination, as the Stoics would have it, of an on-going labour of learning how to die. (. . .) We still have too little sense of the changing ethical and discursive practices that surround suicide and especially the senses in which such practices presuppose suicide as a particular kind of performance with particular kinds of intended effects" (p. 174).

Still, one has to be aware that "to examine images with a view to revealing how cultural attitudes towards suicide are reflected in art, denies the images a creative role" (Brown, 2001, p. 9). Indeed, there seems to be a reciprocal relationship between suicide imagery in the Western art and its concurrent cultural and social meaning(s). Henry Wallis's painting *The Death of Chatterton* (1856) and John Everett Millais's *Ophelia* (1851–52) not only showed romantic suicides, but were artistic milestones contributing to the romantic notion of suicide in the literature and in general public's attitude to self-inflicted death (Fontana, 1998; Marchwinski, 1987). Eduard Manet in *The Suicide* (1877), an image of a lonely a man who had just shot himself, stripped the death of its heroic connotations, presented its realistic details, and did not provide any clues to the question "Why?" thus challenging his contemporary late nineteenth-century audience used to seeing heroic suicides in historical paintings (Ilg, 2002).

An English poet and forger of antiquities, Thomas Chatterton (1752–70) who poisoned himself with arsenic at the age of 17 became a hero of the Romantic Movement. His death became an icon of romantic suicide and was immortalized by Henry Wallis's painting *The Death of Chatterton* (1856) showing the dead body of the beautiful young poet seductively draped over a bed. An earlier image of Chatterton's suicide, John Flaxman's ink drawings *Chatterton Taking the Bowl of Poison from the Spirit of Despair* (or *Despair Offering a Bowl of Poison to Chatterton*,

1775) and its several versions, started the "visual cult of Chatterton" which turned him into a martyr of art and a victim of society guilty of alienating a romantic artist (Brown, 2001; Williams, 1960). Chatterton's death contributed to the debate on causes of suicide by moving focus from reason and intellect linked to heroic suicide to impulse, intuition, mental illness, and depression, an approach flagged in the seventeenth century by Robert Burton in his book *The Anatomy of Melancholy*. The female equivalent of Wallis's *The Death of Chatterton* was John Everett Millais's *Ophelia* (1851–52).[1] This Pre-Raphaelite painting of drowned Ophelia, a heroine of Shakespeare's *Hamlet*, became the iconic prototype of romantic female suicide (Fontana, 1998). Ophelia's death became a popular subject of paintings and drawings, and Cutter (1983) listed eleven artists from mid-eighteenth century to mid-twentieth century who painted it, including Henry Fuseli (1770), Eugène Delacroix (1844), Leonor Fini (1938), and David Irnshaw (1980).

Manet's *The Suicide* (1877), one of his paintings showing the threat of death and loneliness of modern mankind, revolutionalized the Western iconography of suicide (Harris, 2008a; Ilg, 2002). The painting shows a man with indistinct facial features lying on his back on a bed with a revolver, which he had just used to shot himself, still in his hand. Such image of suicide did not fit the rules of academic historical painting which were prevalent at the time and which regarded suicide as a "privilege of a *grand homme*, of the hero, who in this way concluded the irreconcilable clash between his ideals and his convictions on one side, and reality on the other" (Ilg, 2002, p. 181). Manet's anonymous male suicide[2] is very different from the celebrity suicides painted by masters of the historical genre. Unlike David's Seneca or Delacroix's Sardanapalus, he is not a historical figure serving as a didactic example of heroism and virtue, and the viewer is deprived of clues or narrations regarding the motives and circumstances of the death which abound in the other paintings.

Images of suicide have been used across centuries to underline and reinforce moral, social, and political values and ideologies of the time. In antiquity suicide was a part of "iconography of power" (van Hooff, 1990), presenting images of defeated enemies who preferred to kill themselves rather than be captured (*suicides obsidionaux*), such as the famous marble statue of *Ludovisi Gaul and His Wife* (or *Gaul Slaying Himself and His Wife*, c. 220 BC). Centuries later, during the French Revolution, iconic images of suicides of ancient revolutionaries and patriots such as Seneca and Socrates, embodied in the famous paintings by Jacques-Louis David (*The Death of Socrates*, 1787) and Peter Paul Rubens (*The Dying Seneca*, 1608) became praise-worthy examples of Royalist sacrifice, Republican virtue, and liberty (Brown, 2001; Harris, 2014). Of interest, Seneca's and Socrates's deaths are frequently mentioned in recent years in the context of the rational suicide and euthanasia debate (Flemming, 2005; Papadimitriou et al., 2007).

In nineteenth century, not only in England, but also in a broader European context, suicide started to be linked to social and political issues. A French neo-impressionist painter Camille Pissarro, who along other French artists became involved in the socialist-anarchist movement, made a series of twenty-eight drawings entitled *Les Turpitudes Sociales* (1890) (Herbert & Herbert, 1960). The drawings showed images of poverty, hunger, money, the stock exchange, capital, religion, wage slavery, and suicide. The drawing of a hanging man (*Le Pendu*) has an inscription "a millionaire is too heavy, he troubles the harmony of interests, he disrupts the equilibrium of rights, he crushes the poor." The social and political meanings of suicide have continued into the twentieth and the twenty-first centuries, for example, in relation to Indigenous suicides in Australia and suicide bombers in the Middle East. Artistic representations of suicide by hanging can be found in contemporary Australian Indigenous art (Hunter, Reser, Baird, & Reser, 1999). Hanging is not only the most frequent method of suicide used by Aboriginal and Torres Strait Australians, but also a means of death which has acquired over the last two decades deep political and cultural meaning related to the history of oppression and genocide, especially in relation to Aboriginal deaths in custody. "Countless paintings with similar [hanging-related] themes have been painted by young Aboriginal men in custody and hung in similar community exhibitions around Australia. The hanging theme is pervasive, powerful, and immediately resonates with young Aboriginal viewers" (Hunter et al., 1999, p. 44).

In 2013, a controversy was stirred during an exhibition of Ahlam Shibli, a Palestinian artist, who presented in Paris a series of photographs entitled *Death*, including images of domestic shrines to Palestinian suicide bombers (Flavorwire, 2013; Huffington Post, 2013). Similarly, a doll (a child) dressed as a suicide bomber wearing a black balaclava and wired up to explosives (*Little Terror*) by Mason Storm, displayed at an art gallery in North London, provoked controversy and many angry reactions (Daily Mail, 2013). Interestingly enough, such reaction was expected by the artist: "The reason I created the piece *Little Terror* was to get a reaction from some of the narrow-minded locals who have been moaning over certain pieces in the gallery. If you find this piece offensive, have a collection, raise £1000 and donate it to a charity that helps children who have been damaged by war or made to fight wars. When you have done that, I will happily destroy the piece." A decade earlier, a recreation of the scene of a suicide attack which showed Ezzaldin Almasri who killed himself and fifteen people at a Jerusalem restaurant, which was displayed at An-Najal University in the West Bank was closed by Yasser Arafat (BBC News, 2001). In Sweden in 2004, a public display of an artwork depicting a small ship carrying a picture of Islamic Jihad bomber Hanadi Jaradat, who killed herself and twenty-one bystanders in a suicide bombing in Haifa, sailing in a pool of red-colored water (*Snow White and the Madness of Truth* by Israeli-born artist Dror Feiler) was closed following protests from the Simon Wiesenthal Center (CNN News, 2004).

## The Gender of Suicide

One will not find pictures of deaths of people of lower social status, such as plebeians and slaves, among images of heroic suicides, and the low number of female images, in comparison to male suicides reflected in the arts, may imply the same low social status of women (Brown, 2001). In antiquity, mostly male suicides were represented. Men were the ones who had responsibility in the public domain and could die a good death for the sake of the country. Brown pointed out that the woman's position in the famous ancient marble statue of *Ludovisi Gaul and His Wife* is peripheral. Gaul's wife is "just a woman," deprived of any peculiarities of a "Gaul," and she is a passive object of death. It is her husband who is the active party in their murder-suicide.

Images of suicide heroines, such as Lucretia, stressed their courage and devotion to male wishes and values and, according to Cutter (1983), glorification and idealization of their deaths aimed to imprint in women a preference for death over dishonor and to minimize the risk of their promiscuity. There might have been another reason to paint the heroic women—their exemplary behavior gave moral justification to paint semi-nudes, and "while the artist attempted to convey the tragic and moral aspects of suicide, he could not resist the sexual impact of the model on his and his patron's masculine awareness" (Cutter, 1983, p. 168). The popularity of heroic painting of women peaked in the sixteenth century and practically disappeared in later centuries when it gave way to images of stigmatized and irrational suicide (Brown, 2001).

Lucretia was probably the most frequently painted female suicide from Roman history. She was usually considered to be a personification of female honor and the embodiment of virtue (although, in later centuries, the interpretations of motives of her suicide changed, even to the point where she started to be perceived as a comical figure dying an unnecessary death) and a historical figure who, through the means of her death, contributed to the overthrow of monarchy and establishment of the Roman republic (Donaldson, 1982). Although Lucretia's suicide was frequently discussed in early Christianity, there are only a few known images of her death which have survived from the Middle Ages, for instance Pierre Remiet's *The Suicide of Lucretia* (fourteenth century). Only after the advent of the Renaissance and the reawakening of artistic interest in female body did Lucretia and other heroic females from antiquity become a popular object of arts, and more than one hundred artists painted her death from the mid-fifteenth century to the early twentieth century (Cutter, 1983).

There are many paintings showing the scene of Tarquin's rape of Lucretia which led to her suicide, including paintings by Titian (c. 1570) and Tintoretto (c. 1580), and at least three women painters (Artemisia Gentileschi, Elisabetta Sirani, and Angelica Kaufman) painted Lucretia's rape, a subject particularly cogent and traumatic for women (Harris, 2008b; Wolfthal, 1999). Sirani's (1664) and Kaufman's (eighteenth century) renditions of the subject emphasize the feminine perspective, and Sirani's used "gestures [which] seem more classically feminine than a male artist might use. Sirani seems to have chosen a moment after the rape, when Lucretia realizes the full enormity of the outrage (. . .) and is showing the moment at which Lucretia gets the idea to stab herself with Tarquin's knife. Her interpretation is not so much on exhortation to choose death over dishonor, but rather it is a solution for the significant loss of her honor" (Cutter, 1983, p. 176). Artemisia Gentileschi might have been herself a victim of rape perpetrated by her notorious art teacher Agostino Tassi. However, her rendition of the rape scene hardly revealed (perhaps in an attempt to distance herself from the trauma) any personal disturbance or strength gained from the experience (Donaldson, 1982). Gentileschi's *Tarquin and Lucretia* (c. 1645–50) follows the established conventions of the genre, and the "female interpretation does not basically question, disturb, or refashion the predominantly male myth" (Donaldson, 1982, p. 20).

In Victorian England the subject of suicide and contaminated femininity seems to have dominated the discourse of visual arts and literature to the point that "Victorian Londoners were inundated with images of drowned women" (Nicoletti, 2004). Although, from a statistical point of view, suicide was more prevalent among males than females, the images of female suicides permeated social and artistic narrations of the time, while representations of male suicide were scarce (Nicoletti, 2004). For both males and females suicide was linked to moral decline, but there were significant differences between the perceived motives and methods befitting the two genders. In the popular imagination, befitting the moral double standards of the era, suicide was a means for regaining female chastity and a retribution for adultery, sometimes encompassing murder-suicide of a mother and her child (Anderson, 1987; Brown, 2001). While female suicide was linked to sexual dishonor, such as prostitution, adultery, and unwanted pregnancy, male suicide was perceived as an escape from worldly dishonor. "Among women, suicide by drowning was shown as the reluctant last resort of the seduced and abandoned (and therefore starving and despairing); whereas among men, suicide by shooting, throat-cutting, or hanging was presented as the quickly chosen escape of the proud, the weak, or the wicked from financial ruin, disgrace, or retribution" (Anderson, 1987, p. 196). The gendered-patterns of suicide can be illustrated by Thomas Rowlandson's *She Died for Love, He Died for Glory* (1814–16). This color aquatint shows a satirical dissipated version of the story of Hero and Leander—a suicide pact of two lovers with an image of death as a skeleton wiping his brow and watching the scene. The caption under the aquatint points out passivity of death: "Death smiles and seems his dart to hide, when he beholds the suicide." According to Brown (2001), the picture shows in a gendered form two types of suicide: "for the man, a heroic voluntary death and for woman, dolor [sorrow] suicide as a result of irretrievable loss" (p. 137).

Of interest, in the nineteenth century, suicide, especially among the middle classes, became an object of satire and humor, which often focused on men who failed in marriage or in love affairs and hinted at their sexual problems (Brown, 2001). Such satires include English wood engravings *Mr. Mantalini Poisons Himself for the Seventh Time* by Hablot Knight Browne (a.k.a. Phiz) (an illustration for Charles Dickens's *Nicholas Nickleby* [1839]), *A Cure for Love: No cure: No pay* (1819) (a cartoon after Cruikshank), and French lithographs by Honoré Daumier: *Imagination: The Misanthrope Contemplates Various Ways in Which He Might Put an End to His Life* (c. 1838) and *The Drowned One* and *The Hanged One*, from his series *Sentimental Passions* (c. 1850).

Drowning and jumping became two archetypal female suicide methods in Victorian England, and the stereotype was reinforced by real-life cases, images in the visual arts and in the press, and stories told in popular theater plays. The association was so strong that any image of a young woman lingering near deep water (epitomized by Martha in a wood engraving *The River* (1851–82) by Hablôt Knight Browne, a.k.a. Phiz) was immediately linked to suicide as an aftermath of sexual seduction and betrayal, and "a girl standing near a riverside in the early morning might attract casual joking calls of 'What, are you going to drown yourself so early?'" (Anderson, 1987, p. 197). Suicide by drowning reached the notoriety of being a morbid London tourist attraction and, in the early 1870s, John Diprose's book *London and London Life* featured a thwarted drowning suicide attempt as a typical sight one could encounter in London by night (Nicoletti, 2004).

Images of drowned women were omnipresent in the visual culture of England in the 1840s and 1850s, and Gustave Doré's illustration for Thomas Hood's poem *The Bridge of Sights* (1872) "with its darkened arc of a bridge, forlorn female figure, and hulking church dome" (Gates, 1988, p. 138) is a classical example of the genre. Other notable examples include Augustus Egg's *Past and Present* (1858) and George Frederic Watts's *Found Drowned* (1848). The title of the latter painting was a reference to a daily column run by *The Times* which published lists of women, predominantly prostitutes, who were found drowned in London. The scenography of such artistic images of suicides was quite particular. It showed a moonlight sky, a church dome in the distance, a sanitized and esthetically displayed body of the drowned woman, and a bridge arch which framed the woman's body. The arch reinforced the drama of death and might have been either a reference to religious altar paintings or a reminder of a womb or an egg which "encloses women in symbols of their beginnings, their power, or their fall" (Gates, 1988, p. 140). The famous John Everett Millais's *Ophelia* (1851–52) and its French counterpart, *The Christian Martyr* (1855) by Paul de La Roche, are framed in a similar womb-like arch. The theme of a drowned woman can also be found in Russian art in Wassilij G. Perow's *Drowned Woman* (1867) and in Germany in Max Klinger's series of prints *Eine Mutter* (1881) and Käthe Kollwitz's *Suicide by Drowning* (leaf 4, from *Scenes of Poverty*, 1909).

An image of a woman jumping from a height (especially from a bridge), which often bore an uncanny resemblance to an image of a flying angel or a witch, was also very popular in the iconography of female suicide during the Victorian period (Brown, 2001). Unlike drowning, which was associated with passivity, deadness, and lack of will, jumping was perceived as an act of self-assertion and autonomy. Woodcuts showing suicide of Margaret Moyes became prototypes of the genre (Gates, 1988). Margaret Moyes, a twenty-three-year-old middle-class woman, attractive and possibly educated, jumped from London's Monument on September 11, 1838, leaving behind a suicide note saying "You need not expect to see me again, for I have made up my mind to make away with—Margaret Moyes" (Gates, 1988, p. 40). Her suicide, an open statement of despair in a public place, did not fit the suicide stereotype of a "befitting-end-of-a-fallen-woman," and it was rendered sensational and newsworthy by broadsides and newspapers. In Victorian society, it achieved notoriety similar to that of murder cases, and the cheap sensationalist press was full of detailed descriptions of the accident and speculations regarding Moyes's motivation. Such texts were often illustrated with woodcuts showing the deceased young woman and circumstances of her death, for example, *Self-Destruction of a Female by Throwing Herself off the Monument* (1839) and *Particulars of the Coroner's Inquest Held on the Body of Margaret Moyes* (1839). Unfortunately, imitative suicides followed, and their images also could be found in the cheap press, for instance *The Suicide of Robert Hawes* (1839) and *Another Dreadful Suicide at the Monument, by a Young Woman* (1842). The graphic reporting of these deaths led to a public outcry against cheap sensationalist literature and awoke public interest in suicide prevention. As a result London's Monument was caged in and thereby made inaccessible to potential suicides (Gates, 1988; Leonard, 2001). Woodcuts showing Margaret Moyes's suicide became prototypes of images of jumping (or flying) women and probably the most famous of those is George Cruikshank's etching *Suicide of the Drunkard's Daughter* (1848) with a subtitle *The Poor Girl Homeless, Friendless, Deserted, Destitute, and Gin-Mad Commits Self-Murder*. Similar images illustrated popular fiction novels, melodramas, and plays (Gates, 1988).

In Victorian visual arts and literature, suicide was a gender-related behavior, which not surprisingly, a century later, became a feminist issue subjected to literary and feminist critiques and analyses (Anderson, 1987; Brown, 2001; Gates, 1988; MacDonald & Murphy, 1990). Moreover, suicide in Victorian England was strongly embedded in the context of social class. Although, in general, female suicide by drowning was seen as the conventional aftermath of sexual misbehavior, for members of "the middle class, the female suicide was essentially a sinner; for the working class, she was a victim. For the former, suicide was an inevitable final retribution for fornication or adultery" (Anderson, 1987, p. 199), and the way such deaths were presented in visual arts varied accordingly. Realistic images of desperate women facing adversities of life epitomized by George Cruikshank's *Suicide of the Drunkard's Daughter* were found in easily accessible and affordable printed media and fitted the working class sentiments. The massive oil paintings (such as Watt's *Found Drowned*), etchings (e.g., *Bridge of Sights* by Gerald Fitzgerald, in 1858), and engravings which showed sentimentalized, passive and glamorous images, up to the point of having erotic undertones, of the dead bodies of drowned women, were addressed to the middle classes.

## The Esthetics of Suicide

The way the dead or dying body has been presented is closely related to social and religious taboos and attitudes regarding suicide, as well as the artistic conventions and the type of patronage over the arts: private in ancient Rome, public in ancient Greece, Church-dominated in Middle Ages, and private during the Renaissance (Cutter, 1983). Almost all images of suicide derived from ancient sources show estheticized and sanitized deaths and unmutilated bodies (Brown, 2001; Harris, 2014). Images of Ajax impaled on his sword or Lucretia thrusting a dagger through her chest hardly ever realistically show the inevitable wounds or blood. Images of ancient heroic suicides show rather the intent to kill oneself than the mutilated bodies. For example, a drawing of Phaedra by Reinach (derived from ancient sources) pictures her simply standing with a rope in her hand. This is very different from a mid-twentieth-century representation of the cruel lover, such as Leonard Baskin's *Phaedra Hanged* (1967), which does not spare the viewer any of the violence of suicide and the trauma of the onlooker.[3]

An interesting exception to the ancient and neo-classical rule of aesthetics of suicide is an illustration from a fourteenth manuscript by Pierre Remiet *The Suicides of Antony and Cleopatra*, which shows a decomposing and worm-ridden body of the queen. According to Brown (2001), such a composition is not an accident. It is meant to be a contestation of the heroism of pagan deaths and a deprecatory vision of an "abject, worm-ridden body of Cleopatra" (p. 52). Others have suggested that Pierre Remiet's deep, even obsessive fascination with death went beyond the prevailing medieval *memento mori* sentiment and made him a "master of death" showing realistic and gory details of dead bodies (Freeman Sandler, 1998).

Although suicide episodes from the Bible were a frequent subject of medieval art, the gruesome Apocrypha stories such as the story of Razis who attempted suicide by impaling himself on his sword and jumping from a tower, and who finally died by tearing out his entrails, cannot be found in medieval iconography, and "the restriction of ecclesiastical patronage of the church to sacred themes from the Bible and an aversion to such macabre topics may well be the reason" (Brown, 2001, p. 86). It was believed as well that the choice of suicide method revealed its motives and, in antiquity and the Middle Ages, certain means (especially hanging) were perceived as particularly stigmatized and vulgar. Thus a rope was a symbol of Phaedra's and Judas's final demise, while Ajax's and Lucretia's self-stabbing had a flavor of male and heroic deaths (Brown, 2001; van Hooff, 1999).

The association of Judas's death with Jesus's crucifixion made it the most popular theme in the Christian imagery of suicide and "offered the most potent of binaries [comparisons] to the death of Jesus" (Brown, 2001, p. 50). Cutter (1983) listed over one hundred images of the death of Judas in illuminated manuscripts, frescoes, mosaics, sarcophagi, sculpture, and ivory from the fourth century to 1350. Following the progressing secularization of suicide, images of Judas lost their popularity and practically disappeared from visual arts by the end of the fifteenth century. Although the New Testament gives two versions of his suicide (hanging and bursting), his hanging was depicted most often in the visual arts of the Middle Ages. Evolving theological interpretations of Judas's suicide were mirrored in its changing iconography and, in the thirteenth century, his death became related to guilt. An interesting example of this is a drawing from the so-called *Psalter of St Hildegard* (twelfth century) which shows "Judas hanging, not from a tree, but from the gallows. His hair is tousled, falling onto his neck, and ravens are flying around his corpse. What we see is a scene of judgment; nothing about it reminds us of suicide. (. . .) Later in the Middle Ages, the gallows which substituted the hanging-tree, became an iconographic formula for the representation of the scene, especially in the manuscripts of the *biblia pauperum*" (Shnitzler, 2000, pp. 116–118).

As discussed earlier in this chapter, Victorian female suicides might have been perceived as social victims or sinners but, as had happened to their heroic predecessors such as Lucretia and Cleopatra, images of their dead bodies were estheticized and sanitized (Brown, 2001). Nicoletti (2004) points out that, although "Victorian audiences were not ignorant as to the appearance of drowned corpses, yet their visual representations of female suicide never comply. (. . .) Victorian writers and artists transformed their subject's corrupt life and violent death into a peaceful martyrdom. They left the woman's body unscathed because Victorian art and literature constructed suicide as a redemptive act for unchaste women." Despite this, Victorian audiences not always were spared the graphic images of suicide because contemporary newspapers delivered gory images of the pornography of violence (Brown, 2001). The most notorious newspaper was *Illustrated Police News*, one of the earliest British tabloids which featured sensational melodramatic reports of deaths. The "newsworthy" suicide cases were illustrated with graphic wood engravings such as *The Suicide of Two Girls* (1868), *The Suicide of Alice Blanche Oswald* (1872) (both suicides by jumping), *A Man Crucifying Himself* (1869), *The Suicide by a Guillotine* (1876), *Singular Attempt at Suicide* (self-crucifixion; 1876), *An Extraordinary Suicide* (decapitation; 1876), and *Suicide on a Railway* (1877) (Brown, 2001).

## Conclusions

This brief overview of ways in which suicide has been presented and conceptualized in the Western art over the centuries raises an intriguing question. If visual art reflects the way suicide has been conceptualized (and if the artistic presentation of suicide impacts cultural and social understandings of suicide), can the dominating semantics of suicide (and its artistic representation) affect the behavior of an individual? There is overwhelming evidence regarding the impact of nonfictional and fictional media messages, including online material, on suicidal thoughts and behavior (i.e., the "Werther effect") (Pirkis & Nordentoft, 2011). There is some anecdotal evidence that Goethe's *The Sorrows of the Young Werther* (1774) had an impact on real-life suicides (Thorson & Öberg, 2003), and suicide pacts of young lovers influenced the themes of Kabuki plays which in turn led to copycat suicide pacts (Krysinska & Lester, 2006). Still, as far as we know, no suicides traceable to well-known (or obscure) visual artistic representations of suicide have been reported. Nonetheless, it is possible that the gender-related patterns of suicide, its semantics and esthetics, might have some impact on individual's suicidal behavior or at least attitudes toward self-inflicted death and its means. We can explore this possibility from at least three angles.

First, already in antiquity and the Middle Ages, it was believed that the individual's motives affected the choice of suicide method, and some means (such as hanging) were perceived as vulgar, while others (such as self-stabbing) implied a heroic death. This belief has been reflected in numerous art artifacts (Brown, 2001; van Hooff, 1990). The detestable suicide of Judas or Phaedra is thus an antithesis of the noble suicide of Ajax or Lucretia. Centuries later, the cultural meaning still seems to influence the choice of a suicide method, besides its availability and perceived lethality (Clarke & Lester, 2013). It has been suggested that the decrease in suicide by firearm and an increase in suicide by hanging in Australia in the last three decades of the twentieth century, especially among young males, could be partly related to the association between hanging and capital punishment (De Leo, Dwyer, Firman, & Neulinger, 2003). Young Australian males may be more likely to choose hanging as a suicide method than older males. The latter might still remember the last official Australian hanging execution in 1967 and associate this method with punishment, criminality, and public shame. The popularity of hanging as a method of suicide among Australian Indigenous males (including Aboriginal deaths in custody) has also been traced back to the history of oppression and genocide experienced by this population (Hunter et al., 1999).

Second, there is a related issue of gender differences in the most frequently used suicide methods. As discussed in relation to the images of suicide in Victorian England, drowning and jumping were considered to be the suicide methods of choice for women, while hanging, shooting, and throat-cutting were the typical "male" means of suicide (Anderson, 1987). Again, numerous paintings and prints from this era illustrate this sociocultural belief. Interestingly enough, the most popular and convincing explanation of the "gender paradox of suicide," that is, the inverse relationship between suicidal morbidity and mortality in the two genders, seems to be the "socialization theory" or the "cultural script theory" (Canetto & Cleary, 2012; Canetto & Sakinofsky, 1998). According to this theory, the process of gender socialization during the lifespan is likely to affect the type of suicidal behavior one is likely to engage in (i.e., fatal vs. nonfatal suicidal behavior), as well as the choice of a suicide method. Consequently, currently in the United States and Western European countries, some means of suicide, such as hanging or guns ("hard" methods), might be considered more "masculine" than the less lethal ("soft") methods, such as self-poisoning, which are perceived as "feminine" (McKay, Milner, & Maple, 2013).

Third, the increasing popularity and accessibility of the Internet has raised numerous issues regarding the possibilities for prevention of self-harm and suicide as well as risks related to exposure to information on suicide methods, normalization of suicide, imitation, and contagion (Mishara & Kerkhof, 2013). Although the majority of studies in this area has focused on written communication (e.g., Westerlund, 2012), at least one study looked at the contents, accessibility, and viewers' ratings of nonsuicidal self-injury photographs and in-action videos on YouTube (Lewis et al., 2011). The study showed that the graphic videos are frequently accessed, discussed, and rated positively by viewers, including marking it as a "favorite." The authors concluded that, "the nature of nonsuicidal self-injury videos on YouTube may foster normalization of nonsuicidal self-injury and may reinforce the behavior through regular viewing of nonsuicidal self-injury–themed videos" (Lewis et al., 2011, e552).

Unfortunately, no studies provide an answer to the question whether the choice of a favorite "suicide painting" is a reflection of an imagined ideal way by which one could die or take one's own life. Nevertheless, in the words of Berman (1988), "it appears that to the extent there is an imitative effect of fictional presentations of suicide, the effect is interactive. Characteristics of the person, the stimulus, and conditions of the environment, among others, interact to produce the observed effect; and a more microsociological level of analysis is necessary to better understand this phenomenon" (p. 985).

## Notes

1. The painting has its own tragic history: Elizabeth (Lizzie) Siddal, who at the age of 19 modeled for the picture, fell seriously ill, possibly from pneumonia, while posing as a floating Ophelia in a bathtub filled with water and died by laudanum overdose fourteen years later (Harris, 2007).
2. There has been speculation that the picture shows French artist Jules Holtzapffel who shot himself at his home in April 1866 after his works had been rejected by the jury of the Salon, the official art exhibition of the *Académie des Beaux-Arts* in Paris. Alternatively, the suicide of Manet's assistant Alexandre, who hanged himself in 1859 or 1860, might have been an inspiration for the painting (Harris, 2008a; Ilg, 2002).
3. Likewise, Frida Kahlos's *The Death of Dorothy Hale* (1938), Andy Warhol's *Suicide (Purple Jumping Man)* (1971), and Edward Dwurnik's *The Death of a Poet* (1973) show the very scene of suicide and the maimed body without any attempt at concealing the brutality of death.

# References

Anderson, O. (1987). *Suicide in Victorian and Edwardian England*. Oxford: Clarendon Press.

BBC News. (2001). *Arafat closes "suicide bombing" art show*. September 26, 2001. Retrieved July 12, 2014, from http://news.bbc.co.uk/1/hi/entertainment/arts/1564188.stm

Berman, A. L. (1988). Fictional depiction of suicide in television films and imitation effects. *American Journal of Psychiatry, 145*, 982–986.

Brown, R. M. (2001). *The art of suicide*. London: Reaktion Books.

Canetto, S. S., & Cleary, A. (2012). Men, masculinities and suicidal behavior. *Social Science & Medicine, 74*, 461–465.

Canetto, S. S., & Sakinofsky, I. (1998). The gender paradox in suicide. *Suicide & Life-Threatening Behavior, 28*, 1–23.

Clarke, R. V., & Lester, D. (2013). *Suicide: Closing the exits*. New Brunswick, NJ: Transaction.

CNN News. (2004). Sweden objects to Israeli diplomat's action over artwork. January 17, 2004. Retrieved July 12, 2014, from edition.cnn.com/2004/WORLD/europe/01/17/sweden.israel/index.html?iref=allsearch

Cutter, F. (1983). *Art and the wish to die*. Chicago, IL: Nelson Hall.

Daily Mail. (2009). Anger as art gallery shows sculpture of suicide bomber girl. Retrieved July 12, 2014, from http://www.dailymail.co.uk/news/article-1201566/Anger-art-gallery-shows-sculpture-suicide-bomber-girl.html#ixzz378Fa3gAv

De Leo, D., Dwyer, J., Firman, D., & Neulinger, K. (2003). Trends in hanging and firearm suicide rates in Australia: substitution of method? *Suicide & Life-Threatening Behavior, 33*, 151–164.

Donaldson, I. (1982). *The rapes of Lucretia*. Oxford: Clarendon Press.

Edwards, C., & Osborne, T. (2005). Scenographies of suicide. *Economy & Society, 34*, 173–177.

Flavorwire. (2013). Should France censor Ahlam Shibli's photos of suicide bomber "martyrs" in occupied Palestine? Retrieved July 12, 2014, from http://flavorwire.com/401165/should-france-censor-ahlam-shiblis-photos-of-suicide-bomber-martyrs-in-occupied-palestine

Flemming, R. (2005). Suicide, euthanasia and medicine: reflections ancient and modern. *Economy & Society, 34*, 295–321.

Fontana, E. (1998). Pre-Raphaelite suicides. *Journal of Pre-Raphaelite Studies, 7*, 28–38.

Freeman Sandler, L. (1998). Master of death: the lifeless art of Pierre Remiet, Illuminator. by Michael Camille [Review]. *Speculum, 73*, 482–485.

Gates, B. T. (1988). *Victorian suicide: Mad crimes and sad histories*. Princeton, NJ: Princeton University Press.

Harris, J. C. (2007). Ophelia. *Archives of General Psychiatry, 64*, 1114.

Harris, J. C. (2008a). Le Suicide. *Archives of General Psychiatry, 65*, 744.

Harris, J. C. (2008b). Tarquin and Lucretia (Rape of Lucretia). *Archives of General Psychiatry, 65*, 250–251.

Harris, J. C. (2014). The dying Seneca: Peter Paul Rubens. *JAMA Psychiatry, 71*, 742–743.

Herbert, R. L., & Herbert, E. W. (1960). Artists and anarchism: unpublished letters of Pissarro, Signac and others. *Burlington Magazine, 102*, 473–482.

Higgins, C. (2004). *Work of art that inspired a movement . . . a urinal.* December 2, 2004. Retrieved July 12, 2014, from http://www.guardian.co.uk/uk/2004/dec/02/arts.artsnews1

Huffington Post (2013). *Suicide bomber art: Ahlam Shibli, Palestinian photographer, creates controversy in Paris show.* Retrieved July 12, 2014, from http://www.huffingtonpost.com/2013/06/11/suicide-bomber-art-stirs-controversy-with-ahlam-shibli-show_n_3423139.html

Hunter, E., Reser, J., Baird, M., & Reser, P. (1999). *An analysis of suicide in Indigenous communities of North Queensland: The historical, cultural and symbolic landscape.* Canberra, Australia: Mental Health/Health Services Development Branch, Commonwealth Department of Health and Aged Care.

Ilg, U. (2002). Painted theory of art: "Le suicide" (1877) by Edouard Manet and the disappearance of narration. *Artibus et Historiae, 23,* 179–190.

Krysinska, K., & Lester. D. (2006). Comment on the Werther effect. *Crisis, 27,* 100.

Leonard, E. C. (2001). Confidential death to prevent suicidal contagion. an accepted, but never implemented, nineteenth-century idea. *Suicide & Life-Threatening Behavior, 31,* 460–466.

Lewis, S. P., Heath, N. L., St Denis, J. M., & Noble, R. (2011). The scope of non-suicidal self-injury on YouTube. *Pediatrics, 127,* e552–e557.

MacDonald, M., & Murphy, T. R. (1990). *Sleepless souls: Suicide in early modern England.* Oxford: Clarendon Press.

Marchwinski, A. (1987). The romantic suicide and the artists. *Gazette des Beaux-Arts, 109,* 62–74.

McKay, K., Milner, A., & Maple, M. (2013). Women and suicide: Beyond the gender paradox. *International Journal of Culture & Mental Health, 7,* 168–178.

Mishara, B., & Kerkhof, A. (Eds.). (2013). *Suicide prevention and new technologies: Evidence-based practice.* New York: Palgrave Macmillan.

Nicoletti, L. J. (2004). Downward mobility: Victorian women, suicide, and London's "Bridge of Sighs". *Literary London: Interdisciplinary Studies in the Representation of London, 2*(1). Retrieved July 10, 2014, from http://www.literarylondon.org/london-journal/march2004/nicoletti.html

Papadimitriou, J. D., Skiadas, P., Mavrantonis, C. S., Polimeropoulos, V., Papadimitriou, D. J., & Papacostas, K. J. (2007). Euthanasia and suicide in antiquity: viewpoint of the dramatists and philosophers. *Journal of the Royal Society of Medicine, 100,* 25–28.

Pirkis, J., & Nordentoft, M. (2011). Media influences on suicide and attempted suicide. In R. C. O'Connor, S. Platt, & J. Gordon (Eds.), *International handbook of suicide prevention: Research, policy and practice* (pp. 531–544). Chichester: Wiley Blackwell.

Schnitzler, N. (2000). Judas' death: some remarks concerning the iconography of suicide in the middle Ages. *Medieval History Journal, 3,* 103–118.

Shneidman, E. (1985). *Definition of suicide.* Northvale, NJ: Jason Aronson.

TATE Online. (2004). *Andy Warhol: Marilyn Diptych.* Retrieved July 10, 2014, from http://www.tate.org.uk/art/artworks/warhol-marilyn-diptych-t03093

Thorson, J., & Öberg, P. A. (2003). Was there a suicide epidemic after Goethe's Werther? *Archives of Suicide Research, 7,* 69–72.

van Hooff, A. J. L. (1990). *From authothanasia to suicide. Self-killing in classical antiquity.* London: Routledge.

Westerlund, M. (2012). The production of pro-suicide content on the Internet: a counter-discourse activity. *New Media & Society, 14,* 764–780.

Williams, I. A. (1960). An identification of some early drawings by John Flaxman. *Burlington Magazine, 102,* 246–251.

Wolfthal, D. (1999). *Images of rape: The "heroic" tradition and its alternatives.* Cambridge: Cambridge University Press.

# 9

# Suicide in Kabuki Theater

*Karolina Krysinska*

*A Kabuki play is not meant to be a literary work in itself,*
*it is considered in the first place as stage effect.*
—A. C. Scott, *The kabuki theatre of Japan*

The Kabuki theater originated in Japan in the beginning of the seventeenth century. This traditionally all-male theater was started by O Kuni, a ceremonial dancer from the Izumo shrine, who in 1603 "gave a performance on the dry bed of the Kamo River in Kyoto. She danced the *nembutsu odori*, a Buddhist ceremonial dance, but adapted it to variations of her own and became an immediate success" (Scott, 1955, p. 35). Soon joined by other female and male dancers, she expanded the repertoire of her troupe, adapted the traditional Nō theater rituals, and started using a flute and drum accompaniment. This new theater, known as O Kuni's Kabuki, gained wide popularity, and many similar groups appeared, often linked to the practice of prostitution. After O Kuni's death in 1610, the popularity of *Onna Kabuki* (Women's Kabuki) increased further, and attending the performances became very fashionable among the townspeople. Because of the links with prostitution, in 1629 the Tokugawa government banned the appearance of female Kabuki actors as they "disturbed the country, caused deterioration in various ways, and was the cause of calamities" (Asai Ryōi, 1709 [in Shively, 1955, p. 329]).

A new type of Kabuki, *Wakashu* (Young Men's Kabuki) appeared. These troupes were composed of handsome young men, initially appearing on stage together with the attractive female actresses. Again, because of the sexual allure of the young actors, homosexual practices, and prostitution, in 1652 the government banned *Wakashu*, and the actors were forced by law to shave their forelocks to become less physically attractive (Scott, 1955; Shively, 1955).

119

After government bans regarding the performance of female and young male actors, Kabuki evolved again resulting in *Yaro Kabuki* (Fellow's Kabuki), in which only adult male actors appeared on stage. Paradoxically, these bans, and other legal regulations imposed on the theater in the following decades, contributed to the development and maturity of Kabuki (Shively, 1955). No longer able to rely on their youthful charm, the adult male actors had to develop new acting styles, costumes, stage props, and techniques to attract the audience. New plays, including musical performances and dances, were written especially for the Kabuki theater or adopted from the doll theater (*bunraku*), including works of the master playwright, Chikamatsu Monzaemon (1653–1724). As no women could play on the stage, *onnagata* (male actors specialized in playing female roles) appeared and, over time, perfected their acting techniques, make-up, wigs, and costumes (Leiter, 2002; Robertson, 1999). During the Genroku era (1688–1703), Kabuki developed into a mature theater form, reached technical perfection, and gained unsurpassed popularity among its audience, comprising mostly of the rich merchant class. (The ruling class—the samurai—was forbidden by law to attend the Kabuki plays.)

Despite further governmental restrictions, including segregation laws regarding the establishment of special theater quarters which the actors were forbidden to leave and sumptuary laws restricting the Kabuki theater design and costumes, the popularity of Kabuki continued in the eighteenth and the nineteenth centuries. Kabuki actors, along with sumo wrestlers, firemen, and courtesans, became the idols of the lower and middle classes (*chonin*), including farmers, craftsmen, and merchants. The fashionable town ladies imitated the onstage manners, clothes, and hairstyles of the popular *onnagata* actors. Scenes from Kabuki plays and portraits of the famous Kabuki actors were among the favorite themes of the woodblock *ukiyo-e* prints ("pictures of the floating world") from the seventeenth century onwards (Buckland, 2013).

Earning high wages, some of the popular actors adopted flamboyant lifestyles, which sometimes led to financial problems, as well as problems with law (especially, the sumptuary laws), and in one case, to suicide (Scott, 1955). Ichikawa Danjūrō VIII (1823–54), a very popular actor specializing in the roles of young lovers,[1] died by suicide at the age of 32, suffering from massive debts, jealousy of the older actors and, supposedly, the shame of his father's banishment. His father, Ichikawa Danjūrō VII (1791–1859), considered to be the greatest Kabuki actor of the nineteenth century, was arrested for violating the sumptuary regulations and exiled by the Governor of Yedo. In 1854, during a tour of performances in Osaka with his father, Ichikawa Danjūrō VIII was found with his wrists slashed in his room at an inn. After his death more than a hundred obituary portraits were made.[2]

At the end of the eighteenth century, following the period of flamboyant luxury, the taste of the audience and the general condition of the Kabuki theater declined. Fires in the popular theaters led to serious financial difficulties for the theater owners and, in the early 1840s, a powerful government executive tried to ban Kabuki altogether as "the actors and their plays were harmful to the moral interests of the people as well as being a dangerous source of fire" (Scott, 1955, p. 40). Still, Kabuki managed to survive this crisis, only to be faced by another—the Meiji Restoration of 1868 which opened Japan to the influence of the West and new ideas regarding the arts, including theater. Due to the influence of the great Kabuki actors and playwrights of the time, and the deeply rooted popularity of this art form in the Japanese culture and everyday life, Kabuki evolved again. During the Taisho era (1912–26) new style plays were introduced and the audiences' interest in this form of theater continued until the World War II. The destruction of the theater quarters (*Kabuki za*) in Tokyo during the bombing in 1945 was considered to be the symbolic end of Kabuki. Moreover, the censorship during the American occupation of Japan put serious restriction on the number and type of plays which could be performed (Brandon, 2006). Nonetheless, the Kabuki theater proved invincible again. It has survived the competition of television and film, and its prestige has risen. Along with other traditional Japanese theater forms, such as Nō (classical Japanese musical drama) and *kyogen* (traditional comic theater), Kabuki has become a part of Japan's "soft power" (Klett, 2001; Sadler & Atkins, 2010).

## The Art of a Kabuki Play

> The kabuki is artificial, it makes no pretense at being otherwise. Everything is exaggerated, conventionalized and emphasized to make a pattern for the eye and ear.
> —A. C. Scott, *The kabuki theatre of Japan*

In general, there are three types of Kabuki plays: *jidaimono, sewamono,* and *shosagoto,* and some of the plays are played only during a particular time of the year or in a particular order during a day (Brandon & Leiter, 2002a; Scott, 1955). *Jidaimono* are plays with a historical background; the subject of naturalistic *sewamono* plays is contemporary domestic life of ordinary people; and *shosagoto* are dance dramas. The *sewamono* plays include subgenres, such as *keiseigoto* (courtesan plays of Osaka), *yatsushigoto* (tragic love stories of young men and their beloveds), *shinjumono* (lovers' double suicides), and *kizewamono* (adventures of gamblers, thieves, and figures of the underworld). Some of the Kabuki plays were written specifically for the Kabuki theater, while others have been adopted from the Nō theater or the doll theater (*bunraku*). For example, one of the most famous Kabuki plays, *Kana dehon Chushin-gura* (Story of the Forty-Seven Royal Retainers, 1748), was originally written for *bunraku*. The play is based on a historical incident involving forty-seven *ronin* and their vendetta for the death of their lord, Asano Naganori. The two most famous double suicide (*shinju*) plays (*Sone-zaki no shinjū* [The Love Suicides at Sonezaki, 1703] and *Shinjūten no Amijima* [The Love Suicides at Amijima, 1721]) were also originally doll theater plays later adapted to Kabuki (Keene, 1998).

A Kabuki play is primarily visual, centered on a stage effect appealing to the eye (and the ear) of the audience (Scott, 1955). This includes the actors' elaborate costumes, wigs, make-up, and movements, including steps, dances, and exaggerated and emotionally charged poses (*mie*), which are popular subjects of the *ukiyo-e* prints (Buckland, 2013). The rich and colorful scenography and elaborate stage effects and settings, including revolving stages, trap devices, and *hanamichi* (a raised gang-way connecting the rear of the auditorium to the stage, where some of the play action takes place), are integral parts of the Kabuki play setting. The actor's technique and movements are highly conventionalized, and the audience expects from him a conventional recreation of a stage character imbued with his unique individuality and style (Scott, 1955). Regarding the content of the plays, realistic scenes are intermingled with fantasy (including popular ghost scenes) and, although the human affairs and emotions are often presented *in extremis*, the rules of a conventional and highly structured society are not violated. In the colorful words of Scott (1955), "the Kabuki is not concerned with any particular message, it is first and foremost entertainment, designed solely for the ordinary citizen; everything is devoted to making a vivid appeal to the eye and creating atmosphere by all possible artistry to keep the audience enthralled" (p. 33).

Starting in the early sixteenth century, the Tokugawa government issued numerous restrictions and bans concerning the gender, age, and physical appearance of Kabuki actors, the style and location of theaters, the audience allowed to attend, and the stage costumes (Shively, 1955).

As mentioned earlier, the large theaters had to be located in certain parts of the city, the actors were not allowed to leave the theater quarters, and the samurai were forbidden to attend Kabuki performances. Neither realistic sword blades nor expensive theater costumes made from silk, brocade, or other rich materials were allowed on stage. No unauthorized or private performances could be staged, including plays at homes of samurai or rich merchants, which deprived the actors, and the Kabuki theater in general, of the possibility of patronage by the educated and influential classes.

Other official restrictions regarding the Kabuki theater included censorship of the contents of the plays. The censorship aimed at protecting the audience against any subversive political or moral influence (Shively, 1955). Although *jidaimono*, the historical plays, were very popular, plays containing references to recent events were forbidden, and no contents related to the government could be published. The names of the contemporary samurai or any events involving members of this class occurring after 1600 could not be mentioned in Kabuki plays. Nevertheless, some of the playwrights were successful at introducing political satire or presenting recent events in their plays by changing the names of the characters and casting temporary events in the past. *Chushingura* is based on real events which took place between 1701 and 1703. However, in order to make it acceptable to the censors, the authors changed the names of the characters and set the play 350 years earlier. Nonetheless, as Shively (1955) has observed, "the censorship eliminated any possibility of writing plays of real social or political significance" (p. 355). The censorship included also a graphic and opulent portrayal of the pleasure quarters and their courtesans, which frequently served as the setting of history and domestic plays. Double love suicide (*shinju*), a popular subject catching the hearts and the imagination of the Kabuki audience, was banned by the censors for a few years in 1723.

Another attempt at censorship of themes and scenes deemed inappropriate and "undemocratic," including lovers' suicide, *seppuku*, sword fighting, and revenge, was undertaken during the occupation of Japan by American forces in the aftermath of World War II (Brandon, 2006). *Chushingura*, highly praised by the Japanese intellectuals during World War II, was banned by the American censors until November 1947. This play, hailed as the ultimate Kabuki drama of revenge and loyalty and containing a scene of licking blood from the master's suicide dagger by one of the retainers as an oath of vengeance against the deceased lord's enemy, was not acceptable to the American censors who associated the contents and the message of the play with the recent suicide acts of the kamikaze pilots.

## Suicide in Kabuki Plays

The obvious brutality of murder and suicide is counterbalanced by kabuki's passion for stage beauty.

—J. R. Brandon and S. L. Leiter, editors, *Kabuki plays on stage: Darkness and desire, 1804–1864*

Kabuki plays are highly conventionalized, and their scenes, including those depicting murder and suicide (two very popular themes), follow established forms and patterns of action. "Characters in Kabuki have ways of dying as distinctive as the other elements of performance" (Leiter, 1969, p. 147). Although often brutal and violent, the scenes of suicide and murder are highly stylized and are a part of the visual art of Kabuki performance,[3] referred to as the "aesthetics of cruelty" by Brandon and Leiter (2002b, p. 13). Self-inflicted death is a crucial dramatic device in the Kabuki theater and, although *seppuku* (ritual disembowelment) and *shinju* (double suicide) are the two most frequent types of suicide, Kabuki characters take their lives in many other circumstances and using a variety of methods. Kiuchi Sogo, the title character in *Sakura Giminden* (The Martyr of Sakura, 1851), accepts his death and the death of his family as a consequence of his action when he decides to directly petition the shogun on behalf of the village community. Sogo's wife refuses to divorce him to save herself and the children from punishment. Rokurodayu in *Kajiwara Heizo Homare no Ishikiri* (The Stone-Cutting Feat of Kajiwara, 1730) desperately needs money to support a political cause and offers himself as the second body to test the quality of an expensive sword that is supposed be able to cut through human flesh. When the test seemingly fails, Rokurodayu is ready to kill himself with the sword to save his honor. In *Domo Mata* (Matahei the Stutterer, 1708), Matahei, a disciple of the great court painter Tosa no Shōgen, decides to die when his request to be awarded the Tosa name is repeatedly rejected by the master. He is saved from suicide, as well as awarded the honorable title, when his self-portrait, which was meant to be left as a memento, miraculously appears on the other side of a solid granite water basin on which it was being painted (Brandon & Leiter, 2002a).

Reflecting the real-life complexity of *seppuku*, which was permitted only for samurai and their superiors, and the exact method of which depended on the rank of the samurai and the nature of his offence, there are many ways of performing *seppuku* on stage. As Leiter (1969) observed, "a samurai may be forced to commit seppuku as an honorable punishment, as does Enya Hangan in *Chushingura*, or it may be self-imposed as atonement for bad deeds; Kampei of *Chushingura* decides to kill himself to make up for his earlier mistakes" (p. 148). Although women do not commit *seppuku*, they can die by suicide by thrusting a short sword (or a large hair pin) under the heart. Some scenes of seppuku are accompanied by the "wounded memories" (*teoi no jukkai*) acting technique, which is a variation of "reminiscences" (*modori*), in which a dying character delivers a long speech in which he repents for the (seemingly) villainous deeds perpetrated in his life. Although a samurai delivering the *teoi no jukkai* is not a villain or a really bad person, he must have done something calling for final repentance. The suicide of Kampei, one of the forty-seven *ronin* in *Chushingura*, is an atonement for not being at his lord's side at a crucial moment, and Sōkan in *Tenjiku Tokubei Ikoku-Banashi* (The Tale of Tokubei from India, 1804) commits *seppuku* to atone for having allowed a theft of a precious sword (Brandon & Leiter, 2002b; Leiter, 1969).

A Kabuki actor playing a scene of *seppuku* holds a special short sword by the blade, wrapped in a cloth in such a way that only the blade's point is visible, while sitting cross-legged on the floor or kneeling on a white mat (Leiter, 1969). He pulls the sword across his abdomen from left to right, a gesture ended by a quick upward jerk to the blade. As prescribed by ritual for honorable deaths, when a more formal suicide scene is played, the character is allowed to cut his jugular vein. In case of less honorable suicide, an appointed executioner beheads the suicide from behind before he can complete the self-inflicted act, and a symbolic red cloth is thrown over the "severed" head. The lowest form of *seppuku* is performed by forcing the suicide to make the incision with a bamboo dirk. Leiter (1969) illustrates the complexity of *seppuku*, the variety of actors' techniques, and the scenography accompanying the act by contrasting the deaths of two characters in *Chushuingura*: "When Enya Hangan [a righteous lord] performs ritual suicide in *Chushingura*, no blood mars the scene's almost spiritual quality. This scene contrasts sharply with Kampei's [Hangan's retainer] suicide later in the same play, where the squalor of Kampei's surroundings, and the generally less noble tone of the suicide, permits a more realistic approach. Hangan's death takes place in a palace, is attended by the lord's faithful retainers, and is the event which puts the plot of this famous play into motion. From the point of view of his retainers, Hangan suffers virtual martyrdom and, esthetically, his death demands a simplicity and purity of approach which dispels the need for blood" (p. 151). Sometimes the very act of *seppuku*, although a crucial point of action in the play, is not acted on the stage. Although, reflecting the actual historical event, it is obvious to the audience that in the final act of *Chushingura*, the forty-seven royal retainers will commit suicide after achieving their revenge, the scene of mass *seppuku* is omitted from the play.

The plots of plays involving double suicide (*shinju*) are based upon a conflict between obligations (*giri*) and personal feelings (*ninjo*). They involve a couple (usually a middle-class merchant and a prostitute) whose love can never succeed. The suicide scene is often "grotesquely beautiful" (Leiter, 1969, p. 147), and the actors play both sadness and a hope for a better future after death. The scene of the suicide self is generally preceded by a "traveling on the way" dance-mime (*michiyuki*)—the lovers sadly walk together along the *hanamichi*, while grieving for their misfortunes or recalling the past and, after arriving on the stage, they dance and strike melancholy postures (Leiter, 1969).

Among the most famous kabuki plays using the theme of *shinjū* are Chikamatsu Monzaemon's *Sonezaki no shinjū* (The Love Suicides at Sonezaki, 1703) and *Shinjūten no Amijima* (The Love Suicides at Amijima, 1721) (Keene, 1998). *Sonezaki no shinju* was the pioneer of *sewamono* genre. It dramatized contemporary events and everyday life, and popularized *shinju* as a subject of Kabuki and doll theater plays. In "Love Suicides at Sonezaki," the two main characters are Tokubei, a young orphan merchant clerk, and Ohatsu, a courtesan with whom he is in love. Tokubei finds himself in great danger after refusing an arranged marriage and gets into financial difficulties, after which the couple makes a suicide pact. Tokubei binds Ohatsu to a tree at Sonezaki Shrine and cuts her throat before cutting his own. In "The Love Suicides at Amijima," Jihei, a married paper merchant, falls in love with Koharu, a prostitute. Jihei is unable to redeem her, and despite his wife's noble intervention to save her husband's life and the honor of Koharu, Jihei and Koharu pledge to commit suicide together. They escape at night and travel to the Amijima where Jihei kills Koharu with a sword and then hangs himself (Keene, 1998).

The plot of "The Love Suicides at Sonezaki" is based on real events. In April 1703, Tokubei, a clerk to a soy sauce merchant, and his lover Ohatsu, a courtesan, died by suicide together in the forest of Tenjin. A month later, this event was turned into a *bunraku* play and later adapted to the Kabuki stage. It is possible that *Shinjūten no Amijima* was also based on a real incident (a lovers' suicide at the Amijima Diacho Temple in Osaka in November 1720) although it has also been suggested that Chikamatsu based his play on Ki no Kaion's *Umeda shinjū* (The Love Suicides at Umeda, 1706) (Keene, 1998). The romantic and sensational manner of presenting lovers' suicides by Chikamatsu and other playwrights popularized the concept of lovers' union in the afterlife based on the Buddhist doctrine of reincarnation (Halford & Halford, 1956).

## Imitation of Kabuki Suicides

*Shinju* presented on stage were imitated in real life, leading to an epidemic of suicides. Besides the possible imitation and contagion effects (Krysinska & Lester, 2006), the worsening economic situation, including the devaluation of currency in 1706, and natural disasters plaguing Japan at the time could have contributed to these suicides (Keene, 1998). As Keene (1998) has observed, the motivation of Tokubei and Ohatsu to die together might have not been very convincing. However, later love-suicide plots involved financial problems, for example, in the "Love Suicides at Amijima," adding an element of reality.

The government became concerned about the suicides supposedly triggered by the Kabuki *shinju* plays and banned their performance in 1723 (Shively, 1955). In addition, funerals for those who died in suicide pacts were prohibited, the bodies were left in public view at Nihonbashi Bridge for three days and, if one of the lovers survived, he or she was tried for murder (Takahashi & Berger, 1996). Despite these measures, within a few years the plays were written and performed again, and they have remained a favorite theme of Kabuki and *bunraku* repertoire.[4] Lovers' suicides have remained a relatively popular phenomenon in Japan across the centuries (Robertson, 1999) and may be related to the recent spike in Internet-based suicide pacts in Japan (Ozawa-de Silva, 1998).

The theme of love and suicide appears in Kabuki plays not only in the context of *shinju*. In *Suzugamori* (The Execution Ground at Suzugamori, 1823), a courtesan Komurasaki kills herself after the death of her lover, Gonpachi. (In other versions of the play, the two lovers commit suicide together or Gonpachi kills himself.) *Yasuna* (1818), one of the most popular dances in the Kabuki repertory, shows the insanity of the young hero after his mistress's suicide. It presents a visually stunningly scene with "the figure of a handsome young man driven mad by the suicide of his lover, with his hair hanging loose, wearing a beautiful formal robe and long trailing trousers (*nagabakama*) and embracing his lover's garment as he wanders through a field of yellow blossoms" (Brandon & Leiter, 2002b, p. 92).

## Notes

1. Ichikawa Danjūrō VIII was especially popular with female fans: "When he played Sukeroku, in which he had to immerse himself in a barrel of water, the water was subsequently sold at exorbitant cost to avid admirers. Even when he had to appear as Yosaburo with a scarred face, pastry shops sold beanpaste buns with cracked outer skins called 'Yosaburo buns', which were devoured by the actor's fans." (http://www.fitzmuseum.cam.ac.uk/gallery/japan/gallery/textN.htm)
2. http://ve.torontopubliclibrary.ca/Kabuki%20I/image19.htm
3. In the words of Kabuki actor, Ichikawa Ennosuke II (1886–1963): "If you just read the story, cutting off a child's head [in *Terakoya*, "Village School"] is truly cruel. But when you hold in mind that this is a theatrical art, you see a beautiful, splendid performance." (Brandon, 2006, p. 31)
4. The Shinto Shrine *Tsuyu no Tenjinja*, the suicide place of the real-life Tokubei and Ohatsu in 1703, is known as *Ohatsu Tenjin* and the Shrine of Marriage. According to the shrine website (www.tuyutenjin.com/en): "*Sonezaki Shinju* is a dramatization of the double suicide (of a couple in love) that occurred in the *Tenjin no Mori* (Forest) of our shrine (. . .). This piece of work became very popular amongst the people of the generation and a huge number of men and women of all ages came to worship to our shrine. (. . .) Even today, during the memorial service, lots of people who want to make their love bear fruit visit our shrine."

   In July 1972, the local people build a stone monument as a memorial to the tragic lovers and in April 2004 a bronze statue of Tokubei and Ohatsu was erected on the temple grounds. A variety of merchandise is available to the shrine visitors, including lucky charms based on the characters of Ohatsu and Tokubei: "The charms, which come as a pair in two different colors, is said to bring good luck when two people who love each other carry them around." (www.tuyutenjin.com/en/goods.html)

## References

Brandon, J. R. (2006). Myth and reality: A story of Kabuki during American censorship, 1945–1949. *Asian Theatre Journal, 23*, 1–110.
Brandon, J. R., & Leiter, S. L. (Eds.). (2002a). *Kabuki plays on stage: Brilliance and bravado, 1697–1766* (Vol. 1). Honolulu: University of Hawaii Press.
Brandon, J. R., & Leiter, S. L. (Eds.). (2002b). *Kabuki plays on stage: Darkness and desire, 1804–1864* (Vol. 3). Honolulu: University of Hawaii Press.
Buckland, R. (2013). *Kabuki: Japanese theatre prints.* Edinburgh: NMSE Publishing.
Halford, A. S., & Halford, G. M. (1956). *The Kabuki handbook.* Rutland, VT: Charles E. Tuttle.
Keene, D. (1998). *Four major plays of Chikamatsu.* New York: Columbia University Press.
Klett, E. (2001). Sonezaki Shinju (Love Suicides at Sonezaki), and Tsuri Onna (Fishing for a Wife) (Review). *Theatre Journal, 53*, 640–642.

Krysinska, K., & Lester, D. (2006). Comment on the Werther effect. *Crisis, 27*, 100.

Leiter, S. L. (1969). The depiction of violence on the Kabuki stage. *Educational Theatre Journal, 21*, 147–155.

Leiter, S. L. (2002). From gay to *Gei*, the *onnagata* and the creation of Kabuki's female characters. In S. L. Leiter (Ed.), *A kabuki reader: History and performance* (pp. 211–229). Armonk, NY: M. E. Sharpe.

Ozawa-de Silva, C. (2008). Too lonely to die alone: Internet suicide pacts and existential suffering in Japan. *Culture, Medicine, & Psychiatry, 32*, 516–551.

Robertson, J. (1999). Dying to tell: sexuality and suicide in Imperial Japan. *Signs, 25*, 1–35.

Sadler, A. L., & Atkins, P. S. (2010). *Japanese plays: Classic Noh, Kyogen and Kabuki works*. Tokyo, Japan: Tuttle.

Scott, A. C. (1955). *The kabuki theatre of Japan*. London: George Allen & Unwin.

Shively, D. H. (1955). Bakufu versus Kabuki. *Harvard Journal of Asiatic Studies, 18*, 326–356.

Takahashi, Y., & Berger, D. (1996). Cultural dynamics and suicide in Japan. In A. A. Leenaars & D. Lester (Eds.), *Suicide and the unconscious* (pp. 248–258). Northvale, NJ: Jason Aronson.

# Part II

## Theories of Media Impacts

# 10

# Why Media Coverage of Suicide May Increase Suicide Rates: An Epistemological Review

*Charles-Edouard Notredame, Nathalie Pauwels,*
*Michael Walter, Thierry Danel, Jean-Louis Nandrino,*
*and Guillaume Vaiva*

### Introduction

In his 1974 famous seminal paper, David Philips noticed that suicide rates were higher than expected every month a suicide event was reported in one of the most influential American newspapers' headlines (Phillips, 1974). This observation grounded a new field of research by systematically bridging media coverage and actual suicide epidemiology, thus making the first empirical assumption of a causal link between each other. Moreover, the sociologist proposed a suggestion-imitation process as a hypothetical account for the nature of this link (Phillips, 1974). It is not very clear whether the concept of "Werther effect" (WE) that he introduced referred to his epidemiological report or to the related etiological hypothesis. The confusion progressively became pervasive, as the majority of the following studies employed the concept without disentangling the semantic overlap. As a consequence, "WE" became a generic and vague term with limited heuristic value due to an implicit logical telescoping between its factual epidemiological and putative theoretical meanings.

After more than forty years of intensive research, the epidemiological impact of suicide coverage can now reasonably be considered confirmed. First, Philips' initial findings have been repeatedly reproduced all around the world, extended to other media (Pirkis & Blood, 2010;

Sisask & Värnik, 2012; Notredame, In Press), and successfully assessed with more sophisticated statistical procedures (e.g., Chen, Chen, & Yip, 2011; Hagihara et al., 2014). Based on an extensive review of the so-called *media effect studies*, Pirkis and Blood (Pirkis & Blood, 2010) went a step further and argued that the robust correlation that links suicide coverage and suicide rates satisfies enough of the Hill's criteria (Hill, 1965) to be considered causal. Finally, research has refined and characterized the epidemiological dimension of the WE by disclosing the main factors that modulate its magnitude: qualitative (story's frame, writing style, images, etc.) (Niederkrotenthaler & Sonneck, 2007; Niederkrotenthaler et al., 2010; Blood et al., 2001) and quantitative (coverage extent) properties of the media items (Etzersdorfer, Voracek, & Sonneck, 2004; Pirkis et al., 2006; Suh, Chang, & Kim, 2015), nature of the covered event, reader/viewer's predisposition (Chen et al., 2010a), and so on.

In parallel, authors have broadly discussed the causal mechanisms underlying the contagious propensity of suicides in the media. Interestingly, these discussions have their roots in the passionate debate that opposed two of the most influential sociologists of the nineteenth century (Abrutyn & Mueller, 2014). On the one hand, Gabriel Tarde (Tarde, 1903) subsumed suicidal contagion into a more general hypothesis of purely psychological imitation processes. On the contrary, Durkheim (Durkheim, 1897) adopted a broader scope and claimed that suicide should rather be considered a social fact under normative influence. As a consequence, he argued that suicide rates mainly reflect structural qualities of societies rather than singular conditions.

Modern accounts of the WE tend to follow Tarde's footstep and are dominated by psychological hypotheses. It is the case not only in the *media effect studies*, but also in the more general cluster suicide literature. Also referred to as *mass cluster*, WE represents a specific case of cluster suicide, numerically defined as an increase of suicide events limited in time, but not in space (Mesoudi, 2009; Niedzwiedz et al., 2014). Interestingly, cluster suicide approaches do not suffer from the semantic pitfall that we have pointed out, since their definition remains strictly epidemiological (Niedzwiedz et al., 2014; Blasco-Fontecilla, 2013) and allows authors to treat facts and causes distinctly. However, unlike *point clusters* (which are limited in space and time), WE implies indirect contact via media between the index case and the exposed individuals (Pirkis, 2009). This crucial difference probably appeals to theoretical specificities that should be taken into consideration.

Despite considerable attention, the nature of the causal link between suicide coverage and suicide rates remains largely unknown. We see three main reasons for that: (1) The semantic and logical confusion that we described for the WE is also true for the related theoretical concepts. For instance, the terms *contagion, imitation,* or *modeling* are often employed indistinctly (Gould, Wallenstein, & Davidson, 1989; Pirkis, 2009), without clear precision regarding the logical level at which they operate, that is, whether they refer to the epidemiological fact or to the underlying process. This lack of semantic clarity is not suitable for rigorous concept operationalization. (2) As already pointed out by many authors (Pouliot, Mishara, & Labelle, 2011; Sisask & Värnik, 2012; Yang et al., 2013), the vast majority of the *media effect studies* rely on ecological designs at a population level. With such designs, it is neither possible to know whether those who died by suicide were actually exposed to the risky media items, nor possible to study the individual psychological processes that led to this suicide. (3) Integration of the current assumptions is lacking, so that the WE's theoretical background remains fragmental. This lack of epistemological stabilization into a single coherent model is a major obstacle for the experimentalists to generate refutable hypotheses.

This chapter intends to meet the subsequent need for systematization by critically reviewing the theoretical hypotheses that have been raised to account for the WE. On the base of this review, a preliminary effort will be made to semantically clarify the most frequent related terms and concepts. We will then develop each of the main theories that have been put forward to explain the contagious potential of suicide coverage and try to disentangle the epistemological fields to which they belong. Finally, we will propose a general theoretical model, in an attempt to articulate the causes inventoried.

## Methods

The systematic research was carried on the MEDLINE and PsycINFO databases with no time restriction. The flowchart for selection of the analyzed papers is represented figure 10.1.

Following Haw et al. (Haw et al., 2013), we built the research algorithm by inventorying the most frequently evoked theories about the WE on the basis of a preliminary nonsystematic review of the literature. We first screened reports for English papers that focused on the link between media and suicide. For the sake of specificity, we then made the scope narrower by excluding, after full text-assessment, studies about social media or contagion of nonlethal self-harm, which might

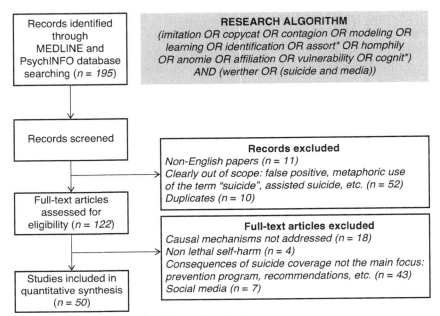

**Figure 10.1.** Selection of articles—flowchart.

involve particularities in their underlying causes. Papers that did not primarily focus on the consequences of media coverage, or without any reference to the causal mechanisms, were also excluded.

## Results

The screening resulted in selection of thirty-two original researches, nine qualitative or quantitative reviews, and nine case reports, editorials, letters, or opinions. Characteristics of the articles are shown in table 10.1.

A preliminary overview urges to clarify the generic terms that are most frequently employed in relation to the WE. This semantic specification is notably necessary to distinguish the purely descriptive expressions from the concepts that merely belong to the interpretative field, in order to stabilize the former and solidly ground the latter.

*Semantic Clarification: Describing the Werther Effect*

*Imitation/Copycat/Modeling.* The majority of the authors employed three main terms (and their declensions) as quasi-synonyms to refer to the epidemiological factuality of the WE: *imitation, copycat,* and *modeling* (cf. table 10.1). Two remarks are worth mentioning about this informal nomenclature: (1) While often used to describe the

**Table 10.1.** Studies that refer to a theoretical background for the Werther Effect: type of paper, design, expression used to refer to the Werther Effect and theories developed.

| Reference | Type of paper | Study design | Expressions used to refer to the Werther effect* | Theories developed** |
|---|---|---|---|---|
| Arendt et al. (2015) | Experimental study | Exposure to articles | Copycat<br>Modeling | Social learning<br>Identification<br>Cognitive effects (influence on implicit suicide cognitions) |
| Koburger et al. (2015) | Epidemiological study | Ecological | Imitation<br>Copycat<br>Modeling | Differential identification<br>Cognitive availability |
| Till et al. (2015) | Experimental study | Exposure to films | Copycat | Identification<br>Vulnerability<br>Emotional and cognitive effects (affective disposition theory, affective and perceptual constriction)<br>Social comparison theory |
| Leon et al. (2014) | Epidemiological study | Ecological | Copycat | Parental identification |
| Schäfer and Quiring (2014) | Epidemiological study<br>Communication study | Ecological<br>Qualitative analysis | Imitation<br>Model/modeling | Social learning<br>Precipitation assumption<br>Grief hypothesis |
| Niederkrotenthaler et al. (2014) | Review | Qualitative | Copycat | Cognitive availability<br>*Accounts for the Papageno effect*<br>Increase of awareness<br>Reduction of stigma<br>Increase of help-seeking |

*(Continued)*

**Table 10.1.** (Continued)

| Reference | Type of paper | Study design | Expressions used to refer to the Werther effect* | Theories developed** |
|---|---|---|---|---|
| Niederkrotenthaler et al. (2014) | Review | Qualitative | Copycat | Cognitive availability *Accounts for the Papageno effect* Increase of awareness Reduction of stigma Increase of help-seeking |
| Lee et al. (2014) | Epidemiological study Communication study | Ecological Qualitative analysis | Imitation Copycat Modeling | Social learning Differential identification Vulnerability |
| Gould et al. (2014) | Epidemiological study | Ecological | Modeling | Differential identification Priming hypothesis Normative pressure |
| Ueda et al. (2014) | Epidemiological study | Ecological | Imitation Copycat | Social learning Differential identification |
| Till et al. (2013) | Experimental | Exposure to films | Imitation Copycat | Identification/identity work Social learning |
| Suh et al. (2014) | Epidemiological study Model fitting | Ecological | Imitation Copycat Contagion | Social learning |
| Ju Ji et al. (2013) | Epidemiological study | Ecological | Imitation Copycat Modeling | Differential identification Vulnerability |
| Kim et al. (2013) | Epidemiological study | Ecological | Imitation | Differential identification |

| Study | | | Terms | Theory / Mechanism |
|---|---|---|---|---|
| Till et al. (2013) | Experimental | Exposure to films | Imitation<br>Copycat | Identification / identity work<br>Social learning |
| Blasco-Fontecilla (2012) | Letter | – | Imitation<br>Copycat<br>Contagion | Imitation (treated as a mechanism)<br>Contagion (treated as a mechanism)<br>Social learning<br>Identification<br>Assortative relating |
| Greenberg and Strous (2012) | Focus/case study | – | Copycat<br>Contagion | Emotional and cognitive effects<br>Disinhibition (related to normative pressure)<br>Social learning |
| Yang et al. (2012) | Epidemiological study | Ecological | Imitation<br>Copycat<br>Modeling<br>Contagion | Contagion (treated as a mechanism) |
| Sisask and Värnik (2012) | Review | Qualitative | Imitation<br>Copycat<br>Modeling<br>Contagion | Learning theory<br>Differential identification<br>Vulnerability<br>Anomie<br>*Accounts for the Papageno effect*<br>Model (treated as a normative pressure) |
| Zarghami (2012) | Editorial | – | Imitation<br>Copycat<br>Modeling<br>Contagion | Social learning<br>Differential identification<br>Vulnerability Homophily |
| Biddle (2012) | Qualitative study | Narrative | Imitation<br>Modeling | Provision of method information |

*(Continued)*

**Table 10.1.** (Continued)

| Reference | Type of paper | Study design | Expressions used to refer to the Werther effect* | Theories developed** |
|---|---|---|---|---|
| Ladwig et al. (2012) | Epidemiological study | Ecological | Imitation Contagion | Social learning Differential identification Modeling (treated as a mechanism related to identification) |
| Pouliot et al. (2011) | Epidemiological study | Analytic | – | Social learning Emotional and cognitive effects Vulnerability |
| Chen et al. (2010) | Epidemiological study Communication study | Ecological Qualitative analysis | Imitation Copycat Modeling | Identification |
| Kunrath et al. (2010) | Epidemiological study Communication study | Ecological Qualitative analysis | Imitation Copycat | Suggestion/attention Normative social pressure |
| Mesoudi (2009) | Computational study | Agent-based simulations | Imitation Copycat Modeling | Social learning Homophily One-to-many transmission Similarity and prestige biases |
| Niederkrotenthaler et al. (2009) | Epidemiological study Communication study | Ecological Qualitative analysis | Imitation Copycat Modeling | Differential identification Social learning |
| Chen et al. (2009) | Epidemiological study | Analytic | Imitation Copycat Modeling | Identification Vulnerability |

| | | | | |
|---|---|---|---|---|
| Ganizadeh (2009) | Case report | – | Imitation<br>Copycat | Social learning |
| Tor et al. (2008) | Commentary | – | Imitation<br>Copycat<br>Modeling | Social learning (treated as an equivalent of modeling)<br>Vulnerability |
| Insel and Gould (2008) | Review | Qualitative | Cluster<br>Imitation (developed in a *Terminology* section)<br>Modeling<br>Contagion | Social learning<br>Normative social pressure<br>Neurobiology |
| Yip and Lee (2007) | Epidemiological study | Ecological | Imitation<br>Copycat<br>Contagion | Cognitive availability and desirability (due to normative pressure)<br>Role of social indicators (socioeconomic conditions) |
| Andriessen (2007) | Letter | – | Imitation | Normative pressure<br>Cultural influence |
| Chotai et al. (2005) | Review | Qualitative | Imitation<br>Copycat<br>Contagion | Vulnerability<br>Activation hypothesis<br>Normative pressure |
| McKenzie et al. (2005) | Epidemiological study | Ecological | Copycat | Imitation (treated as a mechanism) |
| Stack (2005) | Review | Quantitative | Imitation<br>Modeling<br>Copycat | Social learning<br>Differential identification<br>Vulnerability<br>Symbolic interaction |

*(Continued)*

**Table 10.1.** (Continued)

| Reference | Type of paper | Study design | Expressions used to refer to the Werther effect* | Theories developed** |
|---|---|---|---|---|
| Toussignant et al. (2005) | Epidemiological study | Ecological | Imitation<br>Contagion<br>Modeling | Social learning<br>Differential identification<br>Behavioral contagion theory<br>Priming/activation hypotheses<br>Sleeper effect |
| Mishara (2003) | Commentary | – | – | Normative pressure (applied on children) |
| Stack (2003) | Review | Quantitative | Imitation<br>Copycat<br>Modeling | Social learning<br>Differential identification<br>Audience mood |
| Blood et al. (2001) | Review | Qualitative | Imitation | Reception theory<br>Role of social indicators (socioeconomic conditions) |
| | Communication study | Qualitative content analysis | | Attention<br>Cognitive effects<br>Media framing theory |
| Gould et al. (2001) | Review | Qualitative | Imitation<br>Copycat<br>Modeling<br>Contagion (treated as an analogy) | Behavioral contagion theory<br>Social learning<br>Attention<br>Differential identification<br>Cognitive and affective effects<br>Vulnerability<br>Environmental influence |

| Stack (2000) | Review | | Imitation<br>Copycat | Differential identification<br>Normative pressure<br>Audience mood |
|---|---|---|---|---|
| Lester and Schaller (2000) | Commentary | – | Suggestion/imitation | Imitation (treated as a mechanism)<br>*Accounts for the Papageno effect*<br>Psychological reactance theory |
| Stack (1993) | Epidemiological study | Ecological | Suggestion/imitation | Nonadditive model that links structural conditions and audience mood |
| Jonas et al. (1992) | Epidemiological study | Ecological | Imitation<br>Modeling | Disinhibition (related to social learning)<br>Coroner effect<br>Precipitation assumption<br>Grief hypothesis<br>Prior condition hypothesis |
| Stack (1992) | Epidemiological study | Ecological | Imitation<br>Copycat | Imitation (treated as a causal mechanism)<br>Social learning<br>Audience mood/receptivity<br>Symbolic interaction<br>Anomie |
| Taiminen et al. (1992) | Case report | – | Suggestion/imitation<br>Modeling<br>Contagion | Psychotic identification<br>Vulnerability<br>Anomie |
| Schmidtke et al. (1988) | Epidemiological study | Ecological | Imitation | Modeling (treated as a mechanism, related to social learning)<br>Differential identification<br>Precipitation assumption |

*(Continued)*

**Table 10.1.** (Continued)

| Reference | Type of paper | Study design | Expressions used to refer to the Werther effect[*] | Theories developed[**] |
|---|---|---|---|---|
| Stack (1988) | Epidemiological study | Ecological | Imitation | Audience mood, related to anomie<br>Audience receptivity<br>Differential identification |

[*]Expressions are collected in this column when authors use them or their declensions in a merely descriptive sense, without any reference to causal mechanisms.
[**]Theories are collected in this column when specifically developed as hypotheses to account for the Werther effect, being them explicitly labeled or not, supported or challenged. Theories are that are not developed in the manuscript are briefly explained hereafter: *Social comparison theory*: people tend to evaluate themselves by comparing themselves with the depicted character. *Affective disposition theory*: recipients' mood is attuned to the media content. *Grief hypothesis*: suicides are due to the sadness provoked by the celebrity's suicide. *Precipitation assumption*: apparent suicide contagion is due to precipitation of suicides that would have occurred anyway. *Terror management theory*: confrontation to death recruits coping strategies to buffer stress. Mode or reception: distinct and steadily forms of involvement to maintain a certain level of activation or specific mood. *Media framing theory*: the way media content is presented and made understandable directs the reader to attend to what is in the frame and not to what is excluded. *Psychological reactance theory*: situations in which the freedom to act on one's own will is threatened motivate people to restore that freedom by expending extra effort to obtain what was restricted (i.e. life when suicide is depicted). *Coroner effect*: apparent suicide contagion is due to death misclassification by suggestible coroners. *Prior condition hypothesis*: suicide stories may be connected with an increase in suicides.

empirical findings of the *media effect studies*, the meaning of these terms actually implicitly suggest a very first level of interpretation. More precisely, expressions such as "copycat suicides" or "imitative behaviors" insidiously transpose population-based findings to individual-level processes and assume a causal link beyond the correlation. Because causation can only be inferred from the whole ecological studys corpus (see Introduction), words as *imitation, copycat,* and *modeling* introduce ambiguity wherever they are employed in reference to the results of a single study, where a strict descriptive approach is expected. (2) Not only do the terms suggest a causal relationship, but they also have in common to pinpoint, beyond the Hill criteria, a supplementary clue that the index case and the subsequent suicides are causally linked, namely their similarity. It is a robust finding of the *media effect studies* that individuals who share the sex and/or age of the celebrity whose suicide is depicted are overrepresented among the so-called *copycat suicides* (Schmidtke & Häfner, 1988; Chen et al., 2010a; Ju Ji et al., 2014). Similarly, after a celebrity or singular self-death has been reported, suicide methods that are identical to the original case are found more frequent than usual (Chen et al., 2010a; Tousignant et al., 2005; Ladwig et al., 2012; Schäfer & Quiring, 2014). However, even when authors explicitly refer to *imitation, copycat,* or *modeling* as mechanisms to account for these observations, ambiguity remains. Although the similarity cue reinforces the causality assumption, it tells nothing—as long as based on ecological designs—about *how* a covered method might trigger individual use of the same procedure and about *why* people who are similar to the index case might be at higher risk of imitation. As pointed out by Pirkis and Blood (Blood & Pirkis, 2001), this vocabulary may rather mirror the positivist-like approach on which ecological studies are based. Through the stimulus–response model filter, *imitation* can be thought of as the behavioral outcome of exposing one individual to suicide stories, but without any assumption about what is happening in the "black box" that bridges the stimulus and the response.

*Contagion. Contagion* is frequently used as an equivalent for WE. However, the epistemological status of the term deserves special examination. Indeed, unlike the other synonyms, *contagion* more clearly refers to a macro-individual process by which "one suicide facilitates the occurrence of subsequent suicides" (Insel & Gould, 2008). After having reviewed its occurrences across 340 studies, Cheng et al. (Cheng et al.,

2014) identified two meaning strata: *contagion-as-cluster*, that refers to the epidemiological dimension, and *contagion-as-mechanism*. Rather than a meaning overlap, we would argue that the puzzling use of the word reveals confusions in the levels of comprehension by which the WE is assessed. It is noteworthy that *contagion* belongs to the infectious disease vocabulary (Haw et al., 2013; Cheng et al., 2014). In this field of knowledge, the concept represents an explanatory model per se, built to account for both macro-individual observations (epidemics) and micro-individual causes (transmission of pathogenic agents). This twofold dimension makes the model suitable to be transposed in the suicide research field, in order to explain similarities in epidemiological observations. For instance, Yang et al. found that the WE gets stronger with the density of population, as would flu transmission (Yang et al., 2013). However, the infectious model does not allow for any direct inference about the causes of the WE. It should rather be considered as an analogy, a conceptual framework to which WE can be compared to in order to open up and structure lines of research and generate hypotheses (Joiner, 1999). More precisely, the following components of the infectious model can be proposed to analogically help articulating various potential contributors of the WE (Cheng et al., 2014; Haw et al., 2013; Gould, 2001): (1) modes of transmission (direct vs. indirect; Gould, Wallenstein, & Davidson, 1989; *one-to-one* vs. *one-to-many*; Mesoudi, 2009); (2) channels of infection (influence of the type of media that relay the suicide news); (3) host susceptibility (audience vulnerability); (4) incubation and viremic period (dynamic dimension of the WE); (5) degree of virulence (risk related to qualitative aspects of media coverage); (6) dose dependency (risk related to quantitative aspects of media coverage); (7) quarantine and sanitary measures (interventions to prevent the WE).

### Causal Hypotheses: Behind Werther Effect

An overview of our sample revealed a clear dividing line between *social* and *psychological theories*. Social accounts—also referred to as *collective theories*—consider WE to be a consequence of modifications in the way societies are structured and carry shared representations. On the contrary, *psychological* or *individual theories* try to understand the WE through intra-individual mechanisms, by exploring how readers/auditors/viewers emotionally, cognitively, and behaviorally react when exposed to suicide-related media items.

*Psychological Accounts: Social Learning.* Reconsidered in the behavioral theories light, the WE could be summarized by the following question: why may someone acquire an extreme conduct such as suicide, simply by observing it? Obviously, classical or operant conditioning can't apply to this context, since the observer doesn't directly experiment the consequences of a nonreproducible behavior. Bandura's *social learning theory* is frequently used to solve the issue (Bandura, 1977). According to the psychologist, one may learn the behavior of an observed model whenever this behavior leads to some form of reward (Tousignant et al., 2005). In the WE, this pro-social process is thought to become maladaptive (Zarghami, 2012; Suh, Chang, & Kim, 2015). Instead of being considered strongly aversive, lethal behaviors could be interpreted as a way of relieving pain or bringing notoriety, especially when the coverage style is sensationalist, trivial, or romantic (Stack, 1992). Subjectively perceived as a gain, the outcome of the depicted suicide acts as a reinforcer and increases the likelihood of imitation (Insel & Gould, 2008; Ladwig et al., 2012).

When speaking about *observational learning*, some moderating processes should be taken into account (Bandura, 1977; Schäfer & Quiring, 2014). First, factors related to the learner, including, for instance, vulnerability or identification, crucially influence the motivational process described above (see Differential Identification and Vulnerability sections). Attention also has an important role (Bandura, 1977; Schäfer & Quiring, 2014; Gould, Wallenstein, & Davidson, 1989): the more visible and attractive the model (for instance, due to redundancies in stories, large audiences, emphatic style, or use of pictures; Niederkrotenthaler & Sonneck, 2007; Niederkrotenthaler et al., 2010; Schäfer & Quiring, 2014), the more probable the learning process. Additionally, attributes of the model are thought to have a crucial influence. For instance, *social learning theory* predicts that when the outcome of the behavior is uncertain, the learner may estimate its rewarding value on the base of the model social status (Till et al., 2013). Thereby, celebrities could be a priori associated with an implicit reinforcing that increases the risk of copycat behaviors (Tousignant et al., 2005). Finally, this cognitive *prestige bias* has a counterpart according to which individuals preferentially copy the behavior of models that are similar to them, that is, *similarity bias* (Mesoudi, 2009; McElreath & Henrich, 2006).

*Psychological Accounts: Differential Identification.* Since Tarde (Tarde, 1903) and Bandura (Bandura, 1977), *identification* has frequently been presented as a necessary prerequisite for *social learning* to ultimately lead to self-harm imitation (Ladwig et al., 2012; Niederkrotenthaler et al., 2009; Tor, Ng, & Ang, 2008). Because it depends on two distinct dimensions of the model-audience dyad, *identification* is said to be *differential* (Lee et al., 2014; Ju Ji et al., 2014; Sisask & Värnik, 2012; Zarghami, 2012; Stack, 1992). The first dimension is *vertical*. It predicts that identification gets stronger with the extent to which the model is desired (Chen et al., 2010b), admired, or perceived as socially superior (Zarghami, 2012; Niederkrotenthaler et al., 2009; Stack, 1992, 2005). In the *social learning theory, vertical identification* cognitively results in *prestige bias* and helps understanding why celebrities—and more particularly socially approved celebrities (Kim et al., 2013; Stack, 2000)—have been robustly associated to the most manifest WEs. By contrast, the second dimension, namely *horizontal identification*, posits that similarities between the index case and the audience facilitate imitation (Niederkrotenthaler et al., 2009; Lee et al., 2014; Ju Ji et al., 2014; Zarghami, 2012), through the above-mentioned *similarity bias*. Empirical population-based findings specifically validate the statement for the strongest markers of identity, that is, age and sex (Stack, 1991; Sisask & Värnik, 2012). Importantly, *vertical* and *horizontal* dimensions are cumulative (Lee et al., 2014; Zarghami, 2012; Tousignant et al., 2005), so that celebrity suicides have their highest impact on populations of the same age and/or gender (see Section Imitation/Copycat/Modeling).

Some authors more explicitly explored the psychological dimension of the concept. As Haw et al. remind us (Haw et al., 2013), *identification* has psychoanalytic roots into Melanie Klein's theory of identity development (Klein, 1955). Nowadays, psychoanalytic theories have been critically reconsidered and adapted to articulate with cognitive psychology and form more positively testable hypotheses. For instance, Cohen defined *identification* as a tendency not only to share one's emotions and perceptions, but also to adopt his identity and perspective, with a temporary loss of self-awareness (Cohen, 2001). Concerning the WE, this definition helps understanding why *pathological* (Sacks & Eth, 1981) or *psychotic identification* (Taiminen, Salmenperä, & Lehtinen, 1992) may lead to extreme conducts such as suicide. To that respect, Till et al. explored the consequences of presenting films that depict suicide to nonclinical populations. He found that participants who presented with higher suicidality scores more frequently used the films as a support for identity work, that is, active seeking of ideas about how to cope with life events (Till et al., 2013). Interestingly, when exploring the factors that reinforce the *identification* tendency, Till et al. found a strong correlation with the empathy scores (Till et al., 2012, 2013). Although, the authors argue for a causal link, this correlation could also reveal conceptual overlaps between *identification* and the modern understandings of empathy as a complex multifaceted pro-social process (Gonzalez-Liencres, Shamay-Tsoory, & Brüne, 2013).

*Psychological Accounts: Cognitive and Emotional Effects.* Many authors have considered the impacts of suicide media stories in terms of emotional and cognitive disruption. With a quasi case–control study, Pouliot et al. (Pouliot, Mishara, & Labelle, 2011) found suicide scenes to generate transitory distress reactions that could last up to several weeks. Till et al. (2011, 2015) experimentally reproduced the finding by inducing mood deterioration in an euthymic sample through exposure to a fictional suicide. Moreover, the authors found that this effect significantly correlated with the participants' self-reported identification to the story character. In accordance with the *differential identification* theory, the pernicious influence of suicide coverage on mood could thus be seen as the consequence of the reader's excessive propensity to "put himself in the depicted deceased's shoes," to the point of suffering as he did (Till et al., 2010, 2015). This emotional resonance could be attributed to the emotional component of empathy, conceived as an embodied shared representation (Ripoll et al., 2013).

Along with affective impacts, media stories might also act on cognitive schemes. Indeed, media contents about suicide necessarily carry an implicit normative model about how to cope with psychological crisis (see Section Psychological Accounts). Vulnerable recipients who identify with the story character might integrate this model into their own cognitive representations of suicide. If reported incautiously, the death depiction could thus have two main consequences: (1) By linking suicide to a unique cause (Yip & Lee, 2007), giving an impression of familiarity, and, sometimes, providing practical details about the procedure (Biddle et al., 2012), it could foster the idea that suicide is a theoretically and technically accessible solution to relieve suffering—a condition known as *cognitive availability* (Niederkrotenthaler et al., 2014); [2] it could also relay an implicit moral appreciation, by conveying the image of an acceptable, rational, or salutary way of dying (cf. *Social learning theory*). This could generate a more positive and fearless attitude toward suicide and tilt the avoidance/approach decision balance toward copycat behaviors (Cheng et al., 2014).

It is now quite clear that the WE peaks within the three days after the index case coverage, exponentially tails off in about one month (Pirkis & Blood, 2001; Suh, Chang, & Kim, 2015), but can persist for up to several years (Hegerl et al., 2013). These dynamics suggest that the cognitive and emotional effects operate on different timescales. In the most vulnerable ones, media stories may either induce cognitive biases or disinhibit latent preprogrammed cognitive schemes (through *activation* or *priming* processes; Gould et al., 2014; Tousignant et al., 2005) in such a severe way that it precipitates the behavioral component of the *social learning* process (Schäfer & Quiring, 2014; Jonas, 1992) and causes the patient to act out its suicidal ideations (Till et al., 2013). By contrast, when not leading to immediate behavioral consequences, cognitive and emotional disturbances may result in higher vulnerability to ulterior life stressors. In this case, exposure to media stories is thought to predispose to later suicidal behaviors via a *sleeper effect* (Tousignant et al., 2005) or, in Bandura's theory, via an *retention process* (Schäfer & Quiring, 2014) insidiously operating on implicit memory (Arendt, Till, & Niederkrotenthaler, 2015).

*Psychological Accounts: Vulnerability.* WE is considered to require a vulnerable condition preliminary to media exposure. It is common sense—but still, validated by the literature—that suicide imitation is first imputable to general suicidogenic risk factors (Lee et al., 2014; Zarghami, 2012; Tor, Ng, & Ang, 2008). However, it has been discussed whether vulnerability to the WE merely consists in a general predisposition to suicide or to a more specific tendency to imitate suicide stories. Rather than an antagonism, the debate may reveal the multidimensionality of the concept. Beyond a nonspecific vulnerability to suicide, *audience receptivity* (Sisask & Värnik, 2012; Stack, 1992) may qualify the individual proneness to engage in one of the psychological mechanisms that we described above. One example is young populations for whom WE have been found particularly severe (Insel & Gould, 2008; Ju Ji et al., 2014; Chen et al., 2010b; Gould et al., 2014). Although adolescence is considered an at-risk period per se (Gould et al., 2003), teenagers' vulnerability to copycat behaviors could also be explained by their developmental normal tendency to identify with peers and/or icons (Cohen, 2001). Moreover, due to heterosynchronous brain maturation and lack of prefrontal executive control (Blakemore & Choudhury, 2006), adolescents may also be more at risk of overreacting to suicide stories, which could more readily disinhibit latent suicidal cognitive patterns and trigger self-harm behaviors (Insel & Gould, 2008). In the same way, depression was identified early as a candidate for WE potentiation. According to Stack, *audience mood* mediates the effect of suicidogenic socioeconomic conditions on media impact (Stack, 2003, 2005). Through a process of *symbolic interaction*, depression, low self-esteem, or pessimism, all attuned to the general social climate, would facilitate *social learning* (Bandura, 1977) and finally imitation (Taiminen, Salmenperä, & Lehtinen, 1992). More recent individual-level findings tend to confirm the hypothesis. Scheer and Reinemann (Scherr & Reinemann, 2011) found that depression switched the cognitive effect of suicide stories from induction of a "presumed WE," that is, other's risk of imitation estimated higher than own, to induction of a self-centered WE, where recipients fear of engaging themselves in copycat behaviors. Similarly, Chen et al. (Chen et al., 2010b) showed that individuals who just made a suicide attempt are more likely to report influence of media stories when they present with active symptoms of major depression.

Finally, it is worth mentioning that one the most crucial components of *audience receptivity* might be suicidality per se. With an experimental controlled design, Till et al. (Till et al., 2015) recently showed that presentation of a film depicting a suicide tends to increase suicide ideation scores more severely when the baseline scores are higher. Importantly, this later marker significantly interacted with the tendency to identify with the story character, thus suggesting a causal relationship. Presenting with suicide ideas might increase the audience receptivity by disturbing the ability to shift the point of view and distance from the character's experience (Till et al., 2015). This *perceptual constriction* could contribute to the maladaptive reinforcement of identification, thus leading to higher impact of media items (Chen et al. 2010a; Cheng et al., 2007).

*Sociological Accounts: Shared Representations.* When dealing with suicide, media stories not only report events, but also transport an implicit image of what it consists in, what could legitimate or explain it, and what can be its consequences (Niederkrotenthaler et al., 2014). Suicide representations, which are crucially influenced by the editing choices (e.g., relating the suicide to a unique cause vs. revealing prior vulnerability) and the writing style (e.g., cautious vs. sensationalist), could be integrated as a normative model by vulnerable individuals or those who don't know much about its clinical and scientific realities. This *normative pressure* can exert its influence on different levels: [1] by weighting the approach/avoidance balance (see Section Cognitive and Emotional), either toward inhibition if suicide is presented as a medical condition that can be prevented (Niederkrotenthaler et al., 2010) or toward disinhibition when suicide is depicted as an acceptable solution or socially valuable behavior (Gould et al., 2014; Insel & Gould, 2008; Stack, 2000); [2] by influencing collective attitudes toward suicide, thus promoting access to health services or, on the contrary, impeding it by fostering stigma (Niederkrotenthaler et al., 2014).

*Sociological Accounts: Structural Hypotheses.* According to structural hypotheses, suicide clusters should be seen as by-products of more general architectural properties of social networks. For instance, Joiner rejected the idea that imitation accounts for the apparent spatiotemporal contagion of suicide (Joiner, 1999, 2003). He argued that point clusters rather reveal the tendency of similar individuals to group (*assortative relating* or *homophily)* or be found in the same social layers (*assortative susceptibility*). This would result in the formation of high-risk clusters prior to the occurrence of any suicide. Nevertheless, *homophily* doesn't seem to apply for mass clusters, where suicides epidemics are unlimited in space. Another component of Joiner's model seems more relevant to account for the WE, namely the lack of social support. The idea, directly stemming from Durkheim's proposal, is the following: suicide epidemics are directly linked to the degree of organization and structural steadiness of the society. In this view, structural instability undermines social ties, weakens collective norms (a condition called *anomie* (Thorlindsson & Bernburg, 2009; Stack, 2000; Hoffman & Bearman, 2015)), and finally fosters distrust and hopelessness (Taiminen, Salmenperä, & Lehtinen, 1992; Stack, 1992). *Anomie* is a useful concept to enlighten several observations related to the WE. First it reinforces the causal bridge between Stack's concepts of *suicidogenic context* and *audience mood,* by considering that social adverse conditions destabilize societies, which in turn negatively affect individuals' welfare. Then, it allows understanding why unscheduled disorganizing events are associated to waves of suicides, even when they are supposed to have positive consequences (Hoffman & Bearman, 2015). Finally, it plausibly accounts for why young individuals, who are less closely tied to the social fabric than their middle-aged counterparts, are more at risk of WE (Sisask & Värnik, 2012).

## Conclusion: Proposition of Integration

The development of the main hypotheses that have been raised to account for the WE reveals that most of them operate on different levels, either macro-individual for sociological theories or micro-individual for psychological theories. Even within the same level, causal hypotheses involve various interrelated processes (cognitions, emotions, behaviors) or parameters (degree of anomie, socioeconomic conditions). Once the epistemological value of WE-related terms is clarified, that is, purely descriptive or analogical terms are disentangled from causal concepts, an attempt could be made to integrate these concepts into a single model. Our proposal is presented in figure 10.2.

This psychosocial model takes into account the numerous overlaps and bridges that we found in our review by coherently articulating most of the above-mentioned mechanisms. Of course, this proposal is not

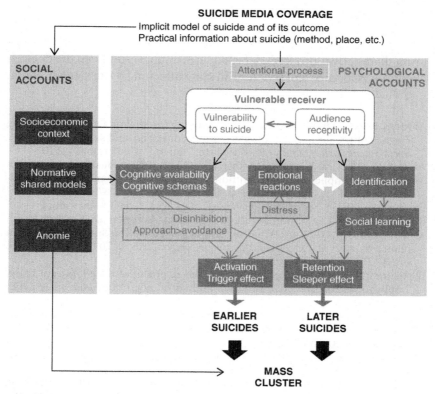

**Figure 10.2.** Hypothetical model of the causal process leading to the WE.

definitive. Rather, it aims to stimulate research by serving as a basis for new hypotheses, orienting the experimental testing of each component in relation to each other, and finally prompting validation and refutation.

Mass cluster suicides probably result from a complex sequence of articulated sociological and psychological mechanisms. On the individual level, imitative behaviors might stem from the encounter between at-risk media items and a vulnerable audience, priorly prone to both suicide and suicide imitation due to interrelated individual and social conditions (anomie, socioeconomic climate, etc.). Under these circumstances, exposure to suicide stories may lead to emotional distress and cognitive endorsement of the normative model implicitly conveyed by the article. These effects may facilitate identification with the story character, which, in turn, may reinforce the cognitive and emotional impacts on the receiver, finally inciting him to adopt imitative self-harm behavior. Given the WE dynamics, the behavioral consequences of the cognitive disinhibition (disequilibrium of the approach/avoidance balance), the emotional distress, and the social learning probably operate on different timescales. While early suicides might be due to an immediate activation effect, later suicides might result from the delayed decompensation of a psychological state affected by the sleeper effect.

## References

Abrutyn, S., & Mueller, A. S. (2014). Reconsidering Durkheim's assessment of tarde: Formalizing a Tardian theory of imitation, contagion, and suicide suggestion. *Sociological Forum, 29*(3), 698–719. http://doi.org/10.1111/socf.12110

Arendt, F., Till, B., & Niederkrotenthaler, T. (2015). Effects of suicide awareness material on implicit suicide cognition: A laboratory experiment. *Health Communication*, 1–9. http://doi.org/10.1080/10410236.2014.993495

Bandura, A. (1977). *Social learning theory.* New York: General Learning Press.

Biddle, L., Gunnell, D., Owen-Smith, A., Potokar, J., Longson, D., Hawton, K., . . . Donovan, J. (2012). Information sources used by the suicidal to inform choice of method. *Journal of Affective Disorders, 136*(3), 702–709. http://doi.org/10.1016/j.jad.2011.10.004

Blakemore, S.-J., & Choudhury, S. (2006). Development of the adolescent brain: Implications for executive function and social cognition. *Journal of Child Psychology and Psychiatry, 47*(3–4), 296–312.

Blasco-Fontecilla, H. (2013). On suicide clusters: More than contagion. *Australian & New Zealand Journal of Psychiatry, 47*(5), 490–491. http://doi.org/10.1177/0004867412465023

Blood, R. W., & Pirkis, J. (2001). Suicide and the media: Part III. Theoretical issues. *Crisis: The Journal of Crisis Intervention and Suicide Prevention, 22*(4), 163.

Blood, R. W., Putnis, P., Pirkis, J., Payne, T., & Francis, C. (2001). Monitoring media coverage of suicide: theory and methodology. *Australian Journalism Review, 23*(1), 57.

Chen, Y.-Y., Chen, F., & Yip, P. S. F. (2011). The impact of media reporting of suicide on actual suicides in Taiwan, 2002–05. *Journal of Epidemiology and Community Health, 65*(10), 934–940. http://doi.org/10.1136/jech.2010.117903

Chen, Y.-Y., Tsai, P.-C., Chen, P.-H., Fan, C.-C., Hung, G. C.-L., & Cheng, A. T. A. (2010a). Effect of media reporting of the suicide of a singer in Taiwan: the case of Ivy Li. *Social Psychiatry and Psychiatric Epidemiology, 45*(3), 363–369. http://doi.org/10.1007/s00127-009-0075-8

Chen, Y.-Y., Tsai, P.-C., Chen, P.-H., Fan, C.-C., Hung, G. C.-L., & Cheng, A. T. A. (2010b). Effect of media reporting of the suicide of a singer in Taiwan: the case of Ivy Li. *Social Psychiatry and Psychiatric Epidemiology, 45*(3), 363–369. http://doi.org/10.1007/s00127-009-0075-8

Cheng, A. T. A., Hawton, K., Chen, T. H. H., Yen, A. M. F., Chang, J.-C., Chong, M.-Y., . . . Chen, L.-C. (2007). The influence of media reporting of a celebrity suicide on suicidal behavior in patients with a history of depressive disorder. *Journal of Affective Disorders, 103*(1–3), 69–75. http://doi.org/10.1016/j.jad.2007.01.021

Cheng, Q., Li, H., Silenzio, V., & Caine, E. D. (2014). Suicide contagion: A systematic review of definitions and research utility.

Cohen, J. (2001). Defining identification: A theoretical look at the identification of audiences with media characters. *Mass Communication & Society, 4*(3), 245–264.

Durkheim, É. (1897). *Le Suicide*. Paris: Alcan.

Etzersdorfer, E., Voracek, M., & Sonneck, G. (2004). A dose-response relationship between imitational suicides and newspaper distribution. *Archives of Suicide Research, 8*(2), 137–145.

Gonzalez-Liencres, C., Shamay-Tsoory, S. G., & Brüne, M. (2013). Towards a neuroscience of empathy: Ontogeny, phylogeny, brain mechanisms, context and psychopathology. *Neuroscience & Biobehavioral Reviews, 37*(8), 1537–1548. http://doi.org/10.1016/j.neubiorev.2013.05.001

Gould, M. S. (2001). Suicide and the media. *Annals of the New York Academy of Sciences, 932*(1), 200–224.

Gould, M. S., Greenberg, T. E. D., Velting, D. M., & Shaffer, D. (2003). Youth suicide risk and preventive interventions: a review of the past 10 years. *Journal of the American Academy of Child & Adolescent Psychiatry, 42*(4), 386–405.

Gould, M. S., Kleinman, M. H., Lake, A. M., Forman, J., & Midle, J. B. (2014). Newspaper coverage of suicide and initiation of suicide clusters in teenagers in the USA, 1988–96: a retrospective, population-based, case-control study. *The Lancet Psychiatry, 1*(1), 34–43.

Gould, M. S., Wallenstein, S., & Davidson, L. (1989). Suicide clusters: A critical review. *Suicide and Life-Threatening Behavior, 19*(1), 17–29.

Hagihara, A., Abe, T., Omagari, M., Motoi, M., & Nabeshima, Y. (2014). The impact of newspaper reporting of hydrogen sulfide suicide on imitative suicide attempts in Japan. *Social Psychiatry and Psychiatric Epidemiology, 49*(2), 221–229. http://doi.org/10.1007/s00127-013-0741-8

Haw, C., Hawton, K., Niedzwiedz, C., & Platt, S. (2013). Suicide clusters: A review of risk factors and mechanisms. *Suicide and Life-Threatening Behavior, 43*(1), 97–108. http://doi.org/10.1111/j.1943-278X.2012.00130.x

Hegerl, U., Koburger, N., Rummel-Kluge, C., Gravert, C., Walden, M., & Mergl, R. (2013). One followed by many?—Long-term effects of a celebrity suicide on the number of suicidal acts on the German railway net. *Journal of Affective Disorders, 146*(1), 39–44. http://doi.org/10.1016/j.jad.2012.08.032

Hill, A. B. (1965). The environment and disease: Association or causation? *Proceedings of the Royal Society of Medicine, 58*(5), 295–300.

Hoffman, M., & Bearman, P. (2015). Bringing anomie back in: Exceptional events and excess suicide. *Sociological Science, 2*, 186–210. http://doi.org/10.15195/v2.a10

Insel, B. J., & Gould, M. S. (2008). Impact of modeling on adolescent suicidal behavior. *Psychiatric Clinics of North America, 31*(2), 293–316. http://doi.org/10.1016/j.psc.2008.01.007

Joiner, T. E. (1999). The clustering and contagion of suicide. *Current Directions in Psychological Science, 8*(3), 89–92.

Joiner, T. E. (2003). Contagion of suicidal symptoms as a function of assortative relating and shared relationship stress in college roommates. *Journal of Adolescence, 26*(4), 495–504. http://doi.org/10.1016/S0140-1971(02)00133-1

Jonas, K. (1992). Modelling and suicide: a test of the Werther effect. *British Journal of Social Psychology, 31*(4), 295–306.

Ju Ji, N., Young Lee, W., Seok Noh, M., & Yip, P. S. F. (2014). The impact of indiscriminate media coverage of a celebrity suicide on a society with a high suicide rate: Epidemiological findings on copycat suicides from South Korea. *Journal of Affective Disorders, 156*, 56–61. http://doi.org/10.1016/j.jad.2013.11.015

Kim, J.-H., Park, E.-C., Nam, J.-M., Park, S., Cho, J., Kim, S.-J., . . . Cho, E. (2013). The Werther Effect of Two Celebrity Suicides: an Entertainer and a Politician. *PLoS ONE, 8*(12), e84876. http://doi.org/10.1371/journal.pone.0084876

Klein, M., & others. (1955). On identification. *The Writings of Melanie Klein, 3*, 141–175.

Koburger, N., Mergl, R., Rummel-Kluge, C., Ibelshäuser, A., Meise, U., Postuvan, V., . . . Hegerl, U. (2015). Celebrity suicide on the railway network: Can one case trigger international effects? *Journal of Affective Disorders, 185*, 38–46. http://doi.org/10.1016/j.jad.2015.06.037

Ladwig, K.-H., Kunrath, S., Lukaschek, K., & Baumert, J. (2012). The railway suicide death of a famous German football player: impact on the subsequent frequency of railway suicide acts in Germany. *Journal of Affective Disorders, 136*(1–2), 194–198. http://doi.org/10.1016/j.jad.2011.09.044

Lee, A.-R., Ahn, M. H., Lee, T. Y., Park, S., & Hong, J. P. (2014). Rapid spread of suicide by charcoal burning from 2007 to 2011 in Korea. *Psychiatry Research, 219*(3), 518–524. http://doi.org/10.1016/j.psychres.2014.06.037

Leon, S., Cloutier, P., Bélair, M.-A., & Cappelli, M. (2014). Media coverage of youth suicides and its impact on paediatric mental health emergency department presentations. *Healthcare Policy | Politiques de Santé, 10*(1), 95–105. http://doi.org/10.12927/hcpol.2014.23940

McElreath, R., & Henrich, J. (2006). Modeling cultural evolution. *RIM Dunvar, & Barret (Eds.), Oxford Handbook of Evolutionary Biology*. Retrieved from http://www2.psych.ubc.ca/~henrich/pdfs/mcelreath_henrich_mce_final.pdf

Mesoudi, A. (2009). The cultural dynamics of copycat suicide. *PLoS ONE, 4*(9), e7252. http://doi.org/10.1371/journal.pone.0007252

Niederkrotenthaler, T., Reidenberg, D. J., Till, B., & Gould, M. S. (2014). Increasing help-seeking and referrals for individuals at risk for suicide by decreasing stigma: The role of mass media. *American Journal of Preventive Medicine, 47*(3), S235–S243.

Niederkrotenthaler, T., & Sonneck, G. (2007). Assessing the impact of media guidelines for reporting on suicides in Austria: Interrupted time series analysis.

*The Australian and New Zealand Journal of Psychiatry, 41*(5), 419–428. http:// doi.org/10.1080/00048670701266680

Niederkrotenthaler, T., Till, B., Kapusta, N. D., Voracek, M., Dervic, K., & Sonneck, G. (2009). Copycat effects after media reports on suicide: A population-based ecologic study. *Social Science & Medicine, 69*(7), 1085–1090. http://doi .org/10.1016/j.socscimed.2009.07.041

Niederkrotenthaler, T., Voracek, M., Herberth, A., Till, B., Strauss, M., Etzersdorfer, E., . . . Sonneck, G. (2010). Role of media reports in completed and prevented suicide: Werther v. Papageno effects. *The British Journal of Psychiatry, 197*(3), 234–243. http://doi.org/10.1192/bjp.bp.109.074633

Niedzwiedz, C., Haw, C., Hawton, K., & Platt, S. (2014). The definition and epidemiology of clusters of suicidal behavior: A systematic review. *Suicide and Life-Threatening Behavior, 44*(5), 569–581. http://doi.org/10.1111 /sltb.12091

Notredame, C.-E. (In Press). Le traitement médiatique du suicide : du constat épidémiologique aux pistes de prévention. *La Presse Médicale.*

Phillips, D. P. (1974). The influence of suggestion on suicide: substantive and theoretical implications of the Werther effect. *American Sociological Review.* Retrieved from http://psycnet.apa.org/psycinfo/1974-32695-001

Pirkis, J. (2009). Suicide and the media. *Psychiatry, 8*(7), 269–271.

Pirkis, J., & Blood, R. W. (2001). Suicide and the media. Part I: Reportage in non-fictional media. *Crisis, 22*(4), 146–154.

Pirkis, J., & Blood, R. W. (2010). Suicide and the news and information media. A critical review. *Mind Frame Media.*

Pirkis, J. E., Burgess, P. M., Francis, C., Blood, R. W., & Jolley, D. J. (2006). The relationship between media reporting of suicide and actual suicide in Australia. *Social Science & Medicine, 62*(11), 2874–2886. http://doi.org/10.1016/j .socscimed.2005.11.033

Pouliot, L., Mishara, B. L., & Labelle, R. (2011). The Werther effect reconsidered in light of psychological vulnerabilities: results of a pilot study. *Journal of Affective Disorders, 134*(1–3), 488–496. http://doi.org/10.1016/j. jad.2011.04.050

Ripoll, L. H., Snyder, R., Steele, H., & Siever, L. J. (2013). The neurobiology of empathy in borderline personality disorder. *Current Psychiatry Reports, 15*(3). http://doi.org/10.1007/s11920-012-0344-1

Sacks, M., & Eth, S. (1981). Pathological identification as a cause of suicide on an inpatient unit. *Psychiatric Services, 32*(1), 36–40.

Schäfer, M., & Quiring, O. (2014). The press coverage of celebrity suicide and the development of suicide frequencies in Germany. *Health Communication, 30*(11), 1149–1158. http://doi.org/10.1080/10410236.2014.923273

Scherr, S., & Reinemann, C. (2011). Belief in a werther effect: Third-Person effects in the perceptions of suicide risk for others and the moderating role of depression: Belief in a Werther effect. *Suicide and Life-Threatening Behavior, 41*(6), 624–634. http://doi.org/10.1111/j.1943-278X.2011.00059.x

Schmidtke, A., & Häfner, H. (1988). The Werther effect after television films: new evidence for an old hypothesis. *Psychological Medicine, 18*(03), 665–676.

Sisask, M., & Värnik, A. (2012). Media roles in suicide prevention: A systematic review. *International Journal of Environmental Research and Public Health, 9*(12), 123–138. http://doi.org/10.3390/ijerph9010123

Stack, S. (1991). Social correlates of suicide by age. In *Life span perspectives of suicide* (pp. 187–213). Springer. Retrieved from http://link.springer.com/chapter/10.1007/978-1-4899-0724-0_14

Stack, S. (1992). The effect of the media on suicide: The Great Depression. *Suicide & Life-Threatening Behavior, 22*(2), 255–267.

Stack, S. (2000). Media impacts on suicide: A quantitative review of 293 findings. *Social Science Quarterly.* Retrieved from http://psycnet.apa.org/psycinfo/2001-14385-003

Stack, S. (2003). Media coverage as a risk factor in suicide. *Journal of Epidemiology and Community Health, 57*(4), 238–240.

Stack, S. (2005). Suicide in the media: A quantitative review of studies based on nonfictional stories. *Suicide and Life-Threatening Behavior, 35*(2), 121–133.

Suh, S., Chang, Y., & Kim, N. (2015). Quantitative exponential modelling of copycat suicides: association with mass media effect in South Korea. *Epidemiology and Psychiatric Sciences, 24*(02), 150–157. http://doi.org/10.1017/S204579601400002X

Taiminen, T., Salmenperä, T., & Lehtinen, K. (1992). A suicide epidemic in a psychiatric hospital. *Suicide and Life-Threatening Behavior, 22*(3), 350–363.

Tarde, G. (1903). The laws of imitation, trans. *EC Parsons.* New York: Henry, Holt.

Thorlindsson, T., & Bernburg, J. G. (2009). Community structural instability, anomie, imitation and adolescent suicidal behavior. *Journal of Adolescence, 32*(2), 233–245. http://doi.org/10.1016/j.adolescence.2008.04.003

Till, B., Niederkrotenthaler, T., Herberth, A., Vitouch, P., & Sonneck, G. (2010). Suicide in films: The impact of suicide portrayals on nonsuicidal viewers' well-being and the effectiveness of censorship. *Suicide and Life-Threatening Behavior, 40*(4), 319–327.

Till, B., Strauss, M., Sonneck, G., & Niederkrotenthaler, T. (2015). Determining the effects of films with suicidal content: a laboratory experiment. *The British Journal of Psychiatry, 207*(1), 72–78. http://doi.org/10.1192/bjp.bp.114.152827

Till, B., Vitouch, P., Herberth, A., Sonneck, G., & Niederkrotenthaler, T. (2013). Personal suicidality in reception and identification with suicidal film characters. *Death Studies, 37*(4), 383–392. http://doi.org/10.1080/07481187.2012.673531

Tor, P. C., Ng, B. Y., & Ang, Y. G. (2008). The media and suicide. *Ann Acad Med Singapore, 37*(9), 797–799.

Tousignant, M., Mishara, B. L., Caillaud, A., Fortin, V., & St-Laurent, D. (2005). The impact of media coverage of the suicide of a well-known Quebec reporter: the case of Gaëtan Girouard. *Social Science & Medicine, 60*(9), 1919–1926. http://doi.org/10.1016/j.socscimed.2004.08.054

Yang, A. C., Tsai, S.-J., Yang, C.-H., Shia, B.-C., Fuh, J.-L., Wang, S.-J., . . . Huang, N. E. (2013). Suicide and media reporting: a longitudinal and spatial analysis. *Social Psychiatry and Psychiatric Epidemiology, 48*(3), 427–435. http://doi.org/10.1007/s00127-012-0562-1

Yip, P. S. F., & Lee, D. T. S. (2007). Charcoal-Burning suicides and strategies for prevention. *Crisis, 28*(S1), 21–27. http://doi.org/10.1027/0227-5910.28.S1.21

Zarghami, M. (2012). Selection of person of the year from public health perspective: Promotion of mass clusters of copycat self-immolation. *Iranian Journal of Psychiatry and Behavioral Sciences, 6*(1), 1.

# 11

# Papageno Effect: Its Progress in Media Research and Contextualization with Findings on Harmful Media Effects

*Thomas Niederkrotenthaler*

Over the last decades, researchers from across the globe have compiled a significant corpus of research about the effects of media on suicidality (Pirkis & Blood, 2010). With the recent groundswell of support internationally for suicide awareness campaigns to tackle the stigma surrounding suicidality and to prevent suicide, the task to complement research on harmful media effects (i.e., suicide contagion) with research on potential benefits of media discourse on suicidality has become a priority on the suicide research agenda (Niederkrotenthaler, Reidenberg, Till, & Gould, M, 2014).

Of particular importance for research on protective media effects is the so-called *Papageno effect*, which denominates suicide-protective effects of media, in contrast to harmful *Werther effects* (Niederkrotenthaler et al., 2010; Phillips, 1974). A synthesis of these two sides of media effects research can considerably contribute to the deepening of our understanding of media roles in suicide and may help identify novel lines of interventions using media as a tool to raise awareness and prevent suicide. Because research on harmful media effects provides a rich and relevant basis for the analysis of potential protective media effects, findings on harmful impacts should always be taken into account when planning and evaluating potentials of protective media effects. Therefore, selected findings on a broad range of media effects as they relate to suicidality have been included in this chapter.

## Research on the Werther Effect: Novel Findings on the Roles of Vulnerability and Identification

Based on more than hundred studies of effects of mainly traditional media types, it is widely accepted today that sensationalist forms of media coverage of suicidal behavior can trigger further suicides (Pirkis & Blood, 2010; Niederkrotenthaler et al., 2014; World Health Organization, 2008). Although the underlying mechanisms are so far only partially understood, it is typically assumed that media contributions presenting suicide as the only possible or likely consequence of negative circumstances increase suicidal tendencies in vulnerable groups and can ultimately trigger suicidal behavior, for example, through model learning (Blood & Pirkis, 2001). As already described in Erwin Ringel's *presuicidale syndrome* (Ringel, 1976) and in Edwin Shneidman's concept of *ten commonalities of suicide* (Shneidman, 1995), suicidal individuals often oscillate between life-sustaining and death-focused impulses before a suicidal act. From this perspective, it seems plausible to assume that messages from the environment, which includes media sources, have a specific relevance for individuals during times of crises. Indirect approaches using experimental designs based on individual data have recently been used to get better insight into factors of relevance for suicide-related media effects and related mechanisms. A recent randomized controlled trial provided some indirect evidence supporting that individuals from the general population who scored above average on suicidality (but were below the cut-off of clinical suicidality) were more likely to search for solutions to own problems when watching a movie culminating in the protagonist's suicide, as compared to individuals with suicidality scores below the sample mean. This finding may indicate that suicidal media content serves a different purpose and is processed in different ways when more vulnerable individuals are exposed to it, as compared to less vulnerable individuals (Till, Vitouch P, Herberth, Sonneck, & Niederkrotenthaler, 2013). Social identification seems to play an important role in these processes (Stack, 1992, Arendt, Till, & Niederkrotenthaler, 2016, Fu & Yip, 2009). Within media and communication studies it has been discussed for a long time that individuals compare themselves with the presented protagonists during media exposures and, depending on the results of this comparison, distance themselves from the content or identify with it, and/or adopt it for themselves (Cohen, 2001). Accordingly, the risk of suicide clusters after coverage of celebrity suicides is significantly increased particularly when social similarities between the model (i.e., the protagonist featured in the media report) and the recipient were present (Niederkrotenthaler, Till, Kapusta, Voracek, Dervic, & Sonneck, 2009). A recent randomized controlled trial which involved the testing of effects of suicide-related movies in clinically non-suicidal individuals was among the first studies which tested this hypothesis for suicide movies (Till, Strauss, Sonneck, & Niederkrotenthaler, 2015). When exposed to a movie culminating with the main protagonist's suicide ('Night Mother, USA, 1986), study participants responded with an increase in suicidal ideation, but this effect was only present in participants who had above-average suicidality scores before watching the movie, highlighting the impact of vulnerability on the effects found. In addition to individual vulnerability, also their identification with the suicidal character featured in the movie played an important role: the more the participants identified with the character, the larger was the effect of their vulnerability on suicidality scores immediately after media consumption. This signals that particularly individuals who were both vulnerable *and* identified with the featured protagonist experienced an increase in suicidality, and the impact of a combination of these factors was stronger than the impact of identification and vulnerability alone. This study highlights that caution is necessary when presenting suicide as a way of problem-solving.

Also repetitive reports of the same suicide, which are often seen in celebrity suicide reporting, need to be avoided whenever possible because vulnerable people could experience an increase in suicidal tendencies when flooded and overwhelmed with information about a particular suicide (Niederkrotenthaler et al., 2010, 2012). In the Austrian print-media, this flooding with information, as reflected in the high quantity of reporting on the same suicide, also tended to include expert opinions and suicide statistics, which were frequently found to be closely intertwined with sensationalist reporting styles (Niederkrotenthaler et al., 2010). Suicide prevention experts therefore need to consider that their information may be put into sensationalist contexts when giving interviews and should promote media recommendations and stories of hope, as well as provide an offer to the journalist to cross-read an article and its graphic layout before finalization and publication. In our experience, this offer is often taken up by media professionals.

Another important point that needs to be kept in mind is that by far not all suicide reports are associated with suicide rates (Niederkrotenthaler et al., 2010; Stack, 2005). Specifically, suicide reports that do not show any sensationalist characteristics but rather focus on the life of the deceased, what he or she contributed to the society and/or arts, seem not to be associated with suicide rates. This finding is of relevance to suicide prevention, because it indicates that suicide *can* be reported without increasing suicide rates if the reporting is consistent with media recommendations (Niederkrotenthaler et al., 2010).

## Changing Media Conversations to Include Perspectives of Suicide Prevention

In order to move the media conversation toward inclusion of suicide-preventive aspects, media recommendations for suicide reporting have been implemented in many countries and have been promoted and issued by the World Health Organization and IASP (World Health Organization, 2008). Austria was among the first countries worldwide to develop and implement media recommendations for suicide reporting back in 1987 (Etzersdorfer & Sonneck, 1998; Etzersdorfer, Sonneck & Nagel-Küss, 1992). These recommendations were developed following an exponential increase in subway suicides in Vienna, which had been widely covered by the local media and had been portrayed in great detail. The launch of the recommendations was followed by repetitive seminars and direct contacts with journalists and editors whenever a sensationalist media report was published, and this "natural experiment" was an unexpected success: Sensationalist coverage of subway suicides showed a significant quantitative decrease, and the suicides in the subway declined by more than 70 percent (Etzersdorfer & Sonneck, 1998; Niederkrotenthaler & Sonneck, 2007; see also chapter by Sonneck and Etzersdorfer in this book). Also the overall reporting on suicide in the Austrian media improved, while essentially no change was found in the overall number of suicide-related reports. Particularly in regions where the media collaboration was strong, suicides showed an immediate decline. Austria has not remained the only country with positive experiences with media recommendations since then (Niederkrotenthaler & Sonneck, 2007). For example, studies from Switzerland, Australia, and Hong Kong have highlighted that media recommendations have had a positive impact, in particular on the quality of reporting (Michel, Frey, Schlaepfer, & Valach, 1995; Pirkis et al., 2009; Sisask & Värnik, 2012). Still, more evaluation work is necessary internationally to determine the impact of various implementation strategies and to assess the effect of specific individual recommendations made in the recommendations.

## Media Work to Actively Prevent Suicide: The Papageno Effect

Changing the media conversation to reporting of suicide prevention is different from actively preventing suicide by media reporting. Nowadays, suicide *prevention* is often one step ahead of suicide *research* when it comes to using media to build awareness for suicide and prevent it: The recent international groundswell of support for awareness campaigns addressing suicide prevention has resulted in the development of a wide range of resources, but still there is little empirical information to inform these campaigns due to the lack of research on protective media effects (Niederkrotenthaler et al., 2014; for some related campaigns, see http://www.lifelineforattemptsurvivors.org; Substance and Mental Health Service Administration, 2012; National Action Alliance for Suicide Prevention, 2014; Pirkis, Machlin, & King, 2014; and Ftanou, Cox, Nicholas, Robinson, Machlin, & Pirkis, in press).

The *Papageno effect*, which describes suicide-protective media effects, is of crucial relevance for these efforts. The seminal study on the *Papageno effect* was published in 2010 and showed that the publication of media reports on individuals coping with adverse circumstances was associated with a decrease in subsequent suicides in regions where the media reached a large audience. Based on Papageno's mastered crisis in Mozart's Magic Flute, this effect was named *Papageno effect* (Niederkrotenthaler et al., 2010; Schikaneder, 1990). Different from sensationalist reports culminating in someone's suicide or portraying suicide as the option, these reports typically featured an individual with lived experience of suicidal ideation who managed to adopt constructive coping strategies.

While the first study on a possible *Papageno effect* assessed associations between the publication of media reports on mastery of crisis/coping with adversities and suicide rates after the publication of media reports, ecological studies like this one have several limitations. Importantly, it is not possible to differentiate individuals who died by suicide but were not exposed to the media reporting, from those who died and were exposed, which means that these studies have a low specificity (Pirkis and Blood, 2001). Therefore, studies using individual data from controlled trials are necessary to test the hypothesis of protective media effects (Niederkrotenthaler et al., 2014). Several recent studies using individual data from randomized controlled trials now indirectly support the Papageno effect. These study designs are typically not suitable to analyze suicide as an outcome variable, but assess the impact of media exposure on variables such as suicidal ideation and other risk factors for suicide. These recent studies indicate that a Papageno effect may occur for various types of media, including film, newspapers, and educative suicide prevention websites. In one randomized controlled trial, where participants from the general population were exposed to movies with suicidal content, it turned out that, different from the effect of a control movie that culminated with the main protagonist's suicide, the film featuring an individual who was suicidal but got better mainly because he fell in love (Elizabethtown, USA, 2005) reduced suicide risk factors in the audience. This effect was most pronounced in the subgroup of the audience who had suicidality scores above the sample median (Till et al., 2015). This finding suggests that more vulnerable individuals may benefit more from positive messages focusing on mastery of crisis than individuals with lowest suicidality scores. However, clinically suicidal individuals were not included in this trial due to safety concerns, and further research is necessary to determine how clinically suicidal individuals respond to movies portraying positive coping.

In another randomized controlled trial which analyzed the effects of an exposure to a newspaper report about an individual who managed to cope with suicidal ideation by seeking professional help from a telephone crisis line, it turned out that exposure to this story resulted in a reduction in suicidal cognitions in a subset of study participants who read the story, but not in the control group, who was exposed to a text not related to mental health but otherwise similar in terms of style, length, and formatting (Arendt, Till, & Niederkrotenthaler, 2016). This positive impact was most pronounced in the subgroup of the audience who did *not* identify with the featured character. This finding may be due to a *contrast effect*: The story focused mainly on the adverse circumstances of the protagonist during his crisis, and much less on his positive experiences in the aftermath of the crisis (Arendt et al., 2015). The study participants, who were all drawn from a general student population, may have evaluated their own lives as better than that of the protagonist, resulting in a reduction of suicide risk factors, which was most pronounced in individuals who did not identify with the character. Further studies are necessary to investigate if clinically suicidal individuals benefit from a media story if they identify with the protagonist or if the benefit is restricted to individuals who do *not* identify with the story. This issue also warrants more research for a different reason: Individuals normally select media input based on their choices from hundreds of different media options, and identification may play a big role in the decision for or against the media product. A recent study showed accordingly that the intention to read suicide-awareness material increased via identification when role model and audience characteristics aligned regarding social traits and the experience of depression (Niederkrotenthaler, Arendt, & Till, 2015). Thus, absence of identification may increase the willingness not to select a suicide-related prevention media product, which may prevent any potential benefit from such material.

Overall, these recent findings indicate that media can make a very relevant contribution to suicide prevention by highlighting that a crisis typically does not represent a fateful disease without any options for positive change and hope, but rather a temporary phase of despair, which can be alleviated by means of practical support of the environment and treatment (Sonneck et al., 2012; Tomandl, Sonneck, Stein, & Niederkrotenthaler, 2014). Particularly reporting on how to cope with suicidality and adverse circumstances at the example of individuals with lived experience may be a powerful, effective component of suicide prevention initiatives. In other medical and public health areas, similar reporting practices have been present in the respective media coverage for a long time: For example, with regard to reports on cancer-related illness, media reports are typically not confined to mortality rates, but a considerable proportion of reporting focuses on various treatment options, positive stories of coping with illness, and positive outcomes. Particularly if reporting about suicidality, this type of coverage may help save lives.

## Research on Online Media: Risk and Opportunities

While the consumption of traditional media like newspapers and television is decreasing in many European countries, the Internet has now reached a penetration of more than 70 percent of the European population, and this global trend continues (http://www. internetworldstats.com). A considerable proportion of suicidal communication nowadays occurs online. Suicidal individuals who use the Internet for suicide-related purposes seem to differ from other suicidal individuals. In particular, suicidal Internet users seem to be more suicidal, as compared to other suicidal individuals, as recent studies have shown (Mok, Jorm, & Pirkis, in press; Haider,

2015; Niederkrotenthaler, Haider, Till, Mok, & Pirkis, in press). This finding highlights that Internet media are of particular relevance for suicide prevention (Reidenberg, 2012).

The Internet comprises diverse media types and includes a wide range of resources related to suicide and prevention. These range from personal experiences of suicidality, to educative professional websites, to other websites where suicide is presented as an appropriate solution (Recupero, Harms, & Noble, 2008, Till & Niederkrotenthaler, 2014). When it comes to enhancing protective potentials of online media, it is therefore of central importance to analyze which contents information seekers find on the Internet and to increase the accessibility of protective contents. In a study comparing web contents identified in Austria and the United States using not only search terms such as "suicide," but also method-related terms (e.g., "how to hang yourself") and help-related terms (e.g., "suicidal thoughts") potentially protective information (e.g., contact details of support services) outnumbered harmful information (e.g., details of suicide methods) by a ratio of 2:1, but the quality of information depended strongly upon the specific search terms used (Till & Niederkrotenthaler, 2014). Method-related search terms, which may reflect advanced stages of the suicidal process, yielded websites with more harmful and less protective characteristics, as compared to searches using the more neutral term "suicide." In contrast, websites retrieved with help-related search terms (e.g., "suicide help") contained more protective and less harmful characteristics. The better a website was ranked in the results list of the search engines, the higher was the number of harmful characteristics on the website and the lower was the number of protective characteristics (Till & Niederkrotenthaler, 2014). These findings demonstrate that prevention efforts need to focus on improving the visibility and accessibility of preventive web contents, particularly for method-related web searches. The adding of suicide-method-related meta-tags and links to other helpful resources on prevention websites may improve the ranking of websites. Further research is warranted to analyze if these measures are effective. In addition, collaborations with large search engine providers are warranted to work on feasible solutions that improve the ranking of suicide prevention websites.

## A Papageno Effect for Educational Suicide Prevention Websites?

A recent randomized controlled trial (Till, Tran, & Niederkrotenthaler, 2015) investigated the effect of educative components of professional suicide prevention websites in a general population sample. Study participants were asked to collect information on suicidality when surfing on a suicide prevention or a control website, and data on suicidal ideation and knowledge related to suicide were measured immediately before and immediately after website exposure, and again one week later. The included prevention websites featured professional resources as well as stories of lived experience of crisis, suicidality, and loss due to suicide. The results indicated that suicide prevention websites had some impact in terms of a reduction of suicidal ideation in those participants with baseline suicidality above the sample median. This effect was present immediately after surfing on the prevention sites and was sustained for one week. In particular, personal beliefs about coping skills increased during the exposure to the prevention websites. Also knowledge related to suicide improved. This finding suggests that educative websites of professional suicide prevention organizations may make a substantial contribution to suicide prevention. Further tests are required to test the impact of such websites on individuals with current suicidal ideation.

## Conclusion

While the evidence for negative effects of sensationalist stories on suicide, particularly repetitive suicide reports and reports on celebrity suicide, has accumulated in recent years, much more research is needed from different countries and settings regarding the protective potentials of media portrayals of suicidality. Stories of lived experience and materials offering treatment and intervention options seem to be most promising when it comes to media-related suicide-protective Papageno effects. In Austria, the reactions of media professionals to the ongoing research on the Papageno effect were very positive, and this research also seems to help promote the media recommendations when it comes to using the media recommendations to prevent potential harmful media effects. Although some progress has been made in recent years, more research in different countries needs to be done to be able to fully understand and utilize protective media potentials for suicide prevention.

## Acknowledgments

The presented research on online media has been funded by the Austrian Science Fund FWF (Project P-23659-B11). Thanks go to national partners, particularly the Wiener Werkstaette for Suicide Research, and Dr. Benedikt Till, as well as to all international collaborators.

# References

Arendt, F., Till, B., & Niederkrotenthaler, T. (2016). Effects of suicide awareness material on implicit suicide cognition: A laboratory experiment. *Health Communication, 31*(6), 718–726.

Blood, R. W., & Pirkis, J. (2001). Suicide and the media. Part III: Theoretical issues. *Crisis, 22*, 163–169.

Cohen, J. (2001). Defining identification: A theoretical look at the identification of audiences with media characters. *Mass Communication & Society, 4*, 245–264.

Etzersdorfer, E., & Sonneck, G. (1998). Preventing suicide by influencing mass-media reporting. The Viennese experience 1980–1996. *Archives of Suicide Research, 4*, 67–74.

Etzersdorfer, E., Sonneck. G., & Nagel Kuess, S. (1992). Newspaper reports and suicide. *New England Journal of Medicine, 327*(7), 502–503.

Ftanou, M., Cox, G., Nicholas, A., Robinson, J., Machlin, A., & Pirkis, J. (in press). Public service announcements (PSAs) designed to prevent youth suicide: Examples from around the world. *Health Communication.*

Fu, K. W., & Yip, P. S. (2009). Estimating the risk for suicide following the suicide deaths of three Asian entertainment celebrities: a meta-analysis approach. *Journal of Clinical Psychiatry, 70*, 869e78.

Haider, A. (2015). Suizid- bezogene Internetnutzung: Charakteristika der UserInnen, Nutzeffekt, und Barrieren beim Offline-Hilfesuchen (Suicide-related internet use: Characteristics of users, effects, and barriers to offline help-seeking. Diploma Thesis (Medicine), MedUni Wien. Supervisor: T. Niederkrotenthaler.

Michel K., Frey C., Wyss K., & Valach L. (2000). An exercise in improving suicide reporting in print media. *Crisis, 21*(2), 71–79.

Mok, K., Jorm, A. F., & Pirkis, J. (2016). Who goes online for suicide-related reasons? *Crisis, 37* (2), 112–120.

National Action Alliance for Suicide Prevention: Suicide Attempt Survivors Task Force (2014). *The way forward: Pathways to hope, recovery, and wellness with insights from lived experiences.* Washington, DC: Author.

Niederkrotenthaler, T., Arendt, F., & Till, B. (2015). Predicting intentions to read suicide awareness stories: The role of depression and characteristics of the suicidal role model. *Crisis, 36*, 399–406.

Niederkrotenthaler, T., Fu, K.-W., Yip, P. S. F., Fong, D. Y. T., Stack, S., Cheng, Q., & Pirkis, J. (2012). Changes in suicide rates following media reports on celebrity suicide: a meta-analysis. *Journal of Epidemiology & Community Health, 66*, 1037–1042.

Niederkrotenthaler, T., Haider A., Till, B., Mok, K., & Pirkis, J (in press). Comparison of suicidal people who use the Internet for suicide-related reasons and those who do not: Survey study in Austria. *Crisis.*

Niederkrotenthaler, T., Reidenberg, D. J., Till, B., & Gould, M. (2014). Increasing help-seeking and referrals for individuals at risk for suicide by decreasing stigma: The role of mass media. *American Journal of Preventive Medicine, 47*, 235–243.

Niederkrotenthaler, T., & Sonneck, G. (2007). Assessing the impact of media guidelines for reporting on suicides in Austria: interrupted times series analysis. *Australian and New Zealand Journal of Psychiatry, 41*, 419–428.

Niederkrotenthaler, T., & Till, B. (2014). *Suicide message boards: Content analysis of 1,200 German and Austrian suicide threads.* Beitrag im Rahmen des 15th

European Symposium of Suicide and Suicidal Behaviour, Tallinn, 27. August 2014, 30. August 2014 (Book of abstracts, S. 165).

Niederkrotenthaler, T., Till, B., Kapusta, N. D., Voracek, M., Dervic, K., & Sonneck, G. (2009). Copycat effects after media reports on suicide: A population-based ecologic study. *Social Science & Medicine, 69*, 1085–1090.

Niederkrotenthaler, T., Voracek, M., Herberth, A., Till, B., Strauss, M., Etzersdorfer, E., Eisenwort, B., & Sonneck, G. (2010). (2010). The role of media reports in completed and prevented suicide – Werther versus Papageno effects. *British Journal of Psychiatry, 197*, 234–243.

Phillips, D. P. (1974). The influence of suggestion on suicide: Substantive and theoretical implications of the Werther effect. *American Sociological Review, 39*, 340–354.

Pirkis, J., & Blood, W. (2010). Suicide and the news and information media: a critical review. http://www.mindframe-media.info/__data/assets/pdf_file/0016/5164/Pirkis-and-Blood-2010-Suicide-and-the-news-and-information-media.pdf

Pirkis, J., Dare, A. R., Blood, W., Rankin, B., Williamson, M., Burgess, B., & Jolley, D. (2009). Changes in media reporting of suicide in Australia between 2000/01 and 2006/07. *Crisis, 30*, 25–33

Pirkis, J., Machlin, A., & King, K. (2014). Harnessing the potential of the media to encourage help-seeking in men. Oral presentation at the 15th European Symposium of Suicide and Suicidal Behaviour, Tallinn, Estonia, August 27–30, 2014 (Book of abstracts, p. 163).

Recupero, P. R., Harms, S. E., & Noble, J. M. (2008). Googling suicide: surfing for suicide information on the Internet. *Journal of Clinical Psychiatry, 69*, 878–888.

Reidenberg, D. (2012). *Suicide prevention: Making the most of new technologies.* Community suicide prevention presentation, Bemidji MN, 26. April 2012.

Ringel, E. (1976). The presuicidal syndrome. *Suicide Life Threatening Behavior, 6(3)*, 131–149.

Schikaneder, E. (1990). The Magic Flute: Libretto. Metropolitan Opera Guild.

Shneidman, E. S. (1995). *Suicide as psychache: A clinical approach to self-destructive behavior.* Northvale, NJ: Aronson.

Sisask, M., & Värnik, A. (2012). Media roles in suicides prevention: A systematic review. *International Journal of Environmental Research and Public Health, 9*, 123–138.

Sonneck, G., Kapusta, N., Tomandl, G., & Voracek, M. (Eds.). (2012). *Kriseninter- vention und Suizidverhütung.* Vienna: Facultas.

Stack, S. (1992). Social correlates of suicide by age: Media impacts. In A. A. Lee- naars (Ed.), *Life span perspectives of suicide: Time lines in the suicidal process* (pp. 187–214). New York: Plenum.

Stack, S. (2005). Suicide in the media: A quantitative review of studies based on nonfictional stories. *Suicide and Life-Threatening Behavior, 35(2)*, 121–33.

Substance and Mental Health Service Administration (SAMHSA). (2012). Retrieved from http://store.samhsa.gov/product/Stories-Of-Hope-And-Recovery-A-Video-Guide-for-Suicide-Attempt-Survivors/SMA12--4711DVD

Till, B., & Niederkrotenthaler, T. (2014). Surfing for suicide methods and help: Content analysis of websites retrieved with search engines in Austria and in the United States. *Journal of Clinical Psychiatry, 75*, 886–892.

Till, B., Strauss, M., Sonneck, G., & Niederkrotenthaler, T. (2015). Determining the effects of films with suicidal content: A laboratory experiment. *British Journal of Psychiatry, 207*, 72–78.

Till, B., Tran, U. S., & Niederkrotenthaler, T. (2015). *Impact of websites on suicide prevention on users' suicidal ideation and their knowledge about suicide.* IASR/AFSP International Summit on Suicide Research, New York, 11. Oktober 2015, 14. Oktober 2015.

Till, B., Vitouch P., Herberth, A., Sonneck, G., & Niederkrotenthaler, T. (2013). Personal suicidality in the reception of and identification with suicidal film characters. *Death Studies, 37*, 383–392.

Tomandl, G., Sonneck, G., Stein, C., & Niederkrotenthaler, T. (2014). *Leitfaden zur Berichterstattung über Suizid (Media recommendations for the reporting of suicide).* Wien: Kriseninterventionszentrum.

World Health Organization. (2008). *Preventing suicide. A resource for media professionals.* Genf: World Health Organization.

# 12

# The Impact of Suicide Portrayals in Films on Audiences: A Qualitative Study

*Benedikt Till*

## Introduction

The impact of suicide portrayals in the media has been a focal area of interest in social and medical sciences for many years. Evidence suggests that stories on suicide in nonfictional media have the potential to trigger suicidal behavior in the population (Sisask & Värnik, 2012; World Health Organization, 2008). In terms of suicide stories portrayed in fictional films, evidence of copycat behavior is more inconclusive as there are conflicting findings in the existing research (Biblarz, Brown, Biblarz, Pilgrim, & Baldree, 1991; Martin, 1998). Since ecologic research designs were used in these studies, which have many limitations (e.g., ecological fallacy), some researchers analyzed the impact of films with suicidal content on audiences with randomized controlled trials. Biblarz et al. (1991), for example, found increased arousal among viewers of a film concluding with the suicide of the two protagonists, while attitudes toward suicide and aggression were not influenced by the movie.

In a recent randomized controlled trial (Till, Niederkrotenthaler, Herberth, Vitouch, & Sonneck, 2010; Till et al., 2011), 150 adults watched either the original or a censored version of a film concluding with the protagonist's suicide or a drama portraying the protagonist's natural death. The results showed that all films and film versions were linked to both negative and positive effects: on the one hand to a deterioration of mood and an increase in inner tension and depression scores, and on the other hand to a rise in self-esteem and life satis-faction and a reduction in suicidal ideation. The results also revealed that the more viewers were geared to their social environment when coping with a problem in their life (Till et al., 2011) and the higher their baseline suicidality was (Till, Vitouch, Herberth, Sonneck, & Niederkrotenthaler, 2013), the more they used the films to get ideas for own problem solving, which amplified the negative film effects (Till et al., 2010, 2011). A follow-up study demonstrated an increase of suicidal ideation among individuals vulnerable to suicide after watching a film concluding with the protagonist's suicide (Till, Strauss, Sonneck, & Niederkrotenthaler, 2015). This effect was greater, the more viewers identified with the suicidal protagonist. The authors noted that more research to investigate the impact of films with suicidal content and explore the pathways between different determinants and effects are warranted (Till et al., 2015).

Hjelmeland and Knizek (2010, 2011) pointed out that qualitative research is essential in moving the suicidological field forward and highlighted its strengths in focusing on *understanding* suicidality (in contrast to *explaining*) and accounting for its complexity, but noted that qualitative studies are scarce in suicide research. Therefore, this study aimed to examine the impact of suicide films used in previous studies (Till et al., 2010, 2011, 2013) on audiences by employing a qualitative approach.

## Method

### Design and Material

A qualitative study was conducted consisting of ten groups of partici-pants, five groups with either three to four men or three to four women, respectively, who were randomly assigned to one of five test conditions (one group with male participants and one group with female partic-ipants to each of the five conditions). The protagonist in the film *It's My Party* (USA, 1996; test condition #1) is a young, homosexual man who is dying of AIDS. He is increasingly losing cognitive abilities and decides to end his life by using a concoction of poisons. He hosts a party to say good-bye to his family and friends and commits suicide at the end of the party. In *The Fire Within* (France/Italy, 1963; test condition #2) the protagonist is a middle-aged man who suffers from an alcohol addiction and lives in a halfway house. Due to his fears about life on the outside after his release he decides to take his life and eventually commits suicide by firearm. In the censored versions of *It's My Party*

172

and *The Fire Within* (test conditions #3 and #4) the suicidal acts were edited out, but viewers could still tell that the respective protagonist committed suicide. *Phenomenon* (USA, 1996; test condition #5) portrays the protagonist's death due to a brain tumor which boosts his intelligence and cognitive skills. Despite his deadly disease, he embraces life and uses his superhuman capabilities to help others. In the end, the protagonist dies in the arms of his newfound love.

Participation in the study was voluntary and anonymous. Before the film, questionnaires on socio-demographics, depression, and suicidality were completed. For ethical reasons, only individuals with suicidality scores < 40 assessed with a questionnaire designed by Stork (1972) and depression scores < 17 measured with the Erlanger Depression Scale (Lehrl & Gallwitz, 1983) were considered as participants. No individual was excluded from participation in this study. After the film screening, focus groups were conducted following the documentary method (Bohnsack, 1999; Przyborski, 2004). All participants were offered psychological counseling to support coping with stress resulting from film exposure or from answering suicidality questions at the end of the study. The study took place in Vienna, Austria, and was approved by the Ethics Committee of the Medical University of Vienna and the Vienna General Hospital (study protocol 220/2006, date: 2006-05-26).

*Participants*

Participants were thirty-one individuals living in Austria. They were recruited with posters, flyers, and public announcements at facilities of the University of Vienna and the Medical University of Vienna, Austria. Mean age was 24.32 years (Md = 26, SD = 4.54). High school graduation was the average level of education for both women and men. Participants in each group were close friends, which allowed decoding frames of collective orientations based on common experiences of people within a certain social context (Bohnsack, 1999; Pfaff, 2010).

*Data Collection*

Participants' perceptions of the films and their content were assessed by conducting focus groups. Each focus group lasted 30–70 minutes and was recorded with an mp3-recorder. Participants were instructed to talk freely about any thoughts they have related to the films or events portrayed in the plot, but a set of predetermined questions (e.g., "Please describe what you have seen here," "How do you feel, when you watch such films?") were used to start or continue the conversation.

## Data Analysis

The audio recordings were transcribed and analyzed based on the documentary method (Bohnsack, 1999; Przyborski, 2004). The objective of this method is to reconstruct organizing principles of conjunctive realms of experience, which are based on implicit knowledge and reflected in everyday conversations (Bohnsack, 1999). To gain insight into an individual's practical knowledge and habitus, the content of a conversation or text is put in relation to the form in which it is presented (Przyborski & Slunecko, 2011). In line with this approach, data of the focus groups were analyzed by summarizing the content of the conversation in focusing on *what* was said (Przyborski & Slunecko, 2011) and by examining language, discourse, and performance of the conversation in order to reveal the structures of communication and subsequently the implicit meaning of the participant's statements (Przyborski, 2004). The documentary method enables researchers to gain insight into individuals' subconscious emotional and cognitive processes and is therefore particularly suited to collect and analyze data on topics that are hardly accessible for self-disclosure (e.g., media effects) or are subject to stigmatization, such as suicide (Till, 2010).

## Results

### The Impact of Drama Films

All films and film versions impacted the participants' emotional well-being. This impact varied across the focus groups revealing three types of predominant reactions to the drama films. However, these differences were not reflected by the test conditions of the study, as there was no distinctive pattern of emotional reactions across the different films and film versions.

The participants of some groups reported a negative impact of the films on their emotional well-being. The viewers were sadder, unhappier, and more depressed after the film screening than they were before. Concurrently, the negative impact of the films was constantly trivialized by the participants by highlighting that this effect was only temporary or marginal or by underlying that their mood is easily influenced by films in general, showing that participants experienced this negative effect as relatively small. This is illustrated by the following examples:

> Well, there was the question, how we felt . . . kind of depressed, but only slightly. (Male group: The Fire Within—censored)

> Well, I weep easily as you can tell, but one time I was on the verge . . . of crying, if the plot would have continued in such a sad way. (Female group: Phenomenon)

The participants of other groups similarly reported a negative impact on their mood, but at the same time they also enjoyed the sad mood, experienced both positive and negative emotions, or got something positive out of the sad storyline. Participants in these groups seem to experience two opposing emotional processes with the films triggering both positive and negative effects on the emotional well-being at the same time. These opposing effects are illustrated by the following examples:

> I didn't think it [the film] was boring actually—well, at the beginning it was, but then totally depressing and sad, it really touched me . . . I liked the movie. (Male group: It's My Party—original)

> Well, it [the film] is actually kind of funny, as they [the producers] are trying to artistically underline it [the tragedy] . . . yeah, sometimes I get the feeling with these films that they are using some symbols, where they don't know what they mean themselves as long as people are thinking about it and get in a ruminative mood. (Male group: The Fire Within—censored)

In contrast to the previous two types of responses, some groups did not acknowledge or discuss the impact of the movies. The participants in these groups did not report any positive or negative film effects, but chose to not mention their emotional reactions to the films. The participants seemed to be very distant toward the plot and indifferent to the content of the films. However, it remains unclear if this lack of discussion on the impact of the films was a result of not being emotionally affected by the films or not wanting to disclose a potential deterioration of mood.

*Psychological Defense Mechanisms*

There were three different types of approaches of the groups to discuss potentially unpleasant or inconvenient topics, such as suicide, death, or euthanasia. These approaches resembled prevalent psychological defense mechanisms (Vaillant, 1992). The differences in terms of these approaches were not reflected by the test conditions of the study, as each type of approach was found in almost all film groups and there was no distinctive pattern across the different films and film versions.

The participants of some groups showed an excessive use of humor either throughout the entire conversation or when the discussion focused on suicide, death, or euthanasia. Due to the constant jokes and funny remarks the discussion remained in a cheerful mood and contained a lot of laughter despite the sad and tragic content of the films. It is also interesting to note that most conflicts between participants in these groups were solved with humor. It seems that these groups used humor to distance themselves from distressing thoughts by artificially lightening up the mood. Examples for this approach include one group's constant mockery of the country life portrayed in *Phenomenon* (*"His [the protagonist's] only problem was a rabbit," "I can't imagine living in the countryside, haha, in solitude, right out in the sticks, a cow to the left, a sheep to the right, and every morning a rooster wakes me up,"* Female group: *Phenomenon*) or (*"I would go out for a beer with him,"* Male group: *The Fire Within*—original) followed by 18 seconds of collective laughter as a reply to one participant's question on what to do with protagonist in *The Fire Within*, who is an alcoholic contemplating suicide.

The participants of other groups used denial to dissociate from tragic events portrayed in the films. These groups highlighted the differences between the portrayed individuals/events in the films and themselves by referring to irrelevant details and underlining that they are different kinds of persons in different situations, even though that actually may have not been the case. The participants in these groups also constantly stated that it was impossible for them to identify with the suicidal protagonist or be emotionally involved in the film. Any parallels between the protagonists' and their own lives were denied and negated. The denial helped the participants to label the tragic events as personally irrelevant. The following examples illustrate this defense mechanism:

> In terms of identification, well, it was a little bit hard for me. I mean, of course I was touched, . . . but it was still a little bit hard with this setting. He [the protagonist] is gay, the other one is gay, and if you are not gay, maybe it is a little bit more difficult to generate that kind of sympathy. (Male group: It's My Party—original)

> Yeah, of course, as stable individuals with high school degrees we cannot . . . imagine this. (Male group: It's My Party—censored)

Some groups avoided the discussion of inconvenient topics by focusing on irrelevant aspects during the conversation. Instead of discussing personal experiences related to suicide or death, the participants abruptly changed the perspective and started to philosophize about these phenomena. For example, in one group a conversation that originally focused on personal opinions regarding suicide changed quickly to a discussion about the meaning of suicide and the "*meta-opinion toward suicide*," which is the "*opinion toward the opinion toward suicide*" (Male group: *The Fire Within*—censored). In another group (Female group: *It's My Party*—censored) a controversial discussion on the protagonist's suicide in *It's My Party* was solved by giving long monologues that included long and elaborated displays of one's own religious beliefs and the concepts of suicide and death in religions. Both examples illustrate that the discussion of an unpleasant or inconvenient topic was brought to an impersonal level or shifted to a nonthreatening aspect in order to prevent a serious discussion of this topics and avoid experiencing disturbing feelings. This approach of excessive philosophizing of irrelevant aspects of a topic resembles the psychological defense mechanism of intellectualization (see Vaillant, 1992). Table 12.1 provides an overview of the predominant types of emotional reactions to the films and psychological defense mechanisms identified in the discussions across all groups.

**Table 12.1.** Overview of the predominant types of emotional reactions to the films and psychological defense mechanisms across all groups.

| Group | Predominant type of emotional reaction | Predominant type of defense mechanism |
|---|---|---|
| Female group: *It's My Party*—original | Positive–negative | Humor |
| Male group: *It's My Party*—original | Positive–negative | Denial |
| Female group: *It's My Party*—censored | Positive–negative | Intellectualization |
| Male group: *It's My Party*—censored | Indifferent | Denial |
| Female group: *The Fire Within*—original | Indifferent | Humor |
| Male group: *The Fire Within*—original | Positive–negative | Humor |
| Female group: *The Fire Within*—censored | Negative | Denial |
| Male group: *The Fire Within*—censored | Negative | Intellectualization |
| Female group: *Phenomenon* | Negative | Humor |
| Male group: *Phenomenon* | Negative | Denial |

## Discussion

This study showed that individuals reacted differently to the screening of drama films concluding with the protagonist's death. While some viewers experienced a small deterioration of mood, others reported the occurrence of positive and negative emotional reactions to the films at the same time. Similarly, a deterioration of mood and a parallel improvement in life satisfaction and suicidal ideation was found in a previous quantitative study that used the same films of the present investigation as stimulus material (Till et al., 2010, 2011). These findings support the previous conclusion (see Till et al., 2010, 2011) that viewers are sad and depressed due to the negative outcome of the films, as suggested by affective disposition theory (Zillmann, 1996), but, in accordance with social comparison theory (Festinger, 1954), feel better about themselves based on the comparison with the hopeless situation of suicidal protagonist. However, this positive effect may not be present when individuals more vulnerable to suicide watch films concluding with the protagonist's suicide (Till et al., 2010, 2013, 2015).

This study also revealed that individuals used specific types of psychological defense mechanisms (i.e., humor, denial, intellectualization) when dealing with potentially unpleasant or inconvenient topics, such as suicide or death. Similarly, predominant coping styles and involvement in a film were found to be significant determinants of the impact of suicide films on audiences (Till et al., 2011, 2013). Psychological defense mechanisms are unconscious and unintentional techniques to reduce anxiety from potentially harmful impulses (Cramer, 1998). These techniques help individuals to deal with thoughts or topics that may appear threatening to them and seem to play a key role in the processing of portrayals of these topics in films and may determine the subsequent impact of these films. Psychological defense mechanisms were also found to influence preferences for suicide-related films and music (Till, Tran, Voracek, & Niederkrotenthaler, 2016; Till, Tran, Voracek, Sonneck, & Niederkrotenthaler, 2014).

No differences in terms of audience reactions were found between the different films and film versions. The viewers did not react differently to a film concluding with the protagonist's suicide than to films portraying the protagonist's natural death or to films with censored portrayals of the protagonist's suicide, which is consistent with previous research (Till et al., 2010). The ineffectiveness of censorship to reduce negative film effects was also highlighted in other media studies (e.g., Till & Vitouch, 2012).

A limitation of this study is that solely individuals at low risk for suicide as indicated by depression and suicidality scores below established cut-off scores were included in the focus groups. As a result, it remains unclear whether individuals of the high-risk group of clinically suicidal individuals, who are at risk for committing imitative suicides (Fu & Yip, 2007), would react differently to the films. Research on the impact of suicide films on audiences at-risk is needed, provided that these studies are conducted under close supervision and ethical consideration (Till et al., 2010, 2015). Furthermore, studies aiming to investigate the potentially protective impact of films focusing on the successful mastering of adverse circumstances (i.e., Papageno effect; Niederkrotenthaler et al., 2010) with qualitative study designs are warranted.

## Acknowledgments

The author thanks Thomas Niederkrotenthaler, Arno Herberth, Gernot Sonneck, and Peter Vitouch for their support and advice in this study.

## Funding

This work was supported by a DOC-team scholarship from the Austrian Academy of Sciences (grant number 70034).

## References

Biblarz, A., Brown, R. M., Biblarz, D. N., Pilgrim, M., & Baldree, B. F. (1991). Media influence on attitudes toward suicide. *Suicide and Life-Threatening Behavior, 21*, 374–384.

Bohnsack, R. (1999). *Rekonstruktive Sozialforschung: Einführung in die Methodologie und Praxis qualitativer Forschung* [Reconstructive social research. Introduction to methodology and practice of qualitative research]. Opladen, Germany: Leske und Budrich.

Cramer, P. (1998). Coping and defense mechanisms: What's the difference? *Journal of Personality, 66*, 919–946.

Festinger, L. (1954). A theory of social comparison processes. *Human Relations, 7*, 117–140.

Fu, K. W., & Yip, P. S. F. (2007) Long-term impact of celebrity suicide on suicidal ideation: results from a population-based study. *Journal of Epidemiology & Community Health, 61*, 540–546.

Hjelmeland, H., & Knizek, B. L. (2010). Why we need qualitative research in suicidology. *Suicide and Life-Threatening Behavior, 40*, 74–80.

Hjelmeland, H., & Knizek, B. L. (2011). Methodology in suicidological research – Contribution to the debate. *Suicidology Online, 2*, 8–10.

Lehrl, S., & Gallwitz, A. (1983). *Erlanger Depressions-Skala EDS* [Erlangen depression scale EDS]. Vaterstetten, Germany: Vless.

Martin, G. (1998). Media influence to suicide: The search for solutions. *Archives of Suicide Research, 4,* 51–66.

Niederkrotenthaler, T., Voracek, M., Herberth, A., Till, B., Strauss, M., Etzersdorfer, E. . . . Sonneck, G. (2010). The role of media reports in completed and prevented suicide – Werther versus Papageno effects. *British Journal of Psychiatry, 197,* 234–243.

Pfaff, N. (2010). Social distinction in children's peer groups: First results from Brazil and Germany. In R. Bohnsack, N. Pfaff, & W. Weller (Eds.), *Qualitative analysis and documentary method in international education research* (pp. 165–192). Opladen, Germany: Barbara Budrich.

Przyborski, A. (2004). *Gesprächsanalyse und dokumentarische Methode. Qualitative Auswertung von Gesprächen, Gruppendiskussionen und anderen Diskursen* [Discourse analysis and documentary method. Qualitative analysis of interviews, group discussions and other discourses]. Wiesbaden, Germany: VS Verlag für Sozialwissenschaften.

Przyborski, A., & Slunecko, T. (2011). Learning to think iconically in the human and social sciences: Iconic standards of understanding as a pivotal challenge for method development. *Integrative Psychological and Behavioral Science, 46,* 39–56.

Sisask, M., & Värnik, A. (2012). Media roles in suicides prevention: A systematic review. *International Journal of Environmental Research and Public Health, 9,* 123–138.

Stork, J. (1972). *Fragebogentest zur Beurteilung der Suizidgefahr* [Questionnaire for the determination of suicide risk]. Salzburg, Austria: Otto Müller.

Till, B. (2010). *Suizid in Filmen: Über die Wirkung von in Spielfilmen dargestellten Suiziden auf den Rezipienten/die Rezipientin* [Suicide in films: On the impact of suicide portrayals in films on viewers]. (Unpublished doctoral dissertation). University of Vienna, Vienna, Austria.

Till, B., Niederkrotenthaler, T., Herberth, A., Vitouch P., & Sonneck, G. (2010). Suicide in films: The impact of suicide portrayals on non-suicidal viewers' well-being and the effectiveness of censorship. *Suicide & Life-Threatening Behavior, 40,* 319–327.

Till, B., Niederkrotenthaler, T., Herberth, A., Voracek, M., Sonneck, G., & Vitouch, P. (2011). Coping and film reception: A study on the impact of film dramas and the mediating effects of emotional modes of film reception and coping strategies. *Journal of Media Psychology, 23,* 149–160.

Till, B., Strauss, M., Sonneck, G., & Niederkrotenthaler, T. (2015). Determining the effects of films with suicidal content: a laboratory experiment. *British Journal of Psychiatry, 207,* 72–78.

Till, B., Tran, U. S., Voracek, M., & Niederkrotenthaler, T. (2016). Music and suicidality: A study on associations between music preferences and risk factors of suicide. *Omega: Journal of Death and Dying, 72*(4), 340–356.

Till, B., Tran, U. S., Voracek, M., Sonneck, G., & Niederkrotenthaler, T. (2014). Associations between film preferences and risk factors for suicide: An online survey. *PLoS One, 9,* e102293.

Till, B., & Vitouch, P. (2012). Capital punishment in films: The impact of death penalty portrayals on viewers' mood and attitude towards capital punishment. *International Journal of Public Opinion Research, 24,* 387–399.

Till, B., Vitouch P., Herberth, A., Sonneck, G., & Niederkrotenthaler, T. (2013). Personal suicidality in the reception of and identification with suicidal film characters. *Death Studies, 37,* 383–392.

Vaillant, G. E. (1992). *Ego mechanisms of defense: A guide for clinicians and researchers.* Washington, DC: American Psychiatric Press.

World Health Organization. (2008). *Preventing suicide. A resource for media professionals.* Geneva, Switzerland: World Health Organization.

Zillmann, D. (1996). The psychology of suspense in dramatic exposition. In P. Vorderer, H. J. Wulff, & M. Friedrichsen (Eds.), *Suspense: Conceptualizations, theoretical analyses, and empirical explorations* (pp. 199–231). Mahwah, NJ: Erlbaum.

# 13

# Between Werther and Papageno Effects: A Propositional Meta-Analysis of Ambiguous Findings for Helpful and Harmful Media Effects on Suicide Contagion

*Sebastian Scherr and Anna Steinleitner*

## Introduction

The fact that suicides and suicide attempts cluster temporarily and locally (Boyce, 2011) contributed to the notion that suicidality can be explained through imitation. Through this theoretical development, media depictions of suicides were generally qualified as an alternative resource for suicide role models. This has been investigated and labeled as "Werther effect" (Gould, 2001; Niederkrotenthaler et al., 2012; Fu, Chan & Yip, 2009; Hawton & van Heeringen, 2009; Jonas, 1992; Phillips, 1974; Schmidtke & Häfner, 1986; Schäfer & Quiring, 2013a). In recent years, research also cumulated evidence for reverse (i.e., positive or wishful) media effects that were labeled as "Papageno effect" (Niederkrotenthaler, Voracek, Hererth, Till, Strauss & Etzersdorfer, 2010; Ruddigkeit, 2010; Schäfer & Quiring, 2013b). This line of research investigates the qualities of and conditions under which media depictions of suicides prevent consequent copycat suicides. On the one hand, this theoretical extension of the research field is an indicator for the fact that media effects on individual suicidality were misread to a certain degree. On the other hand, the new theoretical development has contributed to a focus on extreme media effects that either help or harm. This conceptual dichotomization does not enhance a focus on less clear or even ambiguous findings (Dickersin, 2005).

Hence, to counteract this development this systematic literature review identifies all studies with ambiguous finding regarding copycat suicides ($n$ = 25). These studies were then analyzed using four theoretically derived criteria. Results show that the identified studies are homogenous with regard to their theoretical foundations and research design and heterogeneous with regard to the media outlets under investigation and the key variables.

The discussion about media effects on individual suicidality in the general population is characterized by the notion of dichotomous media effects that media are either helpful or harmful. Thus, media depictions of suicides either lead to more copycat suicides in the aftermath (*Werther effect*) or—under certain circumstances—media depictions can be suicide preventive (*Papageno effect*) (see also chapters 12 and 13). So far, literature reviews (Gould, 2001) shortly refer to studies with ambiguous findings together with other studies that speak either for a Werther or a Papageno effect, but ambiguous research examples are usually not systematically identified or autonomously analyzed. A recent literature review (Sisask & Värnik, 2012), for example, explicitly enumerates nine studies that provide no clear evidence for copycat suicide effects in the aftermath of suicide depictions in the media without discussing them any further. This chapter builds upon this research gap and systematically identifies and analyzes all studies that were described by their authors themselves as not providing clear evidence for Werther or Papageno effects.

Methodologically, there is an increasing need for meta-research on copycat suicides to keep up with theoretical developments and empirical findings. Associated with this, the scope of empirical studies is always limited to spatial, temporal, social, and methodological contexts which can be regarded as a research restriction (Bonfadelli & Meier, 1984). Regarding ambiguous research findings, conducting meta-research can be problematic, as these studies usually are not reporting any effect sizes, because there often are no effects to report. Hence, we draw on an alternative approach of systematically reviewing literature—a *propositional meta-analysis* (Dahinden, 2006). Therefore, we systematically identify relevant studies in literature databases and make an inventory that includes whether each study includes different predefined criteria (*propositions*) or not. Hence, studies can be compared by these propositions or clusters of them, for example, for different dimensions such as methodology, research design, or included covariates. Effects sizes or other research parameters are neither coded nor quantified. This study aims at systematically reviewing existing literature on copycat suicides that yielded only ambiguous or mixed empirical evidence for a Werther effect. By doing so, we want to make this particular body of literature more visible and accessible for researches and practitioners.

## Method

### Identification of Relevant Studies

To identify studies with ambiguous findings, we conducted a systematic literature search using the online literature databases *Communication & Mass Media Complete, Academic Search Complete, Medline, SocIndex with Full Text, PsycINFO, PsychArticles, PsycBooks,* and *Psyndex: Literature and Audiovisual Media with Psyndex Tests.*

The timescale of this search ranged from the year of the first publication on the role of media for copycat suicides (1967) to September 2012. We only included scientific publications from peer-reviewed journals of which the abstract contains the topics (suicide*), imitation (Werther OR Papageno OR copycat OR imitat* OR contagion*), and media (media OR newspaper* OR radio* OR televis* OR film* OR movie* OR book* OR play* OR internet OR online). By doing so, we identified 148 publications that met all of these inclusion criteria. Additionally, we used the comprehensive meta-analysis of the Task Force Suicide and the Media within the International Association for Suicide Prevention (IASP) to identify other literature ($n$ = 101). This milestone publication especially focuses on copycat effects after celebrity suicides and has been conducted by Niederkrotenthaler et al. (2012). Moreover, we used the references of the identified studies to detect other relevant research ($n$ = 6). The full text of all identified studies was then screened by the authors and studies were included in this analysis if the findings were presented as ambiguous or unclear in the abstract, results section, or discussion by the authors of the respective studies. We based our decision on wordings within the publications that referred to missing statistical significance of findings (e.g., "revealed no significant change"; Motto, 1967, p. 256), that were presented as inconclusive (e.g., "only partial support for the Werther effect"; Hittner, 2005, p. 193), or that were unexpected (e.g., "This result was somewhat surprising..."; Steede & Range, 1989, p. 170). We excluded literature reviews or meta-analyses

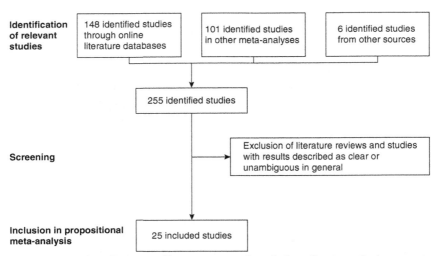

**Figure 13.1.** Flow diagram of literature search and identification of relevant studies.

as well as studies whose global findings were presented as supportive of a Werther or Papageno effect in the abstract, results section, or discussion. In sum, twenty-five studies met all of the inclusion criteria. Figure 13.1 illustrates the process of identifying eligible studies.

*Systematic Analysis of Included Studies*

We used the pioneering work of Phillips (1974) to develop an analytical grid that was used to systematically inventory the identified literature. The grid contained four main criteria that were (1) theoretical mainframe and formulation of hypothesis; (2) research design; (3) medium under investigation; and (4) main variables of interest. The first criterion includes whether the study theoretically builds upon the so-called suggestion hypothesis (Blumenthal & Bergner, 1973) that was used by Phillips mainly describing a simple stimulus–response mechanism or whether other theoretical explanations were used. Moreover, it was coded whether hypotheses were formulated uni- or bidirectional depending on the theoretical framework. The second criterion includes whether studies build upon individual or aggregate data, whether the study used an experimental study design, and whether the content of suicide depictions in the media was elaborately analyzed. Criterion three captures whether the influence of a single medium is observed (as comparable to the pioneer study by

Phillips (1974) who exclusively looked at the influence of front page suicide articles in newspapers on aggregate suicide rates) or whether influences of several media are modeled at the same time such as the influence of television, movies, or other mediums, or whether no medium at all is explicitly mentioned in the study. Criterion four captures whether only completed suicides were used as the dependent variable or whether media influences on suicide attempts or suicidal ideation were also considered as outcome variable. Moreover, we coded whether covariates were included in the analysis without further specification. Table 13.1 gives an overview of all identified and inventoried research articles as well as of the main categories of analysis. The results for each single category will be presented in the following.Table 13.1. Categorization of studies with ambiguous findings on the effects of mass media and suicidality.

## Results

*Theoretical Framework and Formulation of Hypotheses*

Regarding the theoretical foundations used by the studies included in our analysis, one thing becomes pretty obvious: The theoretical foundations of ambiguous studies on copycat suicides are homogeneous in total. All except one study (twenty-four of twenty-five studies) refer to the simple suggestion hypothesis despite the fact that the suggestion hypothesis is more of a description of an empirical phenomenon rather than a theoretical explanation. It remains unclear which processes take place within the recipients evoked by different media content and how they contribute to either an increase or a decrease of individual suicidality (Reinemann & Scherr, 2011). Nevertheless, there are a few studies (six of twenty-five) that build upon other than the suggestion hypothesis to explain their findings. These studies mainly focus on social-cognitive theory by Bandura that includes several intervening variables as moderators of copycat suicides when estimating the probability of imitating a suicide role model (e.g., degree of obviousness of the suicidal act; similarity with the role model; reward for attention; competence of performing an action; positive consequences of behavior). But, complementary theoretical aspects were observed for only five of twenty-five studies.

With regard to the formulation of hypotheses within the identified studies, we found that only one study (Ruddigkeit, 2010) explicitly includes a Papageno effect and therefore the possibility of reversed media effects in the context of individual suicidality. All other studies

187

**Table 13.1.** Catagorization of studies with ambiguous findings on the effects of mass media and suicidality.

| | Motto (1967) [23] | Blumenthal & Bergner (1973) [2] | Stack (1983) [40] | Wasserman (1984) [43] | Horton and Stack (1984) [13] | Kessler and Stipp (1984) [16] | Littmann (1985) [20] | Phillips and Paight (1987) [28] | Platt (1987) [29] | Kessler et al. (1988) [17] | Berman (1988) [1] | Kessler et al. (1989) [18] | Koepping et al. (1989) [19] | Steede and Range (1989) [39] | McDonald and Range (1990) [22] | Stack (1990) [41] | Stack (1992) [42] | Simkin et al. (1995) [37] | Higgins & Range (1996) [10] | Jobes et al. (1996) [14] | Martin & Koo (1997) [21] | Hittner (2005) [11] | Ruddigkeit (2010) [32] | Tsai (2010) [43] | Quinet et al. (2011) [30] | n of studies including a dimension |
|---|---|---|---|---|---|---|---|---|---|---|---|---|---|---|---|---|---|---|---|---|---|---|---|---|---|---|
| *Theoretical framework and foundation of hypotheses* | | | | | | | | | | | | | | | | | | | | | | | | | | |
| Suggestion hypothesis | X | X | X | X | X | X | X | X | X | X | X | X | X | | X | X | X | X | X | X | X | X | X | X | X | 24 |
| Social-cognitive theory | | | | | | | | | X | | | | | X | | | X | | X | | | | X | | X | 6 |
| Complementary theoretical aspects | | | X | | X | | X | | | | | | | | X | | X | | | | | | | | | 5 |
| Formulation of bidirectional hypotheses | | | | | | | | | | | | | | | | | | | | | | | X | | | 1 |
| *Research design* | | | | | | | | | | | | | | | | | | | | | | | | | | |
| Aggregate data | X | X | X | X | X | X | X | X | X | X | X | X | X | | | X | X | X | | X | X | X | X | X | X | 22 |
| Individual data | | | | | | | | | | | | | | X | X | | | X | X | | | | | | | 4 |
| Experiment | | | | | | | | | | | | | | X | X | | | | X | | | | | | | 3 |
| Content analysis | | | | X | | | | | | X | | X | | | | | X | | | | | | X | | | 5 |

*Investigated media*

| | | | | | | | | | | | | | | | | | | | | | |
|---|---|---|---|---|---|---|---|---|---|---|---|---|---|---|---|---|---|---|---|---|---|
| Newspaper | X | X | | X | | | | X | | | | | X | | | X | | X | X | X | 10 |
| TV | | | X | X | | | X | X | | X | | | | X | | | | X | X | | 8 |
| Film | | | | | X | | X | | | | X | | | | | | | | | | 4 |
| Others | | | | | | X | | | X | | | | | | | | X | | | X | 3 |
| Not specified | | X | | | | | | | | | | X | X | | | | | | | X | 4 |

*Key variables*

| | | | | | | | | | | | | | | | | | | | | | |
|---|---|---|---|---|---|---|---|---|---|---|---|---|---|---|---|---|---|---|---|---|---|
| IV nonfictional | X | X | X | | X | | X | X | | X | | | X | X | X | X | | X | X | X | 13 |
| IV fictional | | | X | X | | X | X | X | | X | X | X | X | | | | | | | | 9 |
| DV suicidal behavior | | | X | | X | | | X | X | | X | X | X | | | | | | | | 7 |
| Controls | X | X | X | X | X | X | X | X | X | X | X | X | X | X | X | X | X | X | X | X | 20 |

*Notes*: X, applicable to study; IV, independent variable; DV, dependent variable; controls, control variables.

limit themselves ex ante by simply not considering alternative outcomes such as ambiguous empirical findings as they cannot be theoretically integrated. The theoretical surplus value is a more appropriate description of reality when hypothesizing bidirectional media effect. The qualities of both the media message and the individual are likely to moderate the relationship and the direction of media effects. Basically, these qualities can also neutralize which in turn could result in ambiguous findings (Ruddigkeit, 2010) or indirect media effects (Scherr & Reinemann, 2011).

*Research Design*

Almost all studies (twenty-two of twenty-five studies) build upon aggregate data that are used for correlational analysis. There are no alternative approaches except for a few experimental studies (three of twenty-five studies). The small number of experiments can surely be traced back to ethical concerns of conducting such research. Hence only very few studies de facto investigate the strength and the scope of media effects on individual suicidality. At the same time, strong media effects that affect only very few people (relative to the general population) can only be limitedly tested using aggregate data for causal analysis (Phillips, 1981; Hjelmeland & Knizek, 2010). That's why the approach used by Simkin, Hawton, Whitehead, Fagg, and Eagle (1995)—a combination of individual and aggregate data—can be seen as an innovative research design to test the influence of suicide depictions on individual suicidality: Even if there are no observable media effects on the aggregate level, the accompanying patient survey may show that in individual cases even strong media influences may take effect (e.g., on individual suicidality estimates). Only five studies combined aggregate data ($n = 22$) with a content analysis or with at least some sort of rough estimate for the suicide depiction in the media. For instance, Wasserman (1984) differentiates whether media reports contain a celebrity or a noncelebrity suicide. Studies that only build upon aggregate data cloud the sight of media-induced suicidality the same way as insufficiently developed theoretical explanations for the empirical phenomenon. Regarding the research design, it must be assured that the key influencing variable—suicide reports or suicide depictions in the media—play a crucial role within studies or will be investigated even more in detail. A more detailed view on the qualities of suicide depictions is theoretically rewarding and raises the question how preventive and protective media content have overlapped so far resulting in an interference of their impact and an ambiguous overall effect (Ruddigkeit, 2010).

*Investigated Media*

Studies with ambiguous findings are pretty heterogeneous regarding the media under investigation. Almost all studies with ambiguous findings focused on newspapers (ten of twenty-five studies), but there are almost as many studies on television (eight of twenty-five studies). Less frequent are studies on the impact of movies or other media. Interestingly, only three studies investigate media effects on suicidality using more than one medium. Taken together, a focus on a single medium does not properly reflect the reality of modern media use leading to, strictly speaking, a non sequitur to come to the conclusion of aggregate media effects. Thus, more differentiated studies on the individually used media repertoire would be desirable.

*Key Variables*

Moreover, the key variables within the analyzed studies were heterogeneous: The influence of fictional (nine of twenty-five studies) or nonfictional (thirteen of twenty-five studies) media content on the suicide rate or the individual suicidality (seven of twenty-five studies) is investigated while controlling for relevant covariates (twenty of twenty-five studies). Statistical modeling therefore seems to be heterogeneous in nature offering enough space for observing a wide array of media effects.

## Discussion

Applying a focus on ambiguous findings on copycat suicides, this chapter seeks out to define one important blind spot of this field of research more precisely. Usually, ambiguous findings are only shortly mentioned, often together with other, significant findings. Putting ambiguous findings together should moreover help to acknowledge that media effects on individual suicidality (assessed using either aggregate or individual data) are best described on a media effects continuum that is not only depending on individual predispositions, but is also affected by environmental and social influences. For example, Scherr (2016) recently provided empirical evidence for the complex influence patterns between these variables.

The fact that there is a group of ambiguous research findings between Werther and Papageno effects is expectable from a test-theoretical point of view, but has not been reflected by scientific publication routines: Actually, ambiguous findings represent the shades of gray that lay between the extremes of a media effects continuum. Thereby, ambiguous findings also strengthen the research perspective of a media effects continuum instead of dichotomous (i.e., helpful or harmful) media effects which is by far more appropriate from a mass communication research perspective. On the continuum of media effects on individual suicidality, Werther and Papageno effects mark both extremes with all (more or less) ambiguous findings in between. It seems most likely that particularly inappropriate research designs are responsible that academic and practical research on copycat suicides has not gathered more paces over the last years—despite the remarkably important impulse of reverse (i.e., helpful) media effects (Niederkrotenthaler et al., 2010). This theoretically new perspective should also be used to integrate research findings by elaborating more on overarching theoretical concepts. For instance, Scherr (2016) uses an integrative behavioral model based on the Theory of Planned Behavior (TPB) (Ajzen, 1991) to integrate individual predispositions as well as social and environmental factors and individual suicidality that explains both helpful and harmful media effects. The focus on studies with ambiguous findings also points to the fact that some results also of earlier studies were disregarded although they could have been used as an argument for developing more differentiated theoretical frameworks to explain the impact of media depictions of suicide.

In this sense, this chapter also wants to encourage the publication of empirical findings between a Werther and Papageno effect concomitant with their theoretical foundation between the two extremes—we collected relevant other studies as reference points here that are also in between these extremes. Finally, positive and negative effects may evolve at the same time but for different people leading to overall null findings in aggregate data—this is the typical scenario for cumulative media effects and, thus, should be investigated as differential media effects may show up in dependence of important individual predispositions such as depression in the context of suicidality (Scherr, 2016).

Finally, our study has important implications: Media-induced suicidality poses both new theoretical and practical challenges. While research tends to dichotomize media effects on individual suicidality by only differentiating between helpful and harmful media effects, several empirical studies collected and systematically analyzed here contradict this notion. By doing so, this study raises the question what factors contribute to shifting ambiguous findings into directions that are helpful or harmful for individual suicidality. Future studies should seek out to finding answers to this open research question.

Against the backdrop of this study, we also have some important therapeutic implications: For instance, it seems promising for therapists to talk about individually relevant or especially moving media content and to ensure that such media content has been elaborated in a way that does not jeopardize therapy success. Put differently, excluding specific media content from therapy seems as negligent within modern therapies as to oversimplify media effects when modeling media impacts on individual suicidality. Media play a crucial role in individual suicidal crises—this has been a pretty robust finding of empirical research cumulated until today. Beyond this, this chapter showed that the continuum of media effects between Werther and Papageno effects is likely to be wider than assumed to date.

## References

Ajzen, I. (1991). The theory of planned behavior. *Organizational Behavior and Human Performance, 50*, 179–211.

Berman, A. L. (1988). Fictional depiction of suicide in TV films and imitation effects. *American Journal of Psychiatry, 145*(8), 982–986.

Blumenthal, S., & Bergner, L. (1973). Suicide and newspaper: A replicated study. *American Journal of Psychiatry, 130*(4), 468–471.

Bonfadelli, H., & Meier, W. (1984). Meta-Forschung in der Publizistikwissenschaft: Zur Problematik der Synthese von empirischer Forschung. *Rundfunk und Fernsehen, 32*(4), 537–550.

Dahinden, U. (2006). *Framing. Eine integrative Theorie der Massenkommunikation.* Konstanz: UVK.

Dickersin, K. (2005). Publication bias: Recognizing the problem, understanding its origins and scope, and preventing harm. In H. R. Rothstein, A. J. Sutton, & M. Borenstein (Eds.), *Publication bias in meta-analysis. Prevention, assessment and adjustments* (pp. 11–34). Chichester: Wiley.

Fu, K.-W., Chan, Y.-Y., & Yip, P. S. F. (2009). Testing a theoretical model based on social cognitive theory for media influences on suicidal ideation: Results from a panel study. *Media Psychology, 12*(1), 26–49. doi:10.1080/15213260802669441

Gould, M. S. (2001). Suicide and the media. *Annals of the New York Academy of Science, 932*, 200–224.

Hawton, K., & van Heeringen, K. (2009). Suicide. *The Lancet, 373*(9672), 1372–1381. doi:10.1016/S0140-6736(09)60372-X

Hittner, J. B. (2005). How robust is the Werther effect? A re-examination of the suggestion-imitation model of suicide. *Mortality, 10*, 193–200.

Hjelmeland, H., & Knizek, B. L. (2010). Why we need qualitative research in suicidology. *Suicide and Life-Threatening Behavior, 40*(1), 74–80. doi:10.1521/suli.2010.40.1.74

Horton, H., & Stack, S. (1984). The effect of television on national suicide rates. *The Journal of Social Psychology, 123*, 141–142.

Jobes, D. A., Berman, A. L., O'Carroll, P. W., Eastgard, S., & Knickmeyer, S. (1996). The Kurt Cobain suicide crisis: Perspectives from research, public health, and the news media. *Suicide & Life-Threatening Behavior, 26*(3), 260–271. doi:10.1111/j.1943-278X.1996.tb00611.x

Jonas, K. (1992). Modelling and suicide: A test of the Werther effect. *British Journal of Social Psychology, 31*(4), 295–306. doi:10.1111/j.2044-8309.1992.tb00974.x

Kessler, R. C., Downey, G., Milavsky, J. R., & Stipp, H. (1988). Clustering of teenage suicides after television news stories about suicides: A reconsideration. *The American Journal of Psychiatry, 145*(11), 1379–1383.

Kessler, R. C., Downey, G., Stipp, H., & Milavsky, J. R. (1989). Network television news stories about suicide and short-term changes in total U.S. suicides. *The Journal of Nervous and Mental Disease, 177*(9), 551–555.

Kessler, R. C., & Stipp, H. (1984). The impact of fictional television suicide stories on U.S. fatalities: A replication. *American Journal of Sociology, 90*(1), 151–167.

Koepping, A. P., Ganzeboom, H. B. G., & Swanborn, P. G. (1989). Verhoging van suicide door navolging van kranteberichten. *Nederlands Tijdschrif tvoor de Psychologie, 44*, 62–72. Online abgerufen von http://www.harryganzeboom.nl/suicide/tvptxt.txt

Littmann, S. K. (1985). Suicide epidemics and newspaper reporting. *Suicide and Life-Threatening Behavior, 15*(1), 43–50. doi:10.1111/j.1943-278X.1985.tb00787.x

Martin, G., & Koo, L. (1997). Celebrity suicide: Did the death of Kurt Cobain influence young suicides in Australia? *Archives of Suicide Research, 3*(3), 187–198. doi:10.1080/13811119708258271

McDonald, D. H., & Range, L. M. (1990). Do written reports of suicide induce high-school students to believe that suicidal contagion will occur? *Journal of Applied Social Psychology, 20*(13), 1093–1102. doi:10.1111/j.1559-1816.1990.tb00392.x

Motto, J. A. (1967). Suicide and suggestibility. The role of the press. *American Journal of Psychiatry, 124*, 252–256.

Niederkrotenthaler, T., Fu, K.-W., Yip, P. S. F., Fong, D. Y. T., Stack, S., Cheng, Q., & Pirkis, J. (2012). Changes in suicide rates following media reports on celebrity suicide: A meta-analysis. *Journal of Epidemiology and Community Health, 66*(11), 1037–1042. doi:10.1136/jech-2011-200707

Niederkrotenthaler, T., Voracek, M., Herberth, A., Till, B., Strauss, M., & Etzersdorfer, E. (2010). Role of media reports in completed and prevented suicide: Werther v. Papageno effects. *The British Journal of Psychiatry, 197*, 234–243. doi:10.1192/bjp.bp.109.074633

Phillips, D. P. (1974). The influence of suggestion on suicide: Substantive and theoretical implications of the Werther effect. *American Sociological Review, 39*, 340–354.

Phillips, D. P. (1981). The complementary virtues of qualitative and quantitative research: Reply to Altheide. *Social Forces, 60*(2), 597–599.

Phillips, D. P., & Paight, D. J. (1987). The impact of televised movies about suicide: A replicative study. *New England Journal of Medicine, 317*, 809–811.

Platt, S. (1987). The aftermath of Angie`s overdose: Is soap (opera) damaging to your health? *British Medical Journal, 294*, 954–957.

Queinec, R., Beitz, C., Contrand, B., Jougla, E, Leffondré, K., Lagarde, E., & Encrenaz, G. (2011). Research letter – Copycat effect after celebrity suicides: Results from the French national death register. *Psychological Medicine, 41,* 668–671.

Reinemann, C., & Scherr, S. (2011). Der Werther-Defekt: Plädoyer für einen neuen Blick auf den Zusammenhang von suizidalem Verhalten und Medien. *Publizistik, 56*(1), 89–94. doi:10.1007/s11616-010-0109-y

Ruddigkeit, A. (2010). Der umgekehrte Werther-Effekt: Eine quasi-experimentelle Untersuchung von Suizidberichterstattung und deutscher Suizidrate. *Publizistik, 55*(3), 253–273.

Schäfer, M., & Quiring, O. (2013a). Gibt es Hinweise auf einen „Enke-Effekt"?: Die Presseberichterstattung über den Suizid von Robert Enke und die Entwicklung der Suizidzahlen in Deutschland. *Publizistik, 58*(2), 141–160. doi:10.1007/s11616-013-0172-2

Schäfer, M., & Quiring, O. (2013b). Vorbild auch im Tod?: Neue Hinweise auf einen Werther-Effekt nach Prominentensuiziden. *Suizidprophylaxe, 40*(2), 66–74.

Scherr, S. (2016). *Depression – Medien – Suizid: Zur empirischen Relevanz von Depressionen und Medien für die Suizidalität.* Wiesbaden: Springer VS.

Scherr, S. (2013). Medien und Suizide: Überblick über die kommunikationswissenschaftliche Forschung zum Werther-Effekt. *Suizidprophylaxe, 40*(3), 96–107.

Scherr, S., & Reinemann, C. (2011). Belief in a Werther effect: Third-person effects in the perceptions of suicide risk for others and the moderating role of depression. *Suicide and Life-Threatening Behavior, 41*(6), 624–634. doi:10.1111/j.1943-278X.2011.00059.x

Schmidtke, A. & Häfner, H. (1986). Die Vermittlung von Selbstmordmotivation und Selbstmordhandlung durch fiktive Modelle: Die Folgen der Fernsehserie "Tod eines Schülers." *Nervenarzt, 57,* 502–510.

Simkin, S., Hawton, K., Whitehead, L., Fagg, J., & Eagle, M. (1995). Media influence on parasuicide: A study of the effects of a television drama portrayal of paracetamol self-poisoning. *The British Journal of Psychiatry, 167*(6), 754–759. doi:10.1192/bjp.167.6.754

Sisask, M., & Värnik, A. (2012). Media roles in suicide prevention: A systematic review. *International Journal of Environmental Research and Public Health, 9*(1), 123–138. doi:10.3390/ijerph9010123

Stack, S. (1983). The effect of the Jonestown suicides on American suicide rates. *The Journal of Social Psychology, 119*(1), 145–146. doi:10.1080/00224545.1983.9924456

Stack, S. (1990). The impact of fictional television films on teenage suicide, 1984–1985. *Social Science Quarterly, 71*(2), 391–399.

Stack, S. (1992). The effect of the media on suicide: The great depression. *Suicide and Life-Threatening Behavior, 22,* 255–267.

Steede, K. K., & Range, L. M. (1989). Does television induce suicidal contagion with adolescents? *Journal of Community Psychology, 17,* 166–172.

Tsai, J.-F. (2010). The media and suicide: Evidence-based on population data over 9 years in Taiwan. *Suicide and Life-Threatening Behavior, 40*(1), 81–86. doi:10.1521/suli.2010.40.1.81

Wasserman, I. M. (1984). Imitation and suicide: A reexamination of the Werther effect. *American Sociological Review, 49*(3), 427–436.

# Part III

## Policy

# 14

# Suicide and Mass-Media Reporting: The Very Beginning of the Viennese Experience in the 1980s

*Gernot Sonneck and Elmar Etzersdorfer*

After the opening of the first parts of the Viennese subway system in 1978, it became increasingly acceptable as a means for suicide and suicide attempts, with a sharp increase beginning in 1984. This and the fact that the press reported about these events in a very dramatic way led to the formulation of media guidelines which were launched to the press in mid-1987. The media reports changed immediately and markedly, and the number of subway suicides and attempts decreased by more than 80 percent from the first to the second half of 1987, remaining at a rather low level since. This year was also the turning point from a slightly increasing to a long-lasting decreasing overall suicide rate in Austria.

After starting the subway system in 1978, it became increasingly accepted as a means to commit suicide in the 1980s. This trend is remarkable considering the fact that the Viennese subway system had not been extended during this period nor had the number of passengers risen in a comparable way. The increase in the number of suicide cases in 1984 was also noticed by the print media which published accordingly. Vienna's public transport operator contacted the crisis intervention center because they were afraid that subway suicide was an increasingly favorable suicide method, as was poisoning with city gas, before the poisonous components of the city gas had been removed. Concerning the subway system, all technical security measures had been utilized or were impossible to retrofit. Then we had the idea to take a closer look on media reporting.

Subway suicides are a public way to commit suicide; therefore media are more interested in them than in other methods. The subway line has to be stopped for a while after a suicide; passengers in the station witness it and may be interested to read about it subsequently. A further reason for the dramatic reports in the Viennese mass media in the 1980s might have been that subway suicides and attempts had been novel events, as the whole system had been started only a few years ago. It was recognized that mass media reported about these events in a very dramatic and extensive way (i.e., using large headlines, pictures of the deceased). A working group of the Austrian Association for Suicide Prevention was established to study mass-media reporting. Based on studying the literature on imitative suicide that was available at that time, contacting our colleagues from foreign cities with subways, and studying the actual reports in the Viennese newspapers as well as the clinical experience of the participants, hypotheses of a possible relation between media reports and imitative suicidal behavior were formulated (table 14.1). It was suggested that certain reports, which could be found after the first subway suicides and attempts, could trigger additional suicides. A differentiation was made between aspects that could be a trigger through their expressed attitude on the one hand and aspects of a report that would increase the attention, making it more probable that someone recognizes it on the other hand. We added suggestions about how to reduce the effect, which could be called an advertisement for the idea of life.

The general assumption was twofold: persons in a suicidal crisis are ambivalent and therefore possibly susceptible to suggestions in both directions. A media report which allows identification with the persons described and their suicide and to experience it as support for the (already existing and possibly urging) idea of killing themselves may work as the last trigger for the decision to commit suicide. Another aspect was that persons who are constricted in a severe crisis and cannot think of a way out could find the solution for their unbearable situation presented in the media report.

After formulating these hypotheses a press campaign was launched in mid-1987, informing journalists about possible negative conse-quences of their reporting and offering alternative ways of dealing with those issues. The effect of the campaign was that media reports changed markedly and immediately. Reports on suicidal behavior in general became much more moderate than before, and for the first time several subway suicides were even left unreported. Continuous

**Table 14.1.** Hypotheses used for the media campaign (Sonneck et al., 1994).

*The trigger-effect will be the bigger:*
- the more details of the special methods are reported
- the more suicide is reported as being inconceivable ("he had everything life can give")
- the more the motives are reported to be romantic ("to be forever united")
- the more simplifications are used ("suicide because of bad news")

*The attention will be bigger:*
- if the report is printed on the front page
- if the term "suicide" is used in the headline
- if there is a photograph of the person who died by suicide
- if the attitude of the person is implicitly described as being heroic and desirable ("he had to do that in this situation")

*The effect will be smaller:*
- if more alternatives are shown (where is it possible to find help in such a situation?)
- if there are reports about a crisis that was overcome and did not result in suicide
- if readers are provided with background information on suicidal behavior and suicide in general (such as what to do with someone who expresses suicidal thoughts)

observation of the media reporting allowed subsequent reaction in providing the media with the guidelines again and again.

The results show that following a media campaign in Vienna, which was launched after an increase of suicides and attempts, the subway suicides and attempts decreased and remained on a rather low level since. The preceding increase was not correlated to an extension of the transport system, nor was the drop correlated to a similar decrease in the overall number of suicides in the country. Thus the most probable explanation is that the changed reports led to the drop of subway suicides and attempts (for more details see Sonneck et al., 1994). The overall suicide rate also slightly decreased in Vienna and in Austria in the next years, nevertheless without a sharp decline such as seen with subway suicides. There was no increase in other methods of suicide, pointing to a possible shift of method only. The further development of subway suicides and attempts suggests that some suicides at the peak have occurred additionally. The alternative explanation that they occurred earlier only but would have occurred anyway is not supported by our data, as in this case the numbers in the time before and after the drop should level (for a detailed analysis of this alternative explanation, see Phillips, 1974; or Schmidtke & Häfner, 1988).

A conclusion from our study is that it is possible to change media reports, but it is necessary to state that this is not possible by forcing journalists. Journalists are used to defending their freedom to report about any issue or abstain, and of course it is not possible to forbid reports about suicide totally. Besides, it is not clear whether this really would be the most favorable way to deal with suicides in the mass media or whether there is a preventive potential of reports as well that can be used. Our approach was to inform journalists and leave it up to them and their responsibility to make their own conclusions. Nevertheless we provided guidelines, which offer possible alternative ways of reporting (see table 14.1).

Another experience in the next years was that it is necessary to "refresh" the knowledge or willingness of journalists from time to time. We found that, at least in Austria, often the youngest or inexperienced journalist has to prepare the report about a suicide; someone who may be unaware of possible imitational effects. This has to do with the fact that local stories are at the bottom of the hierarchy of reporting, which again contributes to the fact that the responsibility for these issues often changes. Our strategy in Austria is to be aware of reports in newspapers and, in the case of a report, to send the guidelines, with numerous modifications by now, to the journalist and the newspaper and to ask for discussion. Furthermore we are spreading the information and the guidelines among journalists, whenever members of the Austrian Association for Suicide Prevention get in touch with journalists for whatever reason.

Nearly 25 years later, carrying on investigations on imitative effects we found that the impact of suicide reporting may not be restricted to harmful effects; rather coverage of positive coping in adverse circumstances, as covered in media items about suicidal ideation, may have protective effects, which we call Papageno effects (Niederkrotenthaler et al., 2010).

### References

Niederkrotenthaler, T., Voracek, M., Till, B., Strauss, M., Etzersdorfer, E., Eisenwort, B., & Sonneck, G. (2010). Role of media reports in completed and prevented suicide: Werther v. Papageno effects. *The British Journal of Psychiatry, 197*, 234–243.

Philipps, D. P. (1974). The influence of suggestion on suicide: Substantive and theoretical implications of the Werther effect. *American Sociological Review, 39,* 240–253.

Schmidtke, A., & Häfner, A. (1988). The Werther effect after television films: New evidence for an old hypothesis. *Psychological Medicine, 18,* 665–676.

Sonneck, G., Etzersdorfer, E., & Nagel-Kuess, S. (1994). Imitative suicide on the Viennese subway. *Social Science and Medicine, 38,* 453–457.

# 15

# Development of the US Recommendations for Media Reporting on Suicide

*Daniel J. Reidenberg*

## Brief History

In the United States in April 1994, the first set of Recommendations from a national workshop for media reporting on suicide was developed and published. In response to reporting on a cluster of suicides that occurred in New Jersey in 1987, a small group of experts in suicide prevention collaborated to produce the document that ultimately appeared in the Center for Disease Control and Prevention's *Morbidity and Mortality Weekly Report* (MMWR), Vol. 43, No. 88-6. The Recommendations were evaluated by Jamieson et al. (2003) by looking at 279 published articles on suicide in 1990, 1995, and 1999. The authors found that there was little adherence to the Recommendations in making a connection between a mental illness and suicide and that readers were unlikely to learn the necessity of seeking treatment for a mental health condition to prevent a suicide.

In 2001 a group of experts convened to develop the second set of Recommendations for media reporting on suicide. The group included two suicide prevention organizations as well as the Annenberg Public Policy Center and four federal agencies. It did not include media industry representation. The document produced was a trifold piece with nine pages. On the cover of the document was a typewriter ball, something even at that time was largely outdated, but was included as an attempt to demonstrate engagement of the journalism world.

The document was titled *Reporting on Suicide: Recommendations for the Media* and opened with Suicide Contagion is Real in bold letters on the top of the first page. Within this box was a brief summary of the Vienna study that outlined the reduction in suicides following the release of alternative strategies for reporting on suicide in that country. The formal recommendations followed and included

- Suicide and Mental Illness
- Interviewing Surviving Relatives and Friends
- Language
- Special Situations
- Stories to Consider Covering

The document ended with a full page listing twenty-seven research articles referenced in the document, all of which were at least two years following publication of the journal article, most five to eight years old. While there was no formal study or evaluation following the release of the second version of the Recommendations, two national not-for-profit suicide prevention organizations, Suicide Awareness Voices of Education (SAVE) and the American Foundation for Suicide Prevention (AFSP), distributed over thousand copies to journalists and news outlets across the country. Over a five-year period there was informal follow-up contacts made to over hundred journalists to assess the value, usefulness, and impact of the Recommendations. Overwhelmingly the response was that the document was not very helpful, largely because it was not practical or useful to a reporter on deadline.

Between 2005 and 2009 there was an increase in media reporting on suicide in the United States. SAVE and the AFSP noticed that most of the news reports were not following the Recommendations. There were many sensational headlines and front page stories, graphic details were included in the reports, graphic images became more common-place, and very few reports included the use of suicide prevention experts. During this time social media (social networking platforms and social media bloggers) dramatically increased for the first time, thereby increasing the exposure of suicide stories to many more people rapidly and in more locations. To address the new media (social media) cultural change, the Substance Abuse and Mental Health Services Administration held a New Media Summit in 2009. At that meeting is when I initiated conversations with a small group of people about their interest and willingness to update and revise the (at that time) nearly decade old Recommendations. This was the beginning of the process for creating the new Recommendations.

## Composition of the Task Force

In order to create a task force that was comprehensive and inclusive, it was important that it not be limited in number, geographic region, and area of specialty or expertise, and that it have representation from multiple sectors, most specifically media. A call was put out to the suicide prevention community, prior participants in the earlier guidelines, as well as among the media community. Criteria for being included were an interest and/or expertise in the topic and availability to participate.

The next step was the development of "Tiers" in which task force members would be participating in the process. The first Tier consisted of a small group that included at least one person from a field of expertise. This group was to be the core group that would have the most time involved in the project, be able to access others when and where needed, and assist in major decision making. As in many other task forces or similar structures, there was a need to have a team approach and there needed to be one final decision maker who would be used in the event of a tie in voting or for other key decisions that need to be made to keep the process moving forward.

- Tier 1 included experts in research, public health, nonprofits, federal partners, and media.
- Tier 2 was more broad and expanded on the types of individuals in Tier 1. Their role was to be available for meetings and periodic review and to enlist engagement to an even broader group of constituents and experts as and when needed. Tier 2 had twenty people on it.
- Tier 3 was a larger group. This group was involved and activated only for review of the document and comments. This group was broadened primarily to media (journalists, reporters, news directors, etc.) who would review, edit, and make recommendations on the document.
- The largest of the tiers was Tier 4. This group was involved in ancillary and informal discussions conducted by other task force members. It also included social media champions and bloggers.

## A Consensus Model

The current Recommendations were consensus based, having been agreed to by more than fifty suicide prevention experts, national advocacy organizations, research institutions, media individuals, and organizations from around the world. Further, to determine consensus for inclusion of something in the Recommendations meant the group needed to define how the consensus would be established. Ultimately, the task force arrived at the following:

1. If there was at least one published research article to support a recommendation.
2. If there was at least one evidence-based or best-practice-endorsed program.
3. That there needed to be a majority vote to support the inclusion of a statement.
4. With input from media, their vote was given higher weighting on inclusion of a statement, provided that there were more than one expert and/or research to support it.

## Title of the Document

The initial discussions focused on the title of the document. The task force discussed key ideas or messages we felt were important to convey in the title of the document. These included: media, reporting, guidelines, recommendations, and safety. Once we agreed on the key message of the title, we came up with a large number of options:

- Guidelines for Reporting on Suicide
- Guidelines for Media Reporting on Suicide
- Media Recommendations for Suicide Reporting
- Media Recommendations for Reporting on Suicide
- Recommendations for Media on Suicide Reporting
- Recommendations for Media and Suicide
- Reporting on Suicide
- Reporting on Suicide Safely
- Reporting Safely on Suicide
- Safe Reporting of Suicide
- Safe Reporting of Suicide by the Media

To narrow the list of options, the task force first addressed the issue of "guidelines" versus "recommendations." The experts in suicide prevention felt guidelines was a better word because it had a stronger connotation to it, thus they felt it would more likely be used by the media. On the other hand, the media experts felt the opposite. The media representatives felt strongly that the use of guidelines in the title would be overly strong and thus less likely for media to use it. Further, they expressed that because whatever the final document was, unless it was to be an ethical mandate to be followed, the use of the word recommendations was more accurate in terms of what the document actually was. After running this through the consensus criteria and definition, the task force agreed recommendations would be included in the title.

The next step was to determine the rest of the title. Everyone on the task force expressed an interest that the title be short/brief and directly address what the intent of the document was. The list narrowed down to

- Recommendations for Reporting on Suicide
- Safe Reporting on Suicide

The discussion among the task force was that while both were brief and direct, Safe Reporting on Suicide implied that if media did not follow the document (recommendations) exactly as stated, there was concern among the media that they would be perceived or, worse, criticized for unsafely reporting on suicide. The group determined that there was no sufficient evidence to support that not following the document (recommendations) would constitute unsafe reporting, only that it was believed that if media did follow the recommendations, the reporting on suicide would be done in a safe manner. Thus following a vote, Safe Reporting on Suicide was eliminated.

The final component to the title was working from Recommendations for Reporting on Suicide. There was uniform agreement among the task force members that this title was acceptable. However, there were some media members who expressed that if in fact we were truly developing a tool "for the media," that this should be conveyed in the title. With the consensus criteria giving weight to media's input and with support from the full task force, the final title was selected.

## Document Content, Design, and Layout

To begin, the task force reviewed the 2001 document. Subgroups selected items from each section that we felt should be maintained in the new document (with current updating to that material to be included). The basic items were

- Research findings
- Partners
- Examples

With that determined, the task force began its discussion of what new content should be included. Social media and bloggers, the National Lifeline number as a main resource, and messages of hope were all identified as primary items to be included in the new document.

Another discussion was the length of the document. The media members were very strong in this regard expressing that the document be brief: one page. They talked about the option of it being two pages, but said it should be designed with the most important information conveyed on the front page. Consensus was determined for this format of the content.

With regard to the design, the task force felt the document would benefit from having a color to it (thus not a black and white document), it should include icons and/or graphics to be viewed as current, and it should include an image that media members would resonate with (e.g., keyboard, computer screen).

## Timeline and Milestones

| | |
|---|---|
| May 2009 | The Substance Abuse and Mental Health Services Administration holds a New Media Summit; at the meeting I approach a small group of stakeholders about updating the 2001 Recommendations |
| August 2009 | SAVE facilitates a meeting at Annenberg |
| September 2009 | Reidenberg writes the first draft of the new Recommendations |
| October–November 2009 | Tier 1 works and finishes revisions |
| December 2009 | Reidenberg distributes first draft to Tier 2 (Draft 1) |
| January–February 2010 | Recommendations from Tier 2 are made and became Draft 2 |
| February 2010 | Annenberg conducts focus groups on Draft 2 with The Virginia Pilot staff |
| Early March 2010 | Recommendations from focus groups revisions made and a new format created dropping document to four pages |
| Late March 2010 | Draft 2 distributed to Tiers 2 and 3 |
| April–May 2010 | Feedback received suggested document be summarized "cut and write for media" |
| May 2010 | Light bulb moment: we must create recommendations that were helpful to the media, not to the suicide prevention community (see below for more on this) |
| June 2010 | Reidenberg incorporates recommendations and writes Draft 3 |
| July 2010 | New design created dropping document to two pages and uses formatting suggested by media (Draft 3) |
| Late July 2010 | Reidenberg distributed Draft 3 to Tiers 2, 3, and 4 and includes new media champions |

| August 2010 | Revisions made based on feedback and Drafts 4 and 5 distributed by Reidenberg to Tiers 3 and 4 |
| September–October 2010 | Revisions made based on feedback and Draft 6 created |
| November– December 2010 | Draft 6 distributed to all Tiers; revisions made based on feedback creating Drafts 7 and 8 |
| March 2011 | Draft 8 is used as the final document leading up to a meeting held at the Poynter Institute |
| March 2011 | Final revisions made to the document based on feedback from the meeting |
| April 14, 2011 | Formal release |

### *Key Milestone, May 2010: The Light Bulb Moment*

The key milestone in the development of the current Recommendations came well into the process, drafts, edits, and revisions based on the feedback from the reviews. Up to this point, there was consensus around the major components of the document. The biggest challenges within and between the Tiers was grammar, aesthetic (design), and length. However, on a bright Saturday in May 2010, I printed out every review, comment, suggestion, and edit that was given to me from around the world. The key to this was each one was printed blind (no identifying name to the review). I put each one on the floor, table, bookshelf, and any other available space I had in my office. I then began a modified content analysis of the reviews (comments and recommendations). In doing so I was able to place each review into a pile. After sorting through each one there were clearly two stacks, one much larger than the other (twenty-eight vs. five). In reading through the larger stack of reviews, there were very clear and some strongly written suggestions that almost uniformly and very consistently fell into this content and order:

1. Length: The document needs to be very short. One page would be best, two at the longest.
2. Credibility: The document needs to be seen as credible, having been developed by leading experts in the industry.
3. Format: The document should tell the reader the three most important things that need to be known on the topic and that these can be backed up by research.
   a. The most helpful things to include in the document are what not to do and what to do.

211

4.   Research: Findings are important to researchers and experts in suicide; they are less important to journalists. Those in the media field want to know that research exists to support the Recommendations, but do not take up a lot of space or list outdated research.

5.   Resources: The document should provide the main resource that can be used in all media formats (television, radio, print, social media).

I then went back and determined who gave the feedback for each review. What was remarkable to me and the light bulb moment was that the above 5 sets of recommendations came 100 percent from those in the media industry. It was now clear to me that what had happened with earlier versions of the Recommendations (1994, 2001) and the first drafts of this version was that the authors were listening to the suicide prevention and mental health experts, not the media professionals! I realized that if we wanted a document that was going to be useful to those who were doing the reporting on suicide, we needed to listen to them and what their needs were, as opposed to what we felt was most important. An example of this was on research. This was the main thrust of the 1994 document and the first and last things in the 2001 document. This primary placement of research findings was "our" need, not "theirs," and this needed to change.

With that in mind, I started over completely with what became known as Draft 3. That document was two pages (one piece of paper with printing on both sides). Included at the top was a listing of the partners, giving the document the credibility media asked for. The next section listed the three most important points that we had research to support and, below that, the largest section of page one included "Instead of this" and "Do this" sections. On the back side of the document there was a section included on how to offer and convey hope, as well as a side-bar that had the National Suicide Prevention Lifeline phone number as a uniform resource. The bottom of page two included a website with links to research and a small section on suggestions for new media and bloggers.

## Following the Release

The first update to the Recommendations came in 2012 when we revised the back side (second page) of the Recommendations at the bottom of the document. I received requests to have a space where local resource numbers or websites could be included in the document. As a result, we created a Word version of the Recommendation and added that to the website. Further, we changed the bottom left section of the document to create an open space for people to include local resources.

## Reportingonsuicide.org: The Website to Accompany the Recommendations

To be current and have something easily and quickly accessible to those in the media, a website was necessary to accompany the document. Moreover, because the document was one piece of paper front and back, there was limited area to include everything the task force felt important. Thus a website was developed that included a downloadable version of the Recommendations, current examples of reporting on suicide, a listing of suicide prevention experts available to the media, and a full list of the research on the document. The website was released at the same time as the paper version of the Recommendations.

## Changes to the Website

Since that time there have been two revisions of the website, the most recent taking place in September 2015. That release expanded on the first website, included new examples, and updated research, as well as information on training for media through the Poynter Institute. In addition, the updated website houses the Recommendations translated into other languages (Spanish and German).

## Evaluation

The California Suicide Prevention Social Marketing Project, funded by the voter-approved Mental Health Services Act (MHSA) (Prop. 63), aims to improve reporting on suicide through training individuals in counties on media outreach, providing counties with a guide to media advocacy, conducting forums with journalists and other stakeholders, and disseminating the Recommendations to news media throughout the state. It is overseen by the California Mental Health Services Authority (CalMHSA), an organization of county governments working to improve mental health outcomes for individuals, families, and communities. To measure the effectiveness of this, the project conducted the nation's first study to examine how well news media currently adhere to the Recommendations for Reporting on Suicide. It is important to note that the major limitation of this effort was undertaken in 2011, the same year the Recommendations were released. Nonetheless, the authors created a unique tool to measure California media outlets' adherence and applied it to a sample of more than two hundred recent reports to establish a baseline measure. The report on the findings fell into twelve areas: coverage type; resources; how to help; warning signs and risk factors; attributing suicide to a single condition; reporting on location; reporting on method; sources of quotes; content of suicide notes; language used; reporting on numbers and rates; and visuals.

The results of the study showed that California newspaper and television coverage of suicide during the last six months of 2011 did not consistently adhere to the *Recommendations for Reporting on Suicide*. Although sensational reporting was not the usual practice, it was determined that much more could be done to promote the concepts of preventability, inform the public about available resources, and reduce graphic coverage. California news media showed the strongest degree of adherence to the Recommendations in places where they *discourage* certain reporting practices, such as providing details about method, or using sensational language. Very few articles or broadcasts sensationalized suicide or provided overly graphic descriptions of method. The Recommendations discourage these practices because they can increase the risk for contagion and they provide misinformation about suicide to the community. The lowest degree of adherence to the Recommendations was in areas that *encourage* providing helpful resources and interviewing suicide prevention and mental health professionals as reliable sources of information.

A similar follow-up study was conducted in 2013 after mass dissemination of the Recommendations, education to messengers on suicide prevention, and forums to reach media professionals. They then sought to measure how well California-based newspaper reporting adhered to the *Recommendations* and whether there were changes after the period of most intensive intervention. Eight of their eleven hypotheses were supported by the findings which show the potential of educating both the media *and* suicide prevention spokespeople.

- There was an increase in the percentage and total number of articles covering the *topic of suicide prevention* and a decrease in the percentage of articles that addressed only a *suicide death* or *attempt.*
- The percentage of articles that provided a suicide prevention *resource* increased by almost threefold.
- The percentage of articles that discussed the *method* of a specific suicide death/attempt, including the weapon used and graphic details, decreased by more than 50 percent.
- The percentage of articles that used more *appropriate language* ("killed himself," "died by suicide") to describe suicide doubled.

- We did not see a large shift in *quotes* by or interviews with suicide prevention experts and saw a slight decrease in quotes by mental health professionals. However, the 2013 analysis showed a greater *diversity* in the roles of people who were quoted, and a decrease in interviews with *family members* of decedents, who often are not versed in prevention messaging.
- In addition, we found *more articles that had been written by suicide prevention practitioners or spokespeople themselves* or who were cited as "special contributors."

The authors concluded that there was both potential and benefit of educating both the media *and* suicide prevention spokespeople on effective messaging and reporting on suicide prevention.

## References

AdEase, Educational Development Center, Inc., Your Social Marketer, Inc. (2014). *Know the signs: Media analysis final report.*

Center for Disease Control and Prevention. (1994). *Morbidity and Mortality Weekly Report.* Vol 43, No 88-6.

Jamieson, P., Jamieson, K. H., & Romer, D. (2003). The responsible reporting of suicide in print journalism. *American Behavioral Scientist, 46,* 1643–1660.

Ly, T., Guard, A., & Black, S. (2012). *CalMHSA suicide prevention social marketing project baseline media analysis.* Waltham, MA: Education Development Center, Inc.

# 16

# Raising Media Awareness in French-Speaking Switzerland: Best Practices

*Irina Inostroza and Joanne Schweizer Rodrigues*

At STOP SUICIDE, we think that appropriate ways to inform about suicide can help prevent suicide.[1] Media coverage has been the focus of numerous studies and discussions in the field of prevention, but there are very few programs active in this area beyond dissemination of the WHO guidelines on coverage of suicides.

Through ongoing funding from the canton of Vaud,[2] STOP SUICIDE has worked since 2011 to *improve the suicide-protective effect* of the media and *limit its copycat effect.* We work closely with media to promote sensitive and appropriate reporting of suicide. STOP SUICIDE's "Media programme" leads three main activities: media observation, briefing editorial staff, and journalism students' training.

This article will provide an overview of our experience with this program. Its aim is to point out the best practices identified during the four years of working with media outlets and journalists.

## Monitoring the Press

### Monitoring Media Coverage

The main task of STOP SUICIDE's Media programme is to monitor on a daily basis how the major French-language print media in French-speaking Switzerland report on suicide (fifteen print and online publications). We assess all articles whose main topic is suicide to ensure that newspapers comply with WHO guidelines on coverage of suicide and with Directive 7.9—Suicide of the Editor's Code of Ethics (Swiss Press Council, 2015).

Directive 7.9 of the Code of Ethics specifically addresses media coverage of suicide. It indicates that journalists should report on suicide if there is a "public need to know" and with "the utmost restraint." In order to avoid suicides by imitation, the general rule is that the media should "not mention any details about the method or product used" (Swiss Press Council, 2015).[3]

In a report published in 2014, STOP SUICIDE assessed four hundred articles published in 2013 in eleven French-language Swiss newspapers. The report underscored the incomplete application of guidelines for suicide coverage in the French-language Swiss media (STOP SUICIDE, 2014).[4]

Every two weeks, we also present the findings of this monitoring process in a fortnightly press review[5] to inform both journalists and prevention professionals.

### Lodging Formal Complaints with the National Media Regulation Authorities

In Switzerland, it is possible to lodge a complaint about Swiss newspapers to the Swiss Press Council, the self-regulatory organization responsible for journalism ethics and standards. Since 2003, the council has made around ten statements on articles addressing suicide, among which five of them were complaints made by STOP SUICIDE. In 2011, STOP SUICIDE lodged a complaint against the daily newspaper *Le Matin* about an article entitled "Death for 60 dollars." According to STOP SUICIDE, this article gave too many details of how a twenty-nine-year-old man killed himself using a "suicide kit" that he had ordered on the Internet. The Swiss Press Council concluded that the publication failed to handle the subject in a "restrained and cautious manner." It considered that reporting of the suicide method was not in the public interest to be disclosed and might "almost" prompt vulnerable individuals to imitate identical social behavior (Swiss Press Council, 2012).

Such formal complaints work to promote responsible reporting of suicide in the press, especially when they are awarded by the positions of the Press Council. The former editor-in-chief of *Le Matin* later stated in the press that reconsidering the article she would not have published it or any article resembling this one (Loersch, 2014). However, complaints are rare because they take time and we prefer to complain on reports showing high levels of details (to avoid weakening the rule if the complaint is not awarded) and to work in close cooperation with media outlets.[6] In the case of the complaint against *Le Matin*, the editor-in-chief invited STOP SUICIDE to brief her about responsible coverage of suicide. Our strategy is to focus on building a long-term dialogue with media and journalists.

### Writing Letters to the Press

When we assess that an article may spark fatal behavior among teenagers or adults, because it doesn't comply with either or both Directive 7.9—Suicide and WHO guidelines, we contact the editorial team directly.[7] In 2014, we contacted thirty-five newspapers and we were able to build a constructive dialogue with seventeen of them after they answered to us. In August 2015, *L'Illustré*, a very popular French-language weekly paper, published an interview with Doctor Erika Preisig in which she expressed support for assisted suicide for youth suffering from depression (not currently legal in Switzerland) (Berney, 2015). This type of discourse might give depressed teens the idea that killing themselves is the easiest way out of their problems instead of seeking help. STOP SUICIDE wrote to the editor and requested a right of reply and *L'Illustré* published our letter (Inostroza, 2015).

In most cases, media outlets are receptive to our program. When we recommend they limit the level of detailed information, especially about the suicide method, for example, in a title or a picture, they are generally ready to modify the online version of the article by changing the title or the picture, or they agree that they would avoid detailed or sensationalist reporting in subsequent articles.[8] Following our clues, editors also remind their team that our job is to answer journalists' enquiries about how to report on suicide. Journalists are increasingly contacting STOP SUICIDE when they are seeking advice on how to portray suicide cases or because they would like us to review their stories.

We also update a list of journalists who have already reported on suicide because they are more susceptible to report again on suicide (in the news section or lifestyle section). According to a Swiss survey, only a minority of journalists has already reported on suicide and although they declare to have better knowledge of guidelines on suicide coverage, only half of them say they are informed about the risk of copycat suicides (Altermatt & Steinmann, 2009).[9] It means that the vast majority of journalists have moderate or rather weak knowledge of these risks and of the guidelines (Altermatt & Steinmann, 2009).[10]

## Meeting Journalists

Following the Swiss experience of Konrad Michel and colleagues (Michel, Frey, Wyss & Valach, 2000), STOP SUICIDE implemented a more proactive and preventative strategy in order to improve media knowledge of the positive and negative impacts of suicide coverage. As media outlets don't have much time and suicide coverage is not a priority for them, STOP SUICIDE chose to offer in-house briefings to foster sustainable and interpersonal relationships with newspaper titles. Media outlets show a relatively high interest in organizing in-house briefings on suicide coverage. Since 2012, we approximately organized ten of those meetings with newspapers per year. Journalists are asking fort short trainings and they invite us either at lunchtime or in the morning just after the first briefing of the day.

### Avoiding Dogma

Many journalists still believe that "it is best not to talk about suicide" in the media. They are generally relieved to hear that there are sensitive ways to report on suicide without sparking copycat suicides. According to the director of the local radio station *Radio Fribourg*, "the briefing of Stop Suicide allowed us to escape from a certain type of dogma surrounding this issue. We notably understood that we can—and even should—talk about suicide, but without going into details of what motivated the person to such extremes."

Most editorial teams welcome our main message even among journalists who think that covering suicide is not dangerous. It is especially the case for "tabloids" as it seems more difficult for them to implement the media guidelines for suicide. Editors-in-chief generally see our briefings as "constructive." They say that they don't feel like we had come to tell them "what to do" (Loersch, 2013) and that they are "open to critical thinking" about their reporting on suicide.

Media outlets ask for our strong expertise in the field of suicide prevention. Most of them want to learn about theoretical aspects of copycat suicides and how they can engage in the prevention of suicide. They appreciate that we rely on facts and on clinical-based insights. One editor-in-chief used to say STOP SUICIDE is "not ideological" but rather "pragmatic, based on field experience." They also appreciate the way we deliver the guidelines: with articles, with practical examples, and on a case-by-case basis.

*Influencing Suicide Coverage Before Publishing*

Journalists are also interested in STOP SUICIDE providing guidance on reporting of suicide. In 2014, we provided guidance to seventeen journalists who had enquiries about portraying suicide resulting in the publication of fourteen "Papageno-friendly" articles. Our strategy is to work *with* journalists and not *against* them[11] and our goal is to reach informed coverage and preventative reporting. Journalists generally call us because they want to report on high-profile, unresolved or "mysterious" cases of suicide, involving prominent people or young individuals, and spectacular or particularly rare methods of suicide. They are also looking for statistics or survivors' stories. When debriefing together we talk about the multifactorial causes of suicide and suggest a sensitive and acceptable level of information without unduly restricting the freedom of the press to report on suicide.

In 2013 a young man killed himself; before dying he posted his picture on instagram with a scotch tape on his mouth. One journalist wanted to run a story about what he thought was the "first case in Switzerland." Following our advice the article focused on youth suicide and on using social media to prevent suicide. The picture was not published and both the online and the print versions of the article informed on various sources of support. The father told the press other young people might think twice before taking their own life because he was devastated. The article was sensitive and avoided honoring suicidal behavior.

In 2015 *L'Illustré* contacted STOP SUICIDE because one journalist of the team wanted to report on the effects of suicide on friends and family members. We met the reporter to brief her and connect her with a suicide attempt survivor, a young woman who was willing to tell her story in a preventive way. In most of the stories friends and family members described the devastating effect of suicide and wanted to prevent further suicides. At the end of the story there was a textbox with numbers of helplines.

Our experience shows that it is possible to influence media coverage toward prevention. In some cases, our briefing successfully changed the focus and the content of an article or a broadcast; we were able to influence the choice of the person/specialist speaking. In some other cases, our briefing was helpful in deciding not to publish an article. But what media need most is to be provided with reliable information and sources.

## Providing Useful Information

Many journalists believe suicide deserves a public discussion, especially in Switzerland where many teenagers die of suicide. Some of them have personal experiences with suicide or have covered suicide cases. They appreciate our briefings because we provide them with useful information (e.g., on statistics, "causes" of suicide) and other news or current topics linked to suicide and prevention (e.g., teenage bullying, Swiss prevention strategy).

Journalists are also interested in our approach essentially oriented toward promoting the Papageno effect, which they welcome as a "paradigm-change". They enquire about means to cover suicides that are both informative and preventative and appreciate to meet specialists in the field. "We do not always know how to address the issue of suicide in a broader context and to talk about prevention," said a journalist from a regional daily newspaper. "Meetings that allow us to understand the issue better and to meet stakeholders are therefore interesting. We get to know who to call, who to turn to when we need to cover the subject, and are able to talk about it" (S. Heiniger, personal communication, October 1, 2015).

## Following Up with Editorial Teams

However, changing old-fashioned reporting practices requires time. And for those journalists who generally "work on suicides," especially the tabloids, it might not be easy to let down sensationalist reporting. The editor-in-chief of the free and daily newspaper *20minutes* opens a window to change, though: "things need to go fast. We do not have a lot of time to sort information through. That is particularly the case with briefs picked up and used directly from abroad. We talk about things because others are doing it and we don't want to look like fools. We should perhaps have the courage not to; to say to ourselves, I won't run this."

To have the greatest impact, it is important to reiterate our briefings with media outlets and journalists. We offer some "refresh" or "review" sessions to follow-up with editorial teams on suicide coverage. In some newspaper titles, STOP SUICIDE's briefing takes place every year. Journalists think that it is beneficial to give regular reminders because suicide is a major public health issue. Over the past four years, we have forged ties of trust with the media and we now work better together. Journalists contact us before producing coverage on the issue of suicide or when they need to find experts and witnesses. These special ties have also improved the coverage of our events and activities aiming at youth suicide prevention, and STOP SUICIDE was also able to develop partnership with youth media such as *tink.ch*.[12]

*Getting to Know the "Who Is Who" of Suicide Coverage*

Other Swiss institutions aim to foster dialogue with regional media outlets. In 2014 and 2015 the canton of Neuchâtel organized two workshops on media coverage of suicide. Together with STOP SUICIDE, they invited journalists, police, mental health and suicide prevention experts, and media school representatives. Following the workshops, the canton published a fact-sheet with useful information and a "ready-to-publish" list with helpline numbers and websites. As a result, two regional media outlets added this list to their articles on suicide.

The workshops also raised ethical and strategic questions regarding the implementation of guidelines on suicide coverage. Questions raised included: "Should media avoid informing on the suicide method although it is of public interest (e.g., in cases of suicides on the railway)?" Moreover, journalists and mental health professionals talked about ethics of journalism in hospital settings. The workshops fostered their mutual understanding and reciprocal ties. As a result, one reporter was able to meet a suicide attempt survivor and published his story. A local psychiatric unit got in contact with a journalist who reported on suicide screening and assessment.

However, because only three journalists participated in the workshops, the canton of Neuchâtel will consider further approaches which are more in line with media working environments. This includes participation in in-house meetings together with STOP SUICIDE, building editorial partnerships with health section editors and journalists, and strengthening ties with journalism schools.

## Targeting the Journalists of the Future

To be effective on the long term, we work together with schools of journalism to directly meet their students. This is a way to change practices and raise awareness at the same time.

*Addressing Fears and Raising the Curiosity of Students*

Young journalists are often afraid to report on suicide. They fear "getting it wrong, being sensationalist or sparking an undeniable copycat effect," explains the Director of the Academy of Journalism and Media in Neuchâtel (AJM) (A. Dubied, personal communication, October 1,

2015). According to her, it's important to include suicide in the "baggage given to future journalists" because students are often "tempted by silence," just like many experienced journalists.

In March 2015 three students from this school dared to organize a workshop on the challenges of covering suicide in the media with us. The goal of the workshop was to go beyond such stereotypes, to foster dialogue and train students in this type of "poorly regarded" subject in the profession (e.g., offbeat news, celebrity life).

### Asking the Right Questions

Since 2012, STOP SUICIDE has also been involved twice a year with the other French-language Swiss school of journalism, the Centre de formation au journalisme et aux médias (CFJM). During our sessions, we use a mind-mapping tool to help students ask the correct questions before, during,, and after they report on suicide. We provide tools to help them find a balance between respect for private life and public interest.

### Giving "Case-by-Case" Examples

We display available scientific data on the Werther and Papageno effects to students, as well as the WHO and the Swiss "*Points de repère*" guidelines. But students (like journalists) often feel that such information is contradictory and ask them to "inform about suicide, while omitting some facts." We show them articles which illustrate that it is possible to avoid this paradox by choosing headlines carefully, publishing sensitive images, addressing undercovered topics, and including information on how to seek help. Our goal is to encourage them to seek sensitive ways of breaking the taboo by covering suicide.

### Precious Feedback

According to the student's feedback, what is most interesting about this training is learning concretely how to cover a story on suicide in a balanced and respectful way. They appreciate the tools that we give them, especially one checklist of questions about media coverage. They feel more prepared to cover suicide and mentioned that we helped them in understanding that it was sometimes best to avoid the topic than to address it in an incomplete or "clumsy" manner. Journalism students are generally relieved to know that they can count on STOP SUICIDE's support and to have the helpline numbers. According to one student, "if we don't have enough time to report carefully about suicide, I'd rather not poke this issue."

## Conclusion: It's All in the Approach

STOP SUICIDE's Media programme has developed an innovative and pragmatic approach for suicide prevention over the past four years. Beginning with a systematic monitoring of the press of both positive and negative reactions to media coverage of suicide, we have fostered dialogue with Swiss French-language editorial teams. This dialogue has allowed us to adapt the WHO guidelines to journalists' practices,[13] to create an increasingly appropriate awareness-raising briefing or training, and to "escape from the dogma" that still reigns in the profession: "you cannot talk about suicide." To change common practices, it is essential to work on a long-term perspective, to build trustworthy relationships with journalists, journalism schools, and editorial teams. Starting as early as possible with raising awareness among the journalists of the future is crucial.

### Notes

1. STOP SUICIDE aims to prevent youth suicide in the French-speaking part of Switzerland. Our headquarters are based in Geneva. STOP SUICIDE. (2012). *Introduction.* Retrieved from http://www.stopsuicide.ch/site/content/association

2. Switzerland is a federal state with twenty-six "cantons." French is the official language of French-speaking Switzerland (six cantons, among them Vaud, Neuchâtel, and Geneva) and around 22.5 percent of the population speak French.

3. And it continues as follows: "In all cases, reporting should be limited to what is needed to understand the facts and exclude intimate and personally damaging details."

4. A third of the articles talked about suicide in a simplistic or reductive manner. Twelve percent of all articles included a copycat risk by providing detailed information about the suicide method. Few amount of information addressed the topic of prevention (barely 20 percent of the total number of articles).

5. STOP SUICIDE. (2014). *Informer sur le suicide peut sauver des vies.* Retrieved from www.stopsuicide.ch/site/medias.

6. As such, our strategy is very similar to the Samaritans' one in the United Kingdom (2011).

7. Articles that work toward prevention can also trigger a positive reaction from STOP SUICIDE. STOP SUICIDE. *Revue de presse et des savoirs.* Retrieved from: www.stopsuicide.ch/site/revues-de-presse

8. This approach and its results are in line with other international best practices. Samaritans. (2011). Ibid.

9. In 2009, two students of the University of Northwestern Switzerland released their study on the topic of suicide coverage. They made a survey based on the answers of 222 Swiss-German journalists to an online enquiry. Half of them were working for Swiss daily newspaper. On average they were generally

working under permanent contract and since two years. Only 24 percent of them had experience of reporting on suicide; the majority of them (74 percent) already had to write between one and five articles on suicide. Of those having experience of media coverage, 45 percent had better knowledge of guidelines on media coverage and of the risk of copycat suicides.

10. The authors described the knowledge of the guidelines of all journalists as rather weak (2.5 for inexperienced journalists to 3.0 point for experienced journalists on a scale of 5); 68 percent of all journalists have "some knowledge" of the guidelines.

11. In 2013, STOP SUICIDE worked collaboratively with journalists and other specialists to make WHO media guidelines fit with their practices. This collaboration resulted in a brochure and website. STOP SUICIDE. (2013). *Points de repère à l'usage des journalistes.* Retrieved from http://www.stopsuicide.ch/site/points-de-reperes-journalistes.

12. Tink.ch. Retrieved from www.tink.ch.

13. STOP SUICIDE. (2013). *Points de repère à l'usage des journalistes.* Retrieved from http://www.stopsuicide.ch/site/points-de-reperes-journalistes.

## References

Altermatt, F., & Steinmann, B. (2009). *Berichterstattung über Suizid in Deutschschweizer Zeitungen. Eine suizidpräventive Massnahme für Medienschaffende: Zielgruppenanalyse und Empfehlungen für ein Kursmodul* (Unpublished Bachelor Thesis). University of Applied Sciences and Arts, Northwestern Switzerland FHNW, Olten.

Berney, S. (2015, August 18). Doctoresse Erika Preisig: la femme qui regarde la mort en face. *L'Illustré.* Retrieved from http://www.illustre.ch/illustre/article/doctoresse-erika-preisig-la-femme-qui-regarde-la-mort-en-face

Inostroza, I. (2015, October 17). Suicide assisté: on peut l'éviter! A propos de l'article La femme qui regarde la mort en face. *L'Illustré,* p. 97.

Loersch, A. (2013, June 14). Médias et suicide: délicate pesée d'intérêts, *La Cité,* pp. 18–19.

Loersch, A. (2014). Médias et suicide: une délicate pesée d'intérêts. *Edito+Klartext,* pp. 18–19.

Michel K., Frey C., Wyss K., & Valach L. (2000). An exercise in improving suicide reporting in print media. *Crisis, 21*(2), 71–79.

Samaritans. (2011). *Leveson Inquiry: Culture, Practice and Ethics of the Press.* Retrieved from http://bit.ly/1SGO3ea

STOP SUICIDE. (2014). *La mediatisation du suicide dans la presse écrite romande: Rapport 2013.* Retrieved from http://www.stopsuicide.ch/site/sites/default/files/docs/La%20Mediatisation%20du%20suicide%20en%202013.pdf

Swiss Press Council. (2012, February 17). *No 8/2012: Suicide/Identification/Protection des victimes (Stop suicide c. "Le Matin") Prise de position du Conseil suisse de la presse.* Retrieved from http://www.stopsuicide.ch/site/sites/default/files/docs/No_8_2012.pdf

Swiss Press Council. (2015). *Directives relating to the "Declaration of the Duties and Rights of the Journalist".* Retrieved from www.presserat.ch/Documents/Directives_2015_engl.pdf

# 17

# Promoting Responsible Portrayal of Suicide: Lessons from the United Kingdom and the Republic of Ireland

*Lorna Fraser, Lisa Marzano, and Keith Hawton*

## Summary

Promoting responsible portrayal of suicide is an important priority in national suicide prevention strategies around the world. Samaritans, a suicide prevention charity in the United Kingdom and Republic of Ireland, has extensive experience of achieving this policy objective in practice and is the recognized lead organization on the subject for UK media. Over the years, this has involved a number of proactive initiatives to raise awareness and educate the industry, at all levels; lobbying for change in media regulation; careful and ongoing monitoring and analysis of media reports of suicidal behavior (on average six thousand articles per year); and extensive work with the media and key stakeholders to improve coverage, not least in relation to high-profile stories and programs.

In this chapter, we discuss and reflect on the potential of this multilevel approach to encouraging responsible media portrayal of suicide. Drawing on case examples, we illustrate what can be achieved through this strategy, highlighting key challenges and successes, as well as emerging concerns for research, policy, and practice.

## Promoting Responsible Portrayal to Save Lives: A Multistrand Approach

In the United Kingdom and Republic of Ireland more than six thousand people take their own lives each year, with many thousands more attempting suicide (Office for National Statistics, 2016).

Samaritans, founded in 1953, provides a 24-hour helpline service across the United Kingdom and ROI for people who are struggling to cope with life. This service is delivered by volunteers who respond to more than 5.3 million calls for help each year, from the charity's 201 branches. Because of the proven link between sensationalist or detailed coverage of suicide and imitative behavior (Sisask & Värnik, 2012), Samaritans initiated working proactively with UK media on the portrayal of suicide over two decades ago, to improve standards of reporting and reduce the likelihood of media coverage influencing imitative suicidal behavior.

The need to promote responsible portrayal of suicidal behavior in the media is a core part of the government's suicide prevention policy in England and the equivalent strategy in the Republic of Ireland, as well as the suicide prevention strategies of the devolved administrations in Wales, Scotland, and Northern Ireland (see, e.g., Department of Health, 2012). Samaritans' approach in this context focuses on developing and maintaining good relationships with the media, to enable cooperation and constructive dialogue to raise awareness of the impact inappropriate reporting can have on vulnerable audiences. In line with international guidelines (Pirkis et al., 2006), this approach seeks to promote accurate, responsible, and ethical reporting, not censorship. This work supports Samaritans' vision that fewer people die by suicide.

## Identifying and Promoting Best Practice

There are a number of strands to this area of suicide prevention work, and underpinning all of this is Samaritans' *Media Guidelines for Reporting Suicide* (2013). This is a comprehensive best-practice guide, providing information and advice on how to cover the topic of suicide sensitively and responsibly. The first edition of this guidance was published in 1994. Samaritans' guidelines are widely recognized and used across the UK media industry as a whole. The current edition was developed following wide consultation with academic experts on suicide, the media, and the regulatory bodies. New to the current edition of Samaritans' *Media Guidelines for Reporting Suicide* is the addition of a suite of *supplementary factsheets.* These provide quick-reference guidance for media across a range of mediums (e.g., digital, broadcast, and drama) and covering a range of specific topics, including railway incidents, murder–suicides, and how to work with bereaved families in the aftermath of a suicide. Journalists can quickly refer to these more concise documents when reporting on any of these issues, for specific guidance.

Samaritans has also now published a *Guide for Coroners in England* to support them in their dealings with the press in relation to inquests. In England inquests are generally held as open hearings in a coroner's court. Therefore journalists are able to attend these and report on the case. Due to the nature of this type of investigation inquest hearings do present some unique challenges. The level of detail which is covered during an inquest, particularly in relation to establishing the cause of death, can lead to potentially harmful information being published in media reports (e.g., in 2012–15 the proportion of inquest stories rated by our team as potentially concerning was significantly higher than for reports published pre-inquest (21 percent vs. 16 percent) (data available on request)). This has been particularly problematic with cases involving new, or lesser known, suicide methods.

There have also been a number of difficult cases where a death has occurred while the person was under the care of the state—in a children's home, in psychiatric care, or in custody. In complex cases such as these an appropriate balance between raising a matter of legitimate public interest on the one hand and negatively influencing the behavior of vulnerable audiences on the other can be difficult to achieve.

## Working with Media Regulators

Over the years Samaritans has developed good working relationships with the United Kingdom's media regulatory bodies. These include the Independent Press Standards Organisation (IPSO), Ofcom—the broadcast regulator, the British Board of Film Classification (BBFC), and the Advertising Standards Authority (ASA). All of these bodies have been cooperative in working constructively with Samaritans to encourage responsible coverage of suicide.

In England, mainstream media regulation is divided by print and broadcast: the Ofcom Broadcasting Code for broadcast and IPSO-enforced Code of Practice, framed by the Editors' Code of Practice Committee, for print media. In 2006, following the submission of evidence by Samaritans and other groups to the Code Committee that overt description of suicide by a particular method may lead to increases in actual suicidal behavior involving that method (e.g., Ashton, & Donnan, 1981; Etzersdorfer, Voracek, & Sonneck, 2001, 2004; Veysey, Kamanyire, & Volans, 1999; Hawton et al., 1999), a new sub-clause 5(ii) was added to England's Editors' Code of Practice:

Clause 5 (Intrusion into grief or shock) of the Editors' Code of Practice reads as follows:

> i) In cases involving personal grief or shock, enquiries and approaches must be made with sympathy and discretion and publication handled sensitively. This should not restrict the right to report legal proceedings, such as inquests.

> ii) When reporting suicide, care should be taken to avoid excessive detail about the method used.

Following further revision to the code in January 2016 suicide reporting is now included as a stand-alone clause (5) and the risk of influencing imitative behavior has been incorporated. The revised code now states that "When reporting suicide, to prevent simulative acts care should be taken to avoid excessive detail of the method used, while taking into account the media's right to report legal proceedings."

Ofcom's code for broadcasters also now covers the issue of contagion; its rule 2.5 was updated in July 2015 and states: "This rule reflects a continued concern about the impact of real or portrayed suicide, and self-harm, on those whose minds may be disturbed. Whilst it is always difficult to prove causality, various studies have shown that there may be a short-lived increase in particular methods of suicide portrayed on television. Broadcasters should consider whether detailed demonstrations of means or methods of suicide or self-harm are justified."

Samaritans has also carried out some recent work with the Press Council of Ireland on suicide reporting, requesting the addition of a new clause advising the press to avoid inclusion of excessive details of suicide methods. This was added to its Code of Practice in June 2015.

Approaching the topic of suicide is clearly a challenging area where journalists must balance the pressure to report "of–the-moment" stories which are in the public interest with the responsibility not to publish potentially harmful information or intrude into the grief and shock of those affected. The existence of a code specific to coverage of suicide raises the importance of approaching this complex topic responsibly and supports Samaritans' work in this area.

## Monitoring Media Reports of Suicide

On a daily basis Samaritans monitors press and online news reporting of suicidal behavior (including suicide and attempted suicide) in national, regional, and local publications, assessing around six thousand articles each year. The coding frame used is modeled on previous research in

Australia (Pirkis et al., 2009) and records identifying information (e.g., the name of the specific newspaper and article title), descriptive information (e.g., the date of the article, details on its content and genre), as well as quality ratings for each item, using a set of dimensions that operationalize criteria in media guidelines (e.g., whether the article includes excessive details of the method/s used, inappropriate language, and details of support services and organizations).

This monitoring activity serves a dual purpose. First, it provides valuable data for analysis, to identify trends in reporting over time and continuing to inform Samaritans' work in this area. For example, comparisons of these data with official statistics (e.g., Office for National Statistics publications and online data) and other scientific evidence (e.g., reports of "psychological autopsy" studies (Cavanagh et al., 2003)) enable examination of over- and underreporting of suicidal behavior involving particular groups (including by gender and age) and method used for suicide (e.g., rare vs. common methods, jumping and railway suicides), over time and in different types of media.

In addition, careful and ongoing monitoring of media reports of suicidal behavior enables collaborative working with the press to ensure that the detail reported about a suicide is safe, without unduly affecting the freedom of the press. For example, in cases where a suicide has been poorly reported, this can in part be mitigated by the removal of detailed, potentially harmful content online, to reduce the risk of ongoing coverage influencing imitative behavior.

### Anticipating and Responding to Problematic Press Coverage

When potentially harmful content is identified, Samaritans makes direct contact with editors to request amendments to online stories. Many media outlets are seemingly receptive to Samaritans' approach and respond positively to suggestions to amend articles. Indeed, Samaritans' experience is that media professionals are increasingly aware of the risks and the role the media can potentially have in influencing imitative behavior. We have found editors, by and large, to be receptive to working with us to increase their understanding of the issues surrounding suicidal behavior and to raise the standard of how this is covered. We have witnessed concerted efforts by the press to achieve this and in recent years have seen a marked improvement in media portrayal of suicide (discussed further below).

Despite substantial progress, there are still occasions when the press clearly struggles to rein itself in collectively. This is usually when a suicide involves the death of a well-known public figure or because it involves a particularly newsworthy element—such as a suicide pact or cluster, or a method that is unusual or new to the United Kingdom. News coverage of such cases tends to follow a regular pattern of initial widespread reporting of the incident as the story breaks, often placed on front pages and sensational in tone, fueled by increased pressure to cover the story quickly. Numerous photographs of the deceased are included and details of the suicide method often appear in headlines. This is typically followed by intense media speculation of probable causes over the subsequent days and weeks. Following the initial flurry of intense media activity, Samaritans' experience is that there is often a willingness by the media to engage and take steps to improve how a story is being covered, when made aware that the reporting may have a harmful effect.

In cases where a suicide is likely to attract widespread, potentially *problematic* press coverage Samaritans will immediately publish a confidential media briefing, reminding the press of the need to report responsibly and providing concise and case-specific advice. These briefings were first initiated by the charity in 2009 and are issued relatively infrequently, approximately only half a dozen per year. Samaritans limits publication in this way so as not to diminish the impact when there is a compelling need to brief the media, to effect change in how a story is being covered.

Recent examples of Samaritans' confidential media briefings include:

- The death of Mick Jagger's partner, L'Wren Scott, in March 2014— Samaritans received over three thousand unique visitors to the web page of its media briefing for this case.
- The death of Robin Williams in August 2014. Following a live press conference by the US Coroner, which included a very detailed description of the method of hanging used, some UK news stories reported potentially harmful details.
- The attempted suicide of ex-footballer Clarke Carlisle, reported in 2015.

Our monitoring activity suggests that these media briefings do affect change in the tone and content of reports, influencing subsequent coverage and ultimately reducing the risk of news coverage influencing imitative behavior. In cases where there is a risk of a cluster of suicides forming in a particular location, Samaritans works closely with local media outlets, alerting them of the situation and requesting that they refrain from reporting the method of suicide in great detail and from linking the suicides together. There is of course a risk here of potentially increasing coverage by alerting the media to a situation which they may not have been aware of. However, Samaritans' view is that, on balance, proactive intervention is more likely to prevent inappropriate coverage.

## Media Advisory Service

Much of the work described above is of a reactive nature, including contacting media outlets in response to concerns over coverage. A more proactive element of this work is the media advisory service Samaritans provides to journalists, offering bespoke guidance ahead of publication and transmission. This has proved a very effective way of preventing harmful content appearing in articles and programs in the first place. This advice service spans all media from mainstream news to documentaries, dramas, and soaps.

There is a growing literature suggesting that appropriate, responsible portrayal of suicide in the media can play a vital role in preventing suicides (the "Papageno effect"; Niederkrotenthaler et al., 2010). Programs can help educate the wider public about issues, such as the type of problems which may lead to a person becoming vulnerable and the signs which may indicate they are struggling to cope, and also encourage help-seeking behavior by promoting the benefits of talking. However, achieving this in practice can be a very delicate balance to strike, perhaps particularly when dealing with such a complex topic in a drama. To support this important but challenging task, Samaritans' media advisor works proactively with researchers, script writers, producers, and directors, advising on scripts and scenes to support program makers in creating content that is appropriate and as safe as possible for audiences. In addition, Samaritans provides training for program makers and editorial teams. These sessions offer a useful opportunity for media professionals to learn about the key issues surrounding suicidal behavior and recommended safe approaches to this. They also allow for valuable discussion around the challenges faced by journalists when covering this complex topic, and are often delivered with the support of an academic expert on suicide.

In recent years we have seen a significant increase in program makers using this service, which clearly demonstrates an awareness of the potential risks and a willingness to approach the topic responsibly. By way of illustrating the nature and potential impact of such collaborative work with program makers, some recent examples are described below.

## EastEnders

One of the United Kingdom's most popular soap operas, the BBC's EastEnders has been running since the mid-1980s with viewing figures now reaching over eight million. Over the years EastEnders has run a number of suicide-related storylines and its production team regularly works with Samaritans for guidance. In January 2014 *EastEnders* approached Samaritans with a draft script which included a lead character's suicide attempt. The producers were keen to develop this as safely as possible and shared their script with Samaritans for advice. Character Kat Moon was to attempt to end her life by use of an overdose. This formed part of a longer running storyline where the character struggled to come to terms with her experience of childhood sexual abuse.

Kat's story contained potential for identification with audiences, especially as she is a long-standing character of the soap with a loyal following. Her history of abuse was thought to increase the risk of identification among viewers who may relate to this experience.

Samaritans' media advisor worked with EastEnders' researchers and scriptwriters on the storyline. This advice included

- Not identifying the type of medication used or giving quantities or details of how this drug was obtained;
- Avoiding romanticizing the scenes where the character's husband discovers Kat in a semi-conscious state;
- Not showing immediate recovery after an overdose, and sticking with the reality of this type of suicide attempt by including a follow-up psychological assessment being carried out.

These recommendations were incorporated into revised scripts. Samaritans' helpline number was also given at the end of the episode via the BBC Action Line service, signposting any viewers who were affected by the program to an immediate source of support.

## Panorama: A Suicide in the Family

Producers of a Panorama documentary, Keo Films, contacted Samaritans late in 2014 for advice on a programme covering men and suicide, aware that this would require sensitive handling. The programme makers were keen to minimize any risk to viewers.

The aim was to examine why so many middle-aged men kill themselves, explored through the personal journey of the presenter Simon Jack, BBC Economics Correspondent, who lost his own father to suicide.

Samaritans gave advice around messaging, citing our *Men and Sui-cide: Why It's a Social Issue* report (Samaritans, 2012), and advised on the potential risk areas.

The result was a very powerful film which raised a number of import-ant points, including the potential consequences of suffering in silence and encouraging men to seek help. Sources of support were given at the end of the program.

*A Suicide in the Family* was shortlisted for the 2015 Mind Media awards.

### *Professor Green: Suicide and Me*

During 2015 Samaritans also worked with *Antidote Productions* sup-porting development of a BBC documentary aimed at highlighting the issues of male suicide with a younger audience in mind.

The program was presented by UK rapper Professor Green, aka Stephen Manderson, who lost his father to suicide. The film poignantly examined some of the root causes of suicide, including the psychological impact of loss and the fear among British men of seeking help and talking about emotions. Stephen's quest to uncover the truth behind his father's suicide presented a very personal portrayal of the devastation left behind follow-ing a suicide. Sources of support were given at the end of the program.

### *The Clarke Carlisle Story*

Commercial radio station *Absolute Radio* contacted Samaritans in February 2015 for pre-broadcast advice on a program covering a sui-cide attempt made by ex-footballer, Clarke Carlisle. This was a lengthy interview in which Clarke Carlisle shared his personal emotional struggles, following a number of significant life events, resulting in him attempting to end his life in December 2014.

Aware of the possible risks in covering a suicide attempt and keen to avoid these, Absolute Radio shared their pre-recorded interview piece with Samaritans for review and advice. We recommended a number of edits to the content, all of which were agreed and made. The end result was a candid, thought-provoking interview highlighting the intensity of suicidal feelings, including the sense of complete hopelessness, demonstrating that this can be overcome. Sources of support were signposted at the end of the program and listeners were encouraged to seek help if touched by the content.

This program went on to win a prestigious radio award, *Best Single Programme of the Year*, at the Arqiva Commercial Radio Awards. Absolute Radio included having worked with Samaritans in their award application and this was cited at the awards presentation event.

This collaborative work with program makers ordinarily goes on quietly behind the scenes. However, when a popular soap storyline made headline news in January 2014, Samaritans' media advisory service was thrust into the media spotlight. This was the heavily publicized *Coronation Street* storyline of the suicide of character Hayley Cropper. Samaritans had worked with ITV's production team to help limit the risk of this storyline influencing imitative behavior. Following the transmission of this episode, in January 2014, Samaritans saw a 30 percent increase in calls to its helpline.

In developing this work with the media, both in news and in nonfactual programs, Samaritans has built excellent working relationships with the BBC's and ITV's editorial policy and compliance departments. This has generated opportunities to work collaboratively with news and drama teams, providing expert advice on suicide and self-harm content, ahead of transmission.

Samaritans very rarely takes the route of making formal complaints to the regulators. We believe that the best approach to preventing inappropriate portrayal of suicide is to nurture constructive relationships with the media, providing advice and building understanding about the benefits associated with responsible reporting. Our experience is that journalists and editors appreciate our cooperative and constructive approach, given the complexity of the issues involved. Arguably, a confrontational approach can be counterproductive and therefore best avoided.

## Promising Trends and Future Challenges

A study of UK journalists carried out shortly after the introduction of the 2006 sub-clause on reporting of suicide in the England's Editors' Code of Practice found that many were unfamiliar with relevant guidelines, and less than one in five reported that their workplace had a policy on suicide coverage (Jempson et al., 2007). While a follow-up study is arguably warranted, our experience is that much has changed in the intervening years. More importantly, our monitoring data suggest some clear improvements in how suicidal behavior is portrayed in the UK and ROI media. For example, between 2012 and 2015, the percentage of news reports including details of support helplines has increased year on year (from 6 percent in 2012 to 57 percent in 2015), while the percentage of articles internally rated as potentially concerning (e.g., due to the level of detail provided or because a potential "hotspot" is identified) has dropped from 17 percent in 2012 to 3 percent in 2015.

It is also worth noting that over this period the proportion of articles rated by our media monitoring team as being of poor overall quality has been consistently low (around 2 percent of all reports).

Nonetheless, some aspects of current reporting practice remain problematic. For instance, our data show that the percentage of news headlines which include details of the method(s) used remains high and is increasing (from 21 percent in 2012 to 32 percent in 2015), particularly in relation to specific methods (most notably, suicides involving the railways and jumping from a high place), and that the number of articles focusing on incidents involving women (40 percent) and young people under the age of 25 (33 percent) remains disproportionate compared to official statistics. Also potentially of note is the observed increase in reports featured on pages 1 and 3 (5 percent in 2012 vs. 10 percent in 2015), which may contribute to making suicide more prominent.

In addition, our monitoring data suggest some potentially important changes in how, and where, suicide stories are being reported. For example, in recent years there has been a marked increase in the proportion of online (vs. printed media) suicide news reports (almost 75 percent in 2015 vs. just over 50 percent in 2012), and in stories including one or more photographs of the incident, deceased and/or methods/locations involved (a feature in almost all reports in 2015 vs. 66 percent in 2012). This underscores the need for ongoing research to understand the impact of these changes, if any, on actual suicidal behavior, and to ensure that relevant guidelines and other initiatives to promote responsible portrayal of suicide remain relevant and up-to-date.

There remain a number of specific challenges, including the following:

- New and emerging methods are not sufficiently covered by current media regulation, where minimal detail is enough to influence increases in use (see, e.g., Gunnell et al., 2015).
- High-profile/celebrity suicides continue to attract unprecedented and sensationalized news coverage, where there is greater risk of unintentionally glamorizing suicide (Koburger et al., 2015; Niederkrotenthaler et al., 2012).
- Reports of suicides by young people tend to attract increased media attention and are often more romantically reported, including outpourings of grief and memorials lifted from social media, with intense focus on possible causes (i.e., bullying, pressures of study, and relationship breakdown). It is known that young people are more likely to be influenced by what they see and hear in the media (Phillips & Carstensen, 1986) and at increased risk of imitative suicidal behavior (Haw et al.,

2013; Sisask & Värnik, 2012), and that the risk of imitation is accentuated when the coverage is extensive, prominent, sensationalist, and/or repeated (Pirkis et al., 2007).

Looking to the future our aim is to focus on developing more proactive opportunities, building on educating the media industry as a whole by widely promoting our media advisory service and training program. Following developments in the editorial codes in recent years, media coverage appears to have improved and therefore we see very few actual breaches of the codes. However, in their current form these do not protect against media coverage potentially influencing increases in the use of new suicide methods (e.g., helium, disposable BBQs).

We need to build on research in this field to inform this work going forward and provide evidence for the need to ensure that regulation continues to influence improved coverage of suicide, specifically in relation to preventing the spread of new and emerging methods. More research is also needed to systematically evaluate the impact of such interventions, or combination of interventions, on the nature and quality of media portrayal of suicide and on actual suicidal behavior. Ongoing progress in this field is thus unlikely unless organizations promoting the responsible portrayal of suicide continue working in close collaborative partnership with media outlets and regulators, academics, and other key stakeholders, both nationally and internationally.

## References

Ashton, J. R., & Donnan, S. (1981). Suicide by burning as an epidemic phenomenon: An analysis of 82 deaths and inquests in England and Wales in 1978–79. *Psychological Medicine, 11*, 735–739.

Cavanagh, J. T., Carson, A. J., Sharpe, M., & Lawrie, S. M. (2003). Psychological autopsy studies of suicide: A systematic review. *Psychological Medicine, 33*, 395–405.

Department of Health. (2012). *Suicide prevention strategy for England.* London: Department of Health.

Etzersdorfer, E., Voracek, M., & Sonneck, G. (2001). A dose-response relationship of imitational suicides with newspaper distribution. *Australian and New Zealand Journal of Psychiatry, 35*, 251.

Etzersdorfer, E., Voracek, M., & Sonneck, G. (2004). A dose-response relationship between imitational suicides and newspaper distribution. *Archives of Suicide Research, 8*, 137–145.

Gunnell, D., Coope, C., Fearn, V., Wells, C., Chang, S. S., Hawton, K., & Kapur, N. (2015). Suicide by gases in England and Wales 2001–2011: evidence of the emergence of new methods of suicide. *Journal of Affective Disorders, 170*, 190–195.

Haw, C., Hawton, K., Niedzwiedz, C., & Platt, S. (2013). Suicide clusters: a review of risk factors and mechanisms. *Suicide and life-threatening behavior, 43*(1), 97–108.

Hawton, K., Simkin, S., Deeks, J., O'Connor, S., Keen, A., Altman, D. G., . . . Bulstrode, C. (1999). Effects of a drug overdose in a television drama on presentations to hospital for self-poisoning: time series and questionnaire study. *British Medical Journal, 318,* 972–977.

Jempson, M., Cookson, R., Williams, T., Thorsen, E., Khan, A., & Thevanayagam, P. (2007). *Sensitive Coverage saves lives: Improving Media Portrayal of Suicidal Behaviour.* London: National Institute for Mental Health in England.

Koburger, N., Mergl, R., Rummel-Kluge, C., Ibelshäuser, A., Meise, U., Postuvan, V., . . . Hegerl, U. (2015). Celebrity suicide on the railway network: Can one case trigger international effects? *Journal of Affective Disorders, 185,* 38–46.

Niederkrotenthaler, T., Fu, K. W., Yip, P. S., Fong, D. Y., Stack, S., Cheng, Q., & Pirkis, J. (2012). Changes in suicide rates following media reports on celebrity suicide: a meta-analysis. *Journal of Epidemiology and Community Health, 66,* 1037–1042.

Niederkrotenthaler, T., Voracek, M., Herberth, A., Till, B., Strauss, M., Etzersdorfer, E., Eisenwort, B., & Sonneck, G. (2010). Role of media reports in completed and prevented suicide: Werther v. Papageno effects. *British Journal of Psychiatry, 197*(3), 234–243.

Office for National Statistics. (2016). *Suicide in the United Kingdom – 2014 Registrations.* London: Office for National Statistics.

Phillips, D. P., & Carstensen, L. L. (1968). Clustering of teenage suicides after television news stories about suicide. *New England Journal of Medicine, 315,* 685–689.

Pirkis, J., Blood, R. W., Beautrais, A., Burgess, P., & Skehan, J. (2006). Media guidelines on the reporting of suicide. *Crisis, 27,* 82–87.

Pirkis J, Burgess A, Blood RW, & Francis C. (2007). The newsworthiness of suicide. *Suicide and Life-Threatening Behavior, 37,* 278–283.

Pirkis, J., Dare, A., Blood, R. W., Rankin, B., Williamson, M., Burgess, P., & Jolley, D. (2009). Changes in media reporting of suicide in Australia between 2000/01 and 2006/07. *Crisis, 30,* 25–33.

Press Complaints Commission. (2006). *Editors' Code of Practice.* London: Press Complaints Commission.

Press Complaints Commission. (2016). *Editors' Code of Practice.* London: Press Complaints Commission.

Samaritans. (2012). *Men and suicide – Why it's a social issue.* Ewell: Samaritans.

Samaritans. (2013). *Media Guidelines for Reporting Suicide.* London: Guardian News and Media Limited.

Sisask, M., & Värnik, A. (2012). Media roles in suicide prevention: a systematic review. *International Journal of Environmental Research and Public Health, 9,* 123–138.

Veysey, M. J., Kamanyire, R., & Volans, G. N. (1999). Effects of drug overdose in television drama on presentations for self poisoning: Antifreeze poisonings give more insight into copycat behaviour. *British Medical Journal, 319,* 1131.

# 18

# Implementing International Media Guidelines in a Local Context: Experiences from Hong Kong

*Qijin Cheng and Paul S. F. Yip*

Hong Kong media were notorious for frequently reporting suicide news. In Austria and Australia, only 1–4 percent of suicide cases would be reported by the media (Niederkrotenthaler et al., 2009; Etzersdorfer & Sonneck, 1998; Pirkis, Burgess, Blood, & Francis, 2007). By contrast, the coverage rate in Hong Kong was as high as 47 percent (Au, Yip, Chan, & Law, 2004). In addition, suicide news in Hong Kong (HK) was found to be generally sensational, frequently publishing bloody photos, private information of the deceased and family, and details of suicide methods and locations (Fu, Chan, & Yip, 2011). However, over the years, positive changes are afoot in Hong Kong after our persistent engagement with the media professionals. This chapter will report our experiences and discuss how the local experiences are relevant with international policies and practices in promoting responsible media representation of suicide. We will focus on two versions of recommendations on suicide reporting in HK, published in 2004 and 2015, respectively, to report the contexts and procedures of how we developed and implemented these recommendations, followed by a discussion section.

## 2004 Version

As reviewed by previous studies (Bohanna & Wang, 2012; Pirkis et al., 2006), media guidelines for reporting suicide news vary very little in different countries. The common basis is the guidelines recommended by World Health Organization (2000, 2008). When the HKJC Centre for Suicide Research and Prevention (CSRP) at the University of Hong Kong was founded in 2002, it had already listed introducing the WHO guidelines to local media professionals on its agenda. With the courteous assistance from the Journalism and Media Studies Centre of the University of Hong Kong, the CSRP edited *Suicide and the Media: Recommendations on Suicide Reporting for Media Professionals* and published the booklet in 2004.

The 2004 version was edited in the context that suicide rate in HK reached a historical high in 2003 (18.8 per 100,000 people) and that charcoal-burning suicide had spread in HK from a new and rare method to the second most popular suicide method (CSRP, 2016). During 2003, HK was suffering from the epidemic of severe acute respiratory syndrome (SARS) and also the suicide of a prominent movie star, Mr. Leslie Cheung, who jumped from a hotel window in Central on April 1. Right after his suicide, the number of jumping suicides increased drastically in the first half of April 2003 and the deceased were mostly of similar age as the celebrity. The booklet quoted the charcoal-burning case and the celebrity case as examples that media's prominent and sensational coverage of suicide can lead to copycat effects. Although the booklet also included one section of media as a proactive role, the overall focus was more on the negative impacts that irresponsible reports can result in. The booklet provided three examples of appropriate media reporting, which all came from foreign media, whereas the examples of inappropriate reporting were all from local media. The booklet also highlighted the public outrage toward HK newspapers' reporting of suicide news by quoting the Hong Kong Press Council's denouncement and a community survey's results (CSRP, 2004). In summary, the booklet set a tone toward criticism of HK media's reporting and highlighted what the media should avoid or not do when reporting suicide. To justify the criticism, the CSRP reviewed local newspapers' coverage of suicide news and found that 47 percent of suicide deaths in 2000 were reported by local newspapers and 87.5 percent of the news articles were associated with photos (Au, Yip, Chan, & Law, 2004).

The 2004 booklet was launched through a public seminar and press conference titled *Media and Suicide: Pitfalls and Prevention* in November 2004. In three months after the press conference, around thousand free copies of the booklets were distributed to local media outlets, journalism associations, and schools of journalism by post. The digital copy can be downloaded from the CSRP website.

The introduction of the booklet casted certain impacts on local media suicide news reporting but was not as effective as we expected it would be. When comparing suicide news before and after the introduction (Fu & Yip, 2008), we found that there was a statistically significant decrease in the frequency of publishing photographs (from 92 percent to 90.7 percent) and mentioning problems encountered in the headline (from 65.9 percent to 59.6 percent). However, the frequency of front-page placement, publishing graphical presentation, and mentioning suicide method in the headline remained unchanged. Comparing to Taiwan and mainland China newspapers, HK newspapers were still found to be more frequently publishing suicide news on front page, associating with photos, mentioning suicide method in headline, and less frequently including preventive advice (Fu, Chan, & Yip, 2011).

## 2015 Version

In view of the persisting suicide reporting problem in HK, the CSRP tried to investigate why the booklet did not significantly change local media's practices. We conducted in-depth interviews with seven journalists from local popular newspapers and further organized three focus groups with twenty-four media professionals from local media and correspondence of international media in HK during 2011 and 2012 (Cheng, 2012; Cheng, Fu, Caine, & Yip, 2014). We learned from the participants that the frontline journalists in HK uphold a sense of commitment in improving the society through the media. However, due to the lack of knowledge on how news report can be a potential risk factor for suicide and the urge to chase after more "exciting" news, they overlooked the fact that these suicide news articles can be damaging to vulnerable individuals. Frontline reporters had always struggled between willingness to be socially responsible and pressured from market competition. Young and inexperienced reporters regarded the acceptance of the competitiveness in the media industry as a precondition for working in HK media companies, even if the work ethics conflicted with their own values and professionalism. Many participants also claimed that they were not aware of the 2004 booklet as we did not promote it consistently. The 2004 version booklet was distributed all at once during first publication but then never after. However, local media's employees reported high turnover rates and many frontline journalists are fresh university graduates. Local journalists also commented that the 2004 booklet was outdated as the new media platforms have been rapidly developing and the media ecology, especially social media, has changed since 2004.

To address the participants' concerns and suggestions, we decided to update the booklet through continuous engagement with the media professionals. First of all, we recognized that working styles in local newsrooms combined top-down regulations and also frontline reporter's flexible autonomy. To address the top-down regulations, we proactively reached out to chief editors and senior managers of the media outlets and established regular contacts with them regarding suicide prevention. We were invited to sit in their editorial meetings to learn more about their working procedures in one of the leading newspapers. Certainly, it helps us to have a better understanding of the working culture and mindset among editors in the local newspapers. In addition, we started monitoring local media's suicide-related content on a daily basis. Once noticing any good or poor practice examples, we would immediately contact the media managers to praise their good practice or express our concerns with poor practice and collect their feedback. Through this procedure, we were able to raise the concern to the editors' level and try to lobby for their support from the upstream as well as understand the exact opportunities, challenges, and alternative solutions of applying the media guidelines in the downstream.

After one year of proactive engagement, we started updating the booklet based on our engagement and review of media guidelines in other countries. We used "suicide" AND "media guidelines" as key-words to search on Google and examined the first hundred results to look for relevant ones. The exercise generated thirty-three sets of guidelines recommended by various organizations in the United States, Canada, the United Kingdom, Australia, New Zealand, Ireland, India, Japan, and Korea. We read into their items and absorbed those relevant with the local context into the updates. The updated version was released in July 2015. The copyright of the booklet is in Creative Commons so that other organizations and individuals can freely use and distribute the copies for noncommercial purposes.

A fundamental change in the 2015 version is that we emphasize our respect and treasure of freedom of the press, with no intention whatsoever to interfere with the independence of any media professionals. We, however, hope to recommend and discuss responsible reporting of suicide news solely based on the humanitarian and social responsibility perspective. The media's positive role in suicide prevention is highlighted and we added "practice self-care in the community of media professionals" as one of the three fundamental principles. Another major update to the 2015 version is that we acknowledge the emerging trend of online media outlets and information distribution hubs, such as social networks and search engines. We have therefore written additional three sections on the Internet, search engines, and social networks, respectively, to provide general recommendations for disseminating suicide-related information online.

The tone of the 2015 version booklet was changed to represent partner-style conversations between the suicide prevention field and the media field. The cover of the booklet used brighter color (light blue) to replace the previous heavy color (dark purple). The size was shrunk from 14.8 cm × 21 cm (A5) to 9 cm × 21 cm and the page numbers reduced from 30 pages to 18 pages, which made the updated version much lighter and easier to be carried around. In addition, we archived our comments to local media content, with appreciation and critique, on the CSRP website (csrp.hku.hk/media) so that journalists can find real-life examples of balancing media freedom and suicide prevention.

The distribution of the 2015 version booklets was no longer a one-off post, but through our daily and continuous engagement with the media. Every time we contact the local media to express our appreciation and/or concerns, a hard or soft copy of the 2015 booklet would be attached for reference.

This partner-style engagement has not only created a platform for constructive communication between the media and us, but the media have also responded to our concerns very positively. The chief editor of one local newspaper wrote two editorials that emphasized the importance of communication between the suicide prevention field and the media, and a reminder to all local media outlets about how suicide case should be reported after our visits to each other's offices (Sha, 2014 a&b). An even more heartening news was that some media professionals are willing to take the initiative to learn more about the latest research findings and development on suicide preventions and actively promote suicide prevention to the public, not waiting for another tragedy to strike.

Our constructive engagement with the media showed its effect when a new suicide method (i.e., helium suicide) started spreading in HK in recent years. Based on the established surveillance system that monitors suicide news on a daily basis, we could conveniently extract media content with special emphasis on helium suicide. Thanks to our long-term contact with the media outlets, when we contacted the newsrooms or ISPs addressing our concerns with spreading of this new suicide method, we received positive feedback from the media executives in a timely manner. They removed problematic media content reported by us, started using "gas suicide" to replace "helium suicide" to avoid describing the details of the new method, and even dropped to report some helium suicide cases after receiving our reminders.

It is gratifying to see the media have changed from extensive reporting of suicide cases in the past to a simpler and more objective manner nowadays. The vast majority of these articles also contain professional advices and helpline information and resources. These not only reflect the changes in media professionals, but also show the society as a whole is taking steps toward a more caring and empathetic community. All these require hard work from different stakeholders within the community, and continuous engagement is needed to maintain this dialogue with the media.

## Discussion

Media professionals worldwide responded differently toward the implementation of the suicide reporting guidelines. Some guidelines have been purposely ignored or even backlashed while some have become a success. In Canada, the suicide reporting guidelines were developed by Canadian Psychiatric Association (CPA) in conjunction with medical practitioners and suicide prevention experts dated back in 2009 (Gandy & Terrion, 2015). The guidelines were then distributed through the CPA, Canadian Association for Suicide Prevention, and other government bodies. This introduction of suicide-reporting guidelines created uproar and challenges from media professionals. Not only did they criticize the lack of consultation with the media field during the development stage of the guidelines, but the guidelines failed to reflect the actual culture of the media field. A similar situation was also seen in New Zealand when they first introduced suicide reporting guidelines developed by New Zealand Ministry of Health, without any engagement with the media (Collings & Kemp, 2010). On the other hand, Australia's media reporting guidelines, named the *Reporting Suicide and Mental Illness,* have been successful since their introduction in Australia. One study showed that after the introduction of these media guidelines, there has been a decrease in use of inappropriate language, details of method, and reference to celebrity suicide (Pirkis, 2009). As mentioned before, previous studies showed that the content in media reporting guidelines is mostly similar between one and other (Bohanna & Wang,

2012; Pirkis et al., 2006). Therefore, the acceptance from the media and the outcome effectiveness of implementing the guidelines are more likely to be contributed by the degree to which media professionals have involved in the adaptation and implementation of the guidelines and how much they feel that these guidelines are imposed on them.

The implementation of recommendations on suicide reporting has not been a straight-forward success for Hong Kong either. As we have mentioned, we did not gain as much support from the media professionals for the 2004 version (Fu & Yip, 2008). Nevertheless, through bidirectional communication, providing more solid research findings, and mutual understanding, we have built a collaborative partnership with media professionals to produce the 2015 version—*Recommendations on Suicide Reporting and Online Information Dissemination for Media Professionals*. This bidirectional communication emphasizes a nonhierarchical relationship where both parties see each other equally as partners and participants in the process. Furthermore, the suicide prevention field used to adopt a rather passive role, where we waited to be interviewed, in media engagement. Nowadays, we take on a more active role: rather than encouraging the media to interview the experts, we reach out and actively send reminders or information to the media that concerns the related topic. Our example of helium suicide reporting demonstrated the successful positive relationship between the suicide prevention field and members of the media, with both parties striving to create a win–win situation that places the interest of the public to their utmost priority. This success in collaboration cannot be reached without the support and partnership between the suicide prevention field and different levels of professionals in the media field.

As media is growing from the traditional printed media, television, and radio, to the constantly changing Internet, we have added new media, including web pages, search engines, and social media to our list of recommendations. The growth of the Internet has definitely made an impact on suicide prevention, in terms of raising questions like will it assist in suicide prevention or will it weaken our measures in suicide preventions. On the one hand, social networking has been the most dominant spread of information, especially for young people. If problematic online news are taken down long after being published online, the news hyperlinks or corresponding videos might have already been copied, shared, and reposted on social networking sites. The spread of information on the Internet is much faster than traditional media and this has made it much more difficult to contain any problematic reports of suicide once published. However, on the other hand, as the Internet is a dynamic source of information, it becomes much easier to delete or edit information that has already been published. For example, if we would like to withdraw a photo on a suicide case report, it is just a matter of simple clicks for online media; but if it is on a printed media, there will be no way to withdraw the photo in a cost-effective way. Nevertheless, as we can see, there will always be an upside and a downside to this growing media outlet on the Internet. It is important that both suicide prevention field and media field work together to adapt accordingly to the ever-changing online media outlets. Social media is a double-edged sword and it can go either way; we simply have to be constantly on alert and try to guide this into a direction which produces desirable outcomes.

Last but not the least, we observed a difficulty in media engagement in the case of the emergence of a new suicide method. Taking the helium suicide method for instance, while we need the media's help to raise the public's awareness of the danger of helium, we do not want to spread the knowledge of this new method to the viewers, who might not yet have heard of this method. After careful discussions with our partners, including medical professionals and the regulatory department of compressed gases, we agreed on a holistic response to the situation. On one hand, we urged the media to avoid describing the details of the method (e.g., use "gas suicide" instead of "helium suicide") since the method has not been widely known to the public. On the other hand, when suicides using this method happened, medical professionals would respond to the media enquiry by stressing the negative consequences of suicide instead of describing this method as painless and peaceful. Such responses could prevent this method to be perceived as a desirable suicide method by the public from the early stage (Eddleston et al., 2006; Skopek & Perkins, 1998). In other words, a media engagement approach should be developed to respond at different stages of a suicide epidemic, where restriction of cognitive access to a new suicide method is more urgent and appropriate at the early stage (Chen, Chen, & Yip, 2010; Chen et al., 2016). This experience can serve as a reference for other colleagues when facing a similar dilemma.

## Conclusion

It has been more than a decade since our initial effort to engage with the media in HK. The process was not easy, nor was it a straight-forward success. We have been ignored and challenged along the way, but we learned from our experiences, as well as from those of international colleagues, and always strive for continuous improvement. In recent years, our persistent engagement proved its effect as we received more and more positive feedback from and support and cooperation with the media field. The media professionals have become a strategic partner for suicide prevention. We see the partnership and collaboration with the media need to be maintained while both parties continue to explore more ways to collaborate for the benefit of the public in suicide prevention. We hope that through our persistent engagement, members of the media field can develop a norm in suicide case reporting that considers its impact on suicide prevention. Ultimately, the norms that we collaboratively built can sustainably change the behavior of media professionals, making the future suicide news reports appropriate and prevention-oriented.

## References

Au, J. S., Yip, P. S., Chan, C. L., & Law, Y. W. (2004). Newspaper reporting of suicide cases in Hong Kong. *Crisis: The Journal of Crisis Intervention and Suicide Prevention, 25*(4), 161–168. doi: 10.1027/0227-5910.25.4.161

Bohanna, I., & Wang, X. (2012). Media guidelines for the responsible reporting of suicide: A review of effectiveness. *Crisis: The Journal of Crisis Intervention and Suicide Prevention, 33*(4), 190–198. doi: 10.1027/0227-5910/a000137

Chen, Y.-Y., Chen, F., & Yip, P. S. F. (2010). The impact of media reporting of suicide on actual suicides in Taiwan, 2002–2005. *Journal of Epidemiology and Community Health, 65*(10), 934–940.

Chen, Y.-Y., Tsai, C.-W., Biddle, L., Niederkrotenthaler, T., Wu, K. C.-C., & Gunnell, D. (2016). Newspaper reporting and the emergence of charcoal burning suicide in Taiwan: A mixed methods approach. *Journal of Affective Disorders, 193,* 355–361.

Cheng, Q. (2012). Suicide and the Media in the Chinese Contexts. (Doctoral dissertation). Retrieved from the HKU Scholars Hub: http://hub.hku.hk /handle/10722/180940.

Cheng, Q., Fu, K., Caine, E., & Yip, P. S. F. (2014). Why do we report suicides and how can we facilitate suicide prevention efforts? Perspectives of Hong Kong media professionals. *Crisis: The Journal of Crisis Intervention and Suicide Prevention, 35*(2), 74–81. doi:10.1027/0227-5910/a000241

Collings, S. C., & Kemp, C. G. (2010). Death knocks, professional practice, and the public good: The media experience of suicide reporting in New Zealand. *Social science & medicine, 71*(2), 244–248. doi:10.1016/j.socscimed.2010.03.017

CSRP. (2004). *Suicide and the media: Recommendations on suicide reporting for media professionals.* Hong Kong: Hong Kong Jockey Club Centre for Suicide Research and Prevention, The University of Hong Kong.

CSRP. (2016). *Suicide rate – Proportion by method.* Retrieved January 25, 2016, from http://csrp.hku.hk/statistics/

Eddleston, M., Karunaratne, A., Weerakoon, M., Kumarasinghe, S., Rajapakshe, M., Sheriff, M. R., . . . Gunnell, D. (2006). Choice of poison for intentional self-poisoning in rural Sri Lanka. *Clinical Toxicology (Philadelphia, Pa.), 44*(3), 283–286.

Etzersdorfer, E., & Sonneck, G. (1998). Preventing suicide by influencing mass-media reporting: The Viennese experience 1980–1996. *Archives of Suicide Research, 4,* 67–74.

Fu, K. W., & Yip, P. S. (2008). Changes in reporting of suicide news after the promotion of the WHO media recommendations. *Suicide and Life-threatening Behavior, 38*(5), 631–636. doi:10.1521/suli.2008.38.5.631

Fu, K. W., Chan, Y. Y., & Yip, P. S. (2011). Newspaper reporting of suicides in Hong Kong, Taiwan and Guangzhou: compliance with WHO media guidelines and epidemiological comparisons. *Journal of Epidemiology and Community Health, 65*(10), 928–933. doi:10.1136/jech.2009.105650

Gandy, J., & Terrion, J. L. (2015). Journalism and suicide reporting guidelines in Canada: perspectives, partnerships and processes. *International Journal of Mental Health Promotion, 17*(5), 249–260. doi:10.1080/14623730.2015.1077613

Niederkrotenthaler, T., Till, B., Herberth, A., Voracek, M., Kapusta, N. D., Etzersdorfer, E., Strauss, M., & Sonneck, G. (2009). The gap between suicide characteristics in the print media and in the population. *European Journal of Public Health, 19,* 361–364.

Pirkis, J. E., Burgess, P. M., Blood, R. W., & Fracis, C. (2007). The newsworthiness of suicide. *Suicide and Life-Threatening Behavior, 37,* 278–283.

Pirkis, J. E., Burgess, P. M., Francis, C., Blood, R. W., & Jolley, D. J. (2006). The relationship between media reporting of suicide and actual suicide in Australia. *Social science & medicine, 62*(11), 2874–2886. doi:10.1016/j.socscimed.2005.11.033

Sha, D. (2014a, Sept 22nd). Communication is the most important (最緊要溝通). Apple Daily.

Sha, D. (2014b, Nov 28th). Media should have social responsibility (媒體要有王道). Apple Daily.

Skopek, M. A., & Perkins, R. (1998). Deliberate exposure to motor vehicle exhaust gas: The psychosocial profile of attempted suicide. *Australian and New Zealand Journal of Psychiatry, 32*(6), 830–838. doi:10.3109/00048679809073873

World Health Organization. (2000). *Preventing suicide: A resource for media professionals.* Geneva: Department of Mental Health. Retrieved from http://www.who.int/mental_health/media/en/426.pdf

World Health Organization. (2008). *Preventing suicide: A resource for media professionals.* Geneva: Department of Mental Health and Substance Abuse. Retrieved from http://www.who.int/mental_health/prevention/suicide/resource_media.pdf

# 19

# Conclusion

*Steven Stack and Thomas Niederkrotenthaler*

This volume has covered a range of issues in three areas of work on media and suicide: research, theory, and policy. A summary of selected principal findings was provided in the first chapter. Our conclusion focuses on how selected aspects of issues brought up in the individual chapters, and chapter sets, might help to inform more general issues and discussions on media and suicide. In addition, we provide suggestions for future research, theory, and policy.

## The State of International Research on Traditional Media and Copycat Suicide

The significance of the media as a contributing factor to suicidality is demonstrated by official national documents on suicide prevention. Literally all known national strategies for suicide prevention call for surveillance of the media and contain suicide guidelines for the reporting of the media on suicide (Beautrais & Fergusson, 2012).

The chapters on the effects of traditional media on suicidality are part of a tradition of research dating back to at least 1911 (Hemenway, 1911). There have been over 150 investigations on the impact of exposure to such media outlets as newspapers, television news, magazines, books, and movies on suicidality.

From an international perspective on the generation of knowledge on suicide prevention and the media, it is important to take stock on where the research has taken place. For example, is research concentrated in only a few nations? Do we have adequate knowledge on the link between media and suicidality in nations with the most suicides and/or highest suicide rates? Do trends in research show increases in some nations and decreases in others? Does the world have an adequate research base on the content of media stories on suicide? Do nations with national suicide prevention programs produce more research studies on suicidality and the media than their counterparts?

*Research on Media Effects on Suicide around the Globe*

To address these issues a search was done in *Medline* using two search commands: subject = suicide and keyword = media. A total of 572 studies were found. Studies needed to meet the following criteria to be included: (1) contains a measure of exposure to one or more media stories regarding a suicide death or a suicide attempt and (2) contains a measure of suicidality based on suicide deaths or suicide attempts. Studies where the outcome variable was suicide ideation or a suicide plan were excluded. (3) The study must contain one or more results showing an association or no association between exposure to a media story and a measure of suicidality. Copies of studies that met these criteria were retrieved. The authors of the present book added a number of studies not listed in *Medline* that were found in other sources. These sources included *Sociological Abstracts* and previous reviews of the literature on media and suicide (e.g., Stack 2005, 2009). The total number of studies on media and suicide was calculated for each nation. These study counts were compared with suicide counts in 2012. A measure of the relative amount of work on suicide and the media was calculated: number of research studies to date per thousand suicides in 2012. All eleven nations with known national suicide prevention plans are included. The results are provided in table 19.1.

A total of 152 studies were found. Twenty of the twenty-two nations listed produced at least one study assessing the presence or absence of a copycat effect following media stories on suicide. There was a concentration of research in a few nations. Thirteen of these twenty nations produced only one or two studies. Five nations each accounted for ten or more studies: Austria (ten), South Korea (fourteen), Taiwan (sixteen), the United Kingdom (seventeen), and the United States (fifty-four).

Previous work has noted that only 28 of the 193 member states of the United Nations have a national suicide prevention plan (WHO, 2014), although a list of these 28 is not provided. Reliable suicide data are available for only about half of the world's nearly two hundred nations (Maloney et al., 2014; WHO, 2014). In this context our findings on research on media effects would be expected to come from a small set of the world's nations. In any event, for the vast majority of nations in the world, there is an apparent lack of research on the association between media coverage of suicide and suicide rates.

**Table 19.1.** Number of studies to date on media effects on suicide, number of suicides in 2012, and studies to date per 1,000 suicides.

| Nation | Number of studies to date on copycat suicides | Number of suicides, 2012 (WHO, 2014) | Studies to date per 1,000 suicides in 2012 |
|---|---|---|---|
| Australia* | 5 | 2,679 | 1.866368 |
| Austria* | 10 | 1,319 | 7.581501 |
| Belgium* | 1 | 1,955 | 0.511509 |
| Canada* | 2 | 3,983 | 0.502134 |
| China | 1 | 120,730 | 0.008283 |
| France | 1 | 10,093 | 0.099079 |
| Germany* | 9 | 10,745 | 0.837599 |
| Hong Kong*,** | 3 | 917 | 3.27 |
| Hungary | 3 | 2,519 | 1.190949 |
| India | 1 | 258,075 | 0.003875 |
| Ireland* | 0 | 524 | 0 |
| Israel | 2 | 470 | 4.255319 |
| Japan* | 8 | 29,442 | 0.271721 |
| Netherlands | 1 | 1,666 | 0.60024 |
| Norway* | 0 | 508 | 0 |
| Poland | 1 | 7,848 | 0.127421 |
| Slovenia | 1 | 354 | 2.824859 |
| South Korea | 14 | 17,908 | 0.781774 |
| Switzerland | 2 | 972 | 2.057613 |
| Taiwan** | 16 | 3,766 | 4.25 |
| UK* | 17 | 4,360 | 3.899083 |
| USA* | 54 | 43,361 | 1.245359 |
| Total | 152 | 524,129 | 0.29 |

Notes: * Nation has media reporting guidelines for suicide (Beautrais & Fergusson, 2012). **Used data sources other than the WHO database.

There is some evidence that having a national suicide prevention plan may act as a stimulus to research on media and suicide. Austria and the other 10 nations known to have a national suicide prevention plan produced a total of 109 studies. This is higher than the remaining eleven nations which produced only forty-three studies.

For the twenty nations that have at least one published study on media impacts on suicide, there is considerable variation in the research attention paid to the problem relative to a nation's suicide count. Column 4 of table 19.1 shows that Austria leads with 7.58 studies to date per 1,000 Austrian suicides in 2012. Austria is followed by Israel and Taiwan (4.25 studies/1,000 suicides). Nations at the low end in the relative amount of suicide and media research included China, India, Ireland, and Norway. Each of these had less than 0.01 studies per 1,000 suicides.

In terms of trends, however, most of what we know in the present century (2000 and beyond) about traditional media and suicide is being produced in the Far East. In data not fully described here, since the year 2000 South Korea has produced fourteen investigations, Taiwan sixteen, and Austria eight. All of Taiwan's studies are even more recent and date from 2007, while South Korea's studies date from 2009. The United States, once the leader in such work, trails with only three such investigations, while only two of the United Kingdom's seventeen studies date from 2000. There has been a clear decline in research in most Western nations that do this variety of work. The main exception to this generalization is Austria. In order to assess the impact of the application of suicide media guidelines, work needs to be reinvigorated in the former centers of media effects research.

Another key issue is that there is very little data from less developed nations. For example, there is only one study from India and one from Slovenia. Most of the world's near million suicides each year take place in this group of nations (WHO, 2014). Efforts to assess the impacts of traditional (and new) media on suicide in these nations need to begin as soon as possible.

Importantly, at least two nations known to have media guidelines for the reporting of suicide (Beautrais & Fergusson, 2012) have no studies on possible copycat effects involving traditional media. These are Ireland and Norway. Research is especially needed in such nations to ascertain if the guidelines are working.

Some caution needs to be exercised in interpreting recent findings. Many recent studies are based exclusively on cases of widely publicized celebrity suicides. For example, fully thirteen of the fourteen Korean investigations are limited to celebrity suicides. These suicides are known to be the ones most apt to be associated with a copycat effect (e.g., Stack, 2005; Niederkrotenthaler et al., 2012). In future research it is important to maintain a balance between cases of celebrity suicides and stories regarding the suicides of everyday common people. Most news coverage may be on the latter category, since the suicides of well-known celebrities are relatively rare events. Hence, it is important to assess the extent to which copycat effects exist for noncelebrity cases of suicides. If these tend to minimize copycat effects, suicide prevention efforts might be concentrated on celebrity suicides (Stack, 2005).

*Research on the Content of Media Suicide Stories around the World*

As part of the search for the factors which might increase (Werther effect), decrease (Papageno effect), or have no impact on the probability of a copycat effect, research is needed to assess the content of suicide stories. There has been much work which focuses on the content analysis of suicide stories in the news; the chapter by Canetto and her colleagues is an example. Often this mode of analysis is structured in terms of story compliance with suicide reporting guidelines. There has also been work on other media. For example, there are content analyses on the portrayal of motives for suicide in feature films (Stack & Bowman, 2012). The monitoring of the content of suicide stories has been called for in national strategies for suicide prevention. However, some nations have been more active than others in keeping track of media content on suicide.

Table 19.2 provides data from the *Medline* search and authors' files on studies providing a content analysis of media stories on suicide. A total of sixty-three studies were found. These were done in twenty nations. These are not the same twenty nations as in table 19.1, although most are also included in the former table. Nevertheless, of the 193 reporting nations to the United Nations, only one in ten has assessed the content of their suicide media in at least one study. Not only is the content of suicide narratives unknown in most nations, but trends in the quality of coverage of suicide remain unknown in over 90 percent of the world's nations. Such knowledge is badly needed to assess the effectiveness of suicide guidelines for the media.

Six nations had only one such content analysis. The United States led the world with twelve of the investigations. As in the case of table 19.1's data, there were no studies found on the content of media suicide stories in two nations with a national suicide prevention plan: Ireland and Norway.

Research to ascertain the extent to which media guidelines have been implemented is needed in the vast majority of the world's nations and even in some with a national suicide prevention plan.

As was the case in table 19.1, Austria led the world in the number of studies per 1,000 suicides with 5.3 content analyses to date per 1,000 suicide deaths in 2012. Many nations from table 19.1 had no content analyses. These nations included Belgium, China, and France. Some nations that had no record of a study testing for copycat effects in table 19.1 did have a study on the analysis of the content of suicide stories. These countries were added to table 19.2. They include Columbia, Ghana, and Lithuania, all less developed nations. All had a single content analysis. Finland is added to table 19.2 with one study involving a content analysis of its coverage of suicide.

Importantly, there is a lack of work on the content of media stories in most nations of the world. Only 20 of the 193 reporting countries to the United Nations have at least 1 study. Clearly, much work is necessary to ascertain what type of information on suicide is being communicated to the populations of these 173 nations.

In order to assess trends in adherence to media guidelines, studies are needed in at least two points in time. Such studies need to use similar measures and media samples to facilitate rigorous comparisons. These methodological consistencies are absent in most of the sixty-three investigations in table 19.2. Many investigations are cross-sectional, analyzing media stories only at one point in time. Further, studies by different investigators often differ in the sample of media stories (e.g., newspapers, television news, magazines, or films) and the specific content of the stories under investigation (e.g., specific guideline violations, demographics of suicide victims, or presumed causes of suicide in the stories). There is a need for comparable methodologies across nations and over time to rigorously promote surveillance of the content of media depictions of suicide. In the long run, this would facilitate the extent to which the variation among nations in media coverage of suicide might explain the variation in national suicide rates among nations. Such overtime studies are critical to monitoring any progress in the application of guidelines to the actual presentation of suicide in the media.

Film portrayals have been assessed. The information contained in suicide narratives in major motion pictures is important with respect to audience size. Watching movies is the leading leisure pursuit in many nations, more so than reading newspapers or watching the television news (Stack & Bowman, 2012). Content analyses of suicide stories in feature films are now available in seven recent investigations using data from four nations: Japan, South Korea, the United States, and the United Kingdom (e.g., Stack & Bowman, 2016).

**Table 19.2.** Number of content analyses of media suicide stories to date, number of suicide deaths in 2012, and content analyses to date per 1,000 suicide deaths in 2012.

| Nation | Number of content analyses of media suicide stories | Number of suicide deaths in 2012 | Content analyses to date per 1,000 suicide deaths in 2012 |
|---|---|---|---|
| Australia* | 5 | 2,679 | 1.86 |
| Austria* | 7 | 1,319 | 5.30 |
| Belgium* | 0 | 1,955 | 0 |
| Canada* | 2 | 3,983 | 0.50 |
| China | 0 | 120,730 | 0 |
| Columbia | 1 | 2,517 | 0.39 |
| Finland | 1 | 901 | 1.10 |
| France | 0 | 10,093 | 0 |
| Germany* | 4 | 10,745 | 0.37 |
| Ghana | 1 | 577 | 1.73 |
| Hong Kong*,** | 4 | 917 | 4.36 |
| Hungary | 3 | 2,519 | 1.19 |
| India | 2 | 258,075 | 0.007 |
| Ireland* | 0 | 524 | 0 |
| Israel | 2 | 470 | 4.25 |
| Japan* | 3 | 29,442 | 0.10 |
| Lithuania | 1 | 1,007 | 0.99 |
| Netherlands | 0 | 1,666 | 0 |
| New Zealand | 1 | 459 | 2.17 |
| Norway* | 0 | 508 | 0 |
| Poland | 0 | 7,848 | 0 |
| Slovenia | 0 | 354 | 0 |
| South Korea | 2 | 17,908 | 0.11 |
| Switzerland | 3 | 972 | 3.08 |
| Taiwan** | 3 | 3,766 | 0.80 |
| UK* | 5 | 4,360 | 1.14 |
| USA* | 12 | 43,361 | 0.27 |
| Total | 63 | 529,655 | 0.12 |

Notes: *Nation has media reporting guidelines for suicide according to Beautrais and Fergusson (2012). **Used data sources other than the WHO database. Studies needed to meet the following criteria to be included: (1) an analysis of two or more media depictions of suicidality based on suicide deaths or suicide attempts. (2) The media analyzed are newspapers, television stories, books, plays, novels, related literature, or movies. (3) The analysis provides the presence of themes such as demographics of the suicide victim, presumed causes of suicide, presence of mentions of resources for help for suicidal readers (e.g., helpline numbers), and other themes including violations of suicide guidelines for the media reporting of suicide.

While research is lacking in less developed nations, at present, both tables also find a lack of relevant research in many developed nations. The developed nations for which no studies could be found include France, Iceland, Ireland, Italy, Luxembourg, the Netherlands, Norway, Spain, and Sweden. It is noted, however, that the tables are limited to studies on traditional media. The results need to be replicated for other media.

## The Media's Influence on Suicide Methods: Implications

Previous investigations have often found strong links between the method of suicide used by role models in the media and the method of suicide in subsequent suicides in society. In particular, in the case of the spread of new suicide methods, the influence of media reports is often strong. For example, Chan et al. (2005) found in interviews with persons attempting suicide by a new method (charcoal burning), that nearly all reported that they learned about the method from newspaper reports.

The chapter by Stack and Bowman link the 4:1 male/female gender suicide ratio in the United States to a nearly 4:1 ratio between males and females in the use of a highly lethal suicide method (guns) in American movies. Recent research has found that most suicide attempters report having learned the method that they used in their suicidal behavior from movies (Biddle et al., 2012). Social learning mechanisms are thought to help to account for these social facts.

Anecdotal evidence also shows the influence of movies on suicide. Alan Turing, the famous British mathematician credited with helping to invent the computer, copied the method of death of the witch in *Snow White and the Seven Dwarfs.* That film was known to be Turing's favorite movie for many years. The witch in *Snow White* died eating an apple poisoned with cyanide. Turing used a cyanide-laced apple for his suicide. The apple with a bite out of it, the logo of Apple computers, is believed by some to be a nod to Turing (Leavitt, 2006). The life story of Turing was recently presented in the Academy Award winning movie *The Imitation Game* (2014).

The gender ratio in suicide varies considerably around the world. This variation may be related to the cultural scripts on suicide method presented in film. Perhaps the gender ratio in suicide is, for example, lower in nations where there is less of a difference between males and females in lethal methods of suicide in film. Preliminary analyses suggest that this is the case in two Asian nations, South Korea and Japan (Stack & Bowman, 2016). Firearms are much less available in those nations. However, there is a reversal of the American gender difference in their movies regarding other highly lethal, and available, methods of suicide. These methods include hanging (18 percent females vs. 11 percent of male cinematic suicides), and jumping from high places (36 percent females vs. 24 percent male cinematic suicides). Nations whose films portray relatively more lethal methods of female suicide may have relatively higher rates of female suicide. If so, the film media deserves more attention in explaining the gender ratio in suicide.

### Reflections on the Significance of Historical Artistic Media

The significance of the two chapters on the portrayal of suicide in art history can be gauged, in part, to art's influence on contemporary audiences. For example, many Kabuki plays have been produced into modern feature films. The plot involving the tensions between a near bankrupt paper merchant and his lover, a courtesan, in the modern Japanese feature film, *Double Suicide* (1969), is taken from the old Japanese Kabuki play *The Love Suicides at Amijima* (1721). Other similar Kabuki-based suicide pacts are the subject of Japanese feature films such as *The Double Suicide of Sonezaki* (1978).

The samurai tradition of seppuku—suicide for duty, honor, and/ or atonement—was another theme of Kabuki plays that has lived on through contemporary film. The real historical case of forty-seven ronin (former samurai without a leader) who suicided after murdering an evil lord has been the subject of many feature films in both the East (e.g., *Chushingura Kohen* (1939), *47 Samurai* (1962)) and the West (e.g., *47 Ronin* (2013)). The forty-seven heroes committed mass seppuku as an act of atonement for murdering a treacherous lord, an act forbidden under their code of honor. However, the murder was also necessary for avenging the death and maintaining the honor of their leader, who had been tricked by the lord into suiciding.

The suicides for duty and honor in the samurai code are thought to have influenced many Japanese mass suicides during the end of World War II. As Krysinska points out, the American occupying forces in post-World War II Japan banned renditions of the forty-seven ronin narrative. It was believed to have contributed to the suicides of thousands of Japanese pilots near the end of the war in sacrificial kamikaze attacks. As with the case of the real lovers in the Kabuki play, *The Love Suicides at Sonezaki* (1703), the suicides of the forty-seven ronin have been memorialized in a shrine. The remains of the forty-seven ronin

259

rest there and Japanese school children are taught to respect their actions in the name of honor and duty.

Future research is needed to explore the role of the national memoralization of suicides such as the Japanese case of the forty-seven ronin heroic suicides and the double suicide portrayed in *The Love Suicides at Amijima* (1721). It is not clear how many nations have built shrines or monuments to national heroes or admired persons who died by suicide. It is plausible that nations, such as Japan, that have done so have inadvertently contributed to a high suicide rate. Memorials to suicides can provide positive definitions of suicide. In the United States, in contrast, to the best knowledge of the present authors, there are no major political heroes and others who died by suicide and have had their deaths memorialized. The United States has only an average suicide rate. The memoralization of heroic suicides in art may be a risk factor for suicide.

## Theories of Media Impacts

The four chapters dedicated to various theories of media impacts are relevant to both our understanding of the phenomena described as Werther and Papageno effects and to practical prevention efforts using media as a tool. As highlighted in the chapter by Notredame and colleagues, evidence about the associations between publication of suicide portrayals in the media and subsequent increases of suicides has further accumulated in recent years. In spite of this, there are still important gaps in our understanding of this phenomenon. Their attempt to provide a synthesis of several theories that might be relevant to media effects in the area of suicide and prevention is an important step for evidence-based assessment of media-related phenomena in suicidology and may ultimately be helpful in order to provide more accurate recommendations on reporting.

In a similar vein, the review of studies on negative and ambiguous findings provided by Scherr and Steinleitner may ultimately help to better define helpful and harmful media characteristics, and personal variables that may impact on any media effect. The study by Till constitutes a practical example of a range of recent individual-level studies investigating the impacts of fictional suicide movies qualitatively. This study supports the notion that media effects of suicide portrayals are complex and largely depend on audience characteristics, such as coping mechanisms used when exposed to a suicide portrayal.

This complexity of media effects is also highlighted in the research update on the Papageno effect. While most research since Phillip's first description on the Werther effect has focused on harmful media effects, research on protective potentials of media portrayals has only started to emerge recently. This development can also be contextualized with increased interest within suicide prevention to better understand how media can be used to help actively prevent suicide. While changing the conversation to less sensationalist ways of reporting that take preventive aspects into account has been a relevant focus for a long time, the development of suicide-protective media messages is another challenging, yet extremely relevant task with a huge potential for further research and practical applications that are of direct and immediate relevance to suicide prevention. This research also feeds into the calls of the other authors contributing to this part of the book, to consider a broader-than-ever range of media effects that are relevant to suicide prevention and to develop research designs that are based on and adapted to specific theoretical assumptions rather than vice versa. This section ultimately contributes to the impression that the pieces of the media effects puzzle in suicidology, which have been around for many years, are finally beginning to fall into place. Both content-related and individual factors seem to be relevant to specific media effects that include harmful and protective effects, as well as ambiguous effects.

## Policy Issues

Although many countries have implemented media recommendations for suicide reporting as well as other media collaborations that may help to prevent suicide in recent years, different from empirical research findings on media effects, the experiences with specific models of implementation and collaboration are often left unreported, resulting in a concerning lack of shared experiences with various settings and forms of implementation and a resulting lack of expertise on best-practice models on how to implement research findings into practice.

The five chapters included in this part of the book provide comprehensive insight into regional experiences with various forms of media collaborations and related implementation models. These insights are relevant to policy makers and prevention experts in other parts of the world in order to amend, refine their ongoing initiatives, or implement similar models based on these experiences. The chapter on the Viennese experience by Sonneck and Etzersdorfer revisits experiences from the probably first experiment worldwide to develop and implement media recommendations for suicide reporting. The results of this widely known natural experiment have served as a basis for similar initiatives in many other countries and highlight that practical initiatives need to be accompanied by evaluation research in order to make a true difference for suicide prevention.

Also the United States has had media recommendations for suicide reporting for several years, but, as highlighted by Dan Reidenberg from SAVE, the initial recommendations had not adequately addressed the needs of media professionals, which made the development of novel recommendations by a committee including both suicide prevention and media experts necessary. An initial evaluation of changes in the quality of reporting subsequent to the development of the new recommendations suggests considerable improvements in reporting characteristics, with an increase in the number of articles that were written by suicide prevention practitioners and spokespeople themselves. The media recommendations may thus be effective in educating both the media and suicide prevention experts in effective messaging.

While most of the experiences with media recommendations come from Western countries, there have been several studies recently on particularly sensationalist reporting and subsequent copycat phenomena in some Asian countries. Therefore, the report of Cheng and Yip on the implementation of media recommendations for suicide reporting in Hong Kong is particularly relevant. In comparison to a first version of the recommendations in 2004, which were largely ineffective in changing the mass media conversation about suicide, the development of the 2015 recommendations was based on focus group interviews with media professionals. This experience highlights once again the relevance of engaging media professionals in the implementation process, an experience which was relevant to the Austrian, the US, and the Hong Kong initiatives.

The practical insights into the present policy chapters also highlight that currently ongoing initiatives in media collaborations go far beyond what is probably the most traditional aspect, the provision and promotion of media recommendations for suicide reporting. In the example of Stop Suicide's initiatives to raise media awareness in the French-speaking part of Switzerland, Irina Inostroza gives insight into several working areas of their program, including the screening of media for suicide-related contents, the briefing of editorial staff, and the training of journalism students, which seems particularly relevant based on their experience as well as experience from several other countries which suggest that particularly young journalists are responsible for the coverage of local suicides. Fraser and colleagues report on the multi-level approach of the Samaritans in the United Kingdom and the Republic of Ireland to encourage responsible media portrayal of suicide, drawing on specific case examples that provide very useful, practical insight into internationally ongoing efforts in the subject area.

Present media guidelines have been applied to the analysis of news stories, but have neglected other channels of the media including film and music. Cinematic portrayals of suicidal acts leave little to the imagination. For example, media guidelines discourage news reports from providing the details of a suicide method, omitting pictures of the dead body, and using the word "suicide" in the headline. In cinematic portrayals these and related departures from media guidelines are commonplace. The details of the method of suicide are often quite clear. The actual act of suicide—by gunshot, hanging, drowning, and other methods—is often shown in great detail (Stack & Bowman, 2012). These details are extremely rare in news reports. Given that the films containing cinematic suicides are generally available for replay on DVD, for rental online, and other sources, they are easily retrieved for additional study by suicidal persons. Cumulative exposure to suicide movies is a leading risk factor for suicide attempts (Stack, Kral, & Borowski, 2014). Given these and other considerations, it is imperative for suicide prevention policy to include the surveillance of suicide films along with the standing concern with the news media.

## References

Beautrais, A., & Fergusson, D. M. (2012). Media reporting of suicide in New Zealand. *New Zealand Medical Journal, 125,* 5–10.

Biddle, L., Gunnell, D., Owen-Smith, A., Potokar, J., Longson, D., Hawton, K., . . . Donovan, J. (2012). Information sources used by the suicidal to inform choice of method. *Journal of Affective Disorders, 136,* 702–709.

Chan, K. P., Yip, P. S., Au, J., & Lee, D. T. (2005). Charcoal burning suicide in post transition Hong Kong. *The British Journal of Psychiatry, 186,* 67–73.

Hemenway, H. (1911). To what extent are suicide and other crimes against the person due to suggestion from the press? *Bulletin of the American Academy of Medicine, 12,* 253–263.

Leavitt, D. (2006). *The man who knew too much: Alan Turing and the invention of the computer.* New York: Norton.

Maloney, J., Pfuhlmann, B., Arensmen, E., Coffey, C., Gusmão, R., Poštuvan, V. . . . Schmidtke, A. (2014). How to adjust media recommendations on reporting suicidal behavior to new media developments. *Archives of Suicide Research, 18,* 156–169.

Niederkrotenthaler, T., Fu, K.-W., Yip, P. S. F., Fong, D. Y. T., Stack, S. . . . Pirkis, J. (2012). Changes in suicide rates following media reports on celebrity suicide: A meta-analysis. *Journal of Epidemiology and Community Health, 66*(11), 1037–1042.

Stack, S. (2005). Suicide and the media: A quantitative review. *Suicide & Life Threatening Behavior, 35,* 121–133.

Stack, S. (2009). Copycat effects of fictional suicides: A meta analysis. In S. Stack & D. Lester (Eds.), *Suicide in the creative arts* (pp. 231–244). New York: Nova Science Publishers.

Stack, S., & Bowman, B. (2012). *Suicide movies: Social patterns, 1900–2009.* Cambridge, MA: Hogrefe.

Stack, S., & Bowman, B. (2016). Themes in the presentation of suicidality in the cinema: Japan, South Korea, and the US. Paper presented at the VII Congress of the International Association for Suicide Prevention, Asian-Pacific Division, with the Japanese Association of Suicide Prevention, Tokyo, May 18–20.

Stack, S., Kral, M., & Borowski, T. (2014). Exposure to suicide movies and suicide attempts. *Sociological Focus, 47,* 61–70.

World Health Organization. (2014). *Preventing suicide: A global imperative.* Geneva: WHO.

# About the Authors

**Karl Andriessen**, MA, is an Anika Foundation PhD student at the School of Psychiatry, University of New South Wales, Sydney, Australia, where he pursues a doctoral study on adolescents bereaved by suicide. He worked more than twenty-five years in suicide prevention and postvention, nationally and internationally, in various positions from fieldwork to research and policy development. He has published many peer-reviewed articles and book chapters and coedited four books. He is a Co-Chair of the Special Interest Group on Suicide Bereavement and Postvention of the International Association for Suicide Prevention (until end of 2015) and received the 2005 IASP Farberow Award for outstanding contributions in the field of bereavement and survivors after suicide.

**Dr. Louis Bailey** is a research fellow in Health Inequalities in the SEDA Research Group (Supportive care, Early Diagnosis and Advanced disease), based in the Centre for Health and Population Sciences at the Hull York Medical School, University of Hull. With a background in medical sociology, his research takes in the following themes: social marginalization and stigma; life course, ageing, and end of life. He is the coauthor of the *Trans Mental Health Study* (2012; recipient of the GIRES Research Award) and has published papers on minority stress, disenfranchised grief, suicide ideation, bereavement, and memorialization.

**Dr. Jo Bell** is at the School of Social Sciences at the University of Hull. She has researched and published widely on the subject of young suicide and suicide prevention and postvention. Her current research interests include the role of the Internet in suicidal behavior, how the Internet is changing the experiences of those whose lives are affected by suicidal behavior, and the ways in which health professionals can engage with the online environment to support them.

**Barbara Bowman**, MS, JD, is a researcher at the Center for Suicide Research, Troy, MI, USA. She is coauthor of *Suicide Movies: Social Patterns, 1900–2009* (2012). She has also coauthored ten articles and book chapters including ones in *Suicide & Life Threatening Behavior*, *Suicide & the Creative Arts* (2009) and *Suicide as a Dramatic Performance* (Transaction Books, 2015).

**Dr. Silvia Sara Canetto**, PhD, is full professor with appointments in Psychology, Women's/Ethnic Studies, and Human-Development-ment-and-Family-Studies Departments at Colorado State University, USA. She is author of over two hundred publications, mostly on suicide. Her article "The gender paradox in suicide" is the third most cited in *Suicide and Life-Threatening Behavior*. She received AAS Shneidman Research Award and is Fellow of APA and APS.

**Dr. Qijin Cheng** is a research assistant professor at the HKJC Centre for Suicide Research and Prevention, the University of Hong Kong. She was a journalist before obtaining her PhD and specializes in media studies and mental health promotion. She publishes in peer-reviewed journals such as *The Lancet, BMJ, Journal of Clinical Psychiatry*, and *Journal of Affective Disorders*.

**Dr. Thierry Danel** is a doctor in the Psychiatry Department at the Lille University Hospital. Since 2007, he is head of the Regional Federation for Research in Psychiatry and Mental Health, Nord-Pas-de-Calais (France). He is also a member of the CNRS research unit SCALab (Cognitive and Affective Sciences).

**Dr. Med. Elmar Etzersdorfer**, MD (Medical University of Vienna), is a university professor; specialist in psychiatry, psychosomatic medicine, and psychotherapy; psychoanalyst (Member of Vienna Psychoanalytic and German Psychoanalytical Society, IPA); and Medical Director of Furtbachkrankenhaus, Hospital for Psychiatry and Psychotherapy, Stuttgart, Germany. He is member of the Board of German Association for Suicide Prevention, 2006–2014 chair. He and Manfred Wolfersdorf have written the book *Suizid und Suizidprävention* (2011, Kohlhammer, Stuttgart).

**Lorna Fraser**, leading advisor to UK media on the portrayal of suicide, launched the current edition of Samaritans' *Media Guidelines for Reporting Suicide*. Combining her experience as media professional with her clinical work as a psychodynamic therapist, she manages this area of the charity's work, supporting media to improve standards and reduce the risks of media coverage influencing suicidal behavior.

**Dr. Madelyn S. Gould**, PhD, is a professor of epidemiology in psychiatry at Columbia University, NYC, where she directs a community suicide prevention research unit. She has authored 131 articles and chapters, including articles in high-impact journals such as the *New England Journal of Medicine*, the *Journal of the American Medical Association*, and *Lancet Psychiatry*.

**Dr. Keith Hawton**, DSc, FMedSci, is professor of psychiatry at the Oxford University Department of Psychiatry, United Kingdom, where he is director of the Centre for Suicide Research. His research encompasses epidemiology, causes, treatment and prevention of suicidal behavior, and has resulted in over five hundred publications and a number of international awards. His team has had a long-standing interest in suicidal behavior and the media.

**Irina Inostroza** holds two masters degrees in International Relations (the Graduate Institute Geneva, 2007) and Gender Studies (University of Geneva, 2013). She has worked several times as a human rights defender with various NGOs, in Switzerland and abroad. She is currently employed by Stop Suicide where she manages projects to prevent youth suicide.

**Dr. Karolina Krysinska**, PhD, is a project coordinator and senior research officer at the NHMRC Centre of Research Excellence in Suicide Prevention at the Black Dog Institute, University of New South Wales, Sydney, Australia. Her research interests include risk and protective factors in suicide, suicide prevention, thanatology, psychology of trauma, and psychology of religion. She has been a member of the Media and Suicide Taskforce of the International Association for Suicide Prevention since 2008. She is an author and coauthor of numerous book chapters and peer-reviewed articles on various aspects of suicide, trauma, and bereavement.

**Dr. Lisa Marzano,** PhD, is a senior lecturer in psychology at Middlesex University, specializing in suicide and self-harm research. She works closely with Samaritans on the ongoing monitoring and analysis of media reports of suicidal behaviour in the United Kingdom and has authored a number of publications in the field of suicidology.

**Katherine Mok** is a former PhD student at the School of Population and Global Health, the University of Melbourne. Her work focused on the area of suicide and the Internet. In particular, she was interested in the potential impacts of the Internet on suicide and how the Internet might be used in suicide prevention and intervention.

**Dr. Jean-Louis Nandrino** is professor of psychopathology at the University of Lille 3 (Humanities and Social Sciences). He is head of the laboratory team "Dynamics Emotions and Disease" at the CNRS research unit SCALab (Cognitive and Affective Sciences). His expertise mainly focuses on the contribution of emotional regulation mechanisms in the onset and relapse of mental disorders, addictive behaviors, and at-risk behaviors. He is also psychologist and family therapist for teenagers. Finally, he is interested in the effects of family learning on adolescents' emotional skills and he is implementing specific therapeutic procedures for these emotional disorders.

**Dr. Thomas Niederkrotenthaler**, MD, PhD, is an associate professor and head of the Suicide Research Unit at the Institute of Social Medicine, Center for Public Health, Medical University of Vienna, Austria. He has authored more than sixty-five articles and chapters, mostly on media reporting on suicide, and one book. He is the co-chair of the Media & Suicide Special Interest Group of IASP and the current co-chair of National Representatives to IASP. He has first described the Papageno effect and has received several awards, for example, the Hans Rost Award from the German Association for Suicide Prevention and the E. Ringel Award (both awarded to the interdisciplinary suicidology platform *Wiener Werkstaette for Suicide Research*— www. suizidforschung.at).

**Charles-Edouard Notredame** is a psychiatry resident in the University Medical Center, CHRU de Lille, France. He is member of the steering committee of the *Papageno program,* a French national project that aims in preventing suicide through collaboration with media, with a special focus on psychiatry and journalism learners. He is also responsible for the scientific evaluation of the program's efficacy on journalism students' representations, suicide coverage quality, and suicide rates.

**Michael Olivares** is a research assistant in the Department of Psychiatry of the Columbia University Medical Centers and New York State Psychiatric Institute in New York City. He has been collaborating with

Dr. Madelyn Gould on a federally funded evaluation of crisis center follow-up programs in the United States. He received his Bachelor of Arts with honors in psychology from the University of Pennsylvania in 2012 and intends to pursue a PhD in clinical psychology in 2017. He has previously volunteered as a crisis line respondent at the Samaritans crisis hotline.

**Nathalie Pauwels** is in charge of public relations and media department at the Regional Federation for Research in Psychiatry and Mental Health, Nord-Pas-de-Calais (France). She is head of the Papageno program's implementation committee, a French national project that aims to raise journalism students' and journalists' awareness about their role in suicide prevention.

**Dr. Jane Pirkis** is professor and the director of the Centre for Mental Health at the University of Melbourne. She has worked in the field of suicide prevention for twenty years and has published over two hundred journal articles and book chapters. She is recognized internationally for her work on suicide and the media, having conducted a number of studies in this area. Her work has influenced guidelines for journalists on responsible reporting of suicide, both in Australia and overseas. She is currently the general secretary of the International Association for Suicide Prevention.

**Dr. Daniel J. Reidenberg**, PsyD, is the executive director of SAVE, managing director of the National Council for Suicide Prevention, and the US representative to the International Association for Suicide Prevention. Dr. Reidenberg has authored numerous articles on suicide and mental health issues, speaks internationally on the topic, and led the international team that developed the Media Recommendations for Reporting on Suicide. He also serves on Faculty of the Poytner Institute training journalists from across the United States on safe reporting of suicide, was a lead author of the National Strategy for Suicide Prevention, and serves on the National Action Alliance for Suicide Prevention.

**Dr. Jo Robinson** is a Senior Research Fellow at Orygen, the National Centre of Excellence in Youth Mental Health, where she leads a program of work focused upon the prevention of youth suicide. She is also Australia's national representative to the International Association of Suicide Prevention. Jo currently oversees a number of projects, including a randomized controlled trial testing an Internet-based program on suicidal ideation among secondary school students, and a suite of studies examining the potential utility of social media platforms in suicide prevention. Other studies include the evaluation of an educational program for high-school students and a study of suicide clusters among Australian youth.

**Joanne Schweizer Rodrigues**, after a Masters in Health Psychology (University of Lausanne, 2005), has worked with children and youth people, but also in an association of persons suffering from mental disorders. She's now responsible for the mental health program at the Public Health Service of the Canton of Neuchâtel.

**Dr. Sebastian Scherr**, PhD, is an assistant professor at the Department of Communication Studies and Media Research at LMU, Munich. He has published several articles and a book (2015, Springer, in German) on the interplay of depression, mass media, and suicide (English title: Depression–Media–Suicide: On the Empirical Relevance of Depression and Media for Suicidality).

**Dr. Michael D. Slater** (PhD, Stanford University, 1988; MPA, New York University, 1982; BA, Columbia University, 1974) is Social and Behavioral Science distinguished professor at the School of Communication, Ohio State University. His research includes theory-building efforts in message effects, persuasion, narrative influences, and dynamic processes of media selection, media effects, and maintenance of personal and social identity, with a particular interest in health outcomes, with over 150 publications. He is a Fellow of the ICA and was named the 2013 Outstanding Health Communication Scholar jointly by the Health Communication Divisions of the International Communication Association and the National Communication Association (NCA).

**Dr. Gernot Sonneck**, MD, is professor emeritus, University of Vienna. He is the founding father of the Viennese Crisis Intervention Center, the Austrian Association for Suicide Prevention, and the Wiener Werkstätte for Suicide Research; main initiator of the National Austrian Suicide Prevention Plan; and former secretary of IASP. He has authored 402 publications in the field of suicide prevention and has a long-standing international reputation in the field of suicide prevention, with a strong emphasis on crisis intervention and media research. Under his leadership, Austria became the first country worldwide to implement media guidelines for the reporting of suicide, which are now used across the world and recommended by international organizations such as the WHO/IASP.

**Steven Stack,** PhD, is professor at Wayne State University with appointments in the psychiatry and criminology departments. He is the author of 320 articles and chapters and 3 books (*Suicide Movies: Social Patterns*; *Suicide as a Dramatic Performance*; and *Suicide and the Creative Arts*), mostly on the risk and protective factors for suicide. He serves on five editorial boards including *Archives of Suicide Research, Crisis, Sociology,* and *Suicide & Life Threatening Behavior*. He was the recipient of the Louis Dublin Award for lifetime contributions to suicidology by the American Association of Suicidology.

**Anna Steinleitner,** MA, graduated at Ludwig Maximilian University (Munich, Germany) on the topic of media usage and perception of recipients suffering from depressive symptoms/disorder. She already has coauthored articles on the Werther effect in psychiatry and communication science journals. She now is working as a qualitative market and social researcher (inter alia) with focus on public affairs. Still she is regularly coworking and publishing with communication scientists from LMU, Munich.

**Phillip T. Tatum** is a graduate student at the Colorado State University, Fort Collins, CO, USA.

**Dr. Benedikt Till**, DSc, is an assistant professor in the Suicide Research Unit, Institute of Social Medicine, Center for Public Health, Medical University of Vienna, Austria. He is a founding member of the Wiener Werkstaette for Suicide Research and has authored thirty publications on suicide. In 2011, he received the Star Award of the International Academy of Suicide Research.

**Guillaume Vaiva** is a French expert in Suicide and Emergency Psychiatry and an active member of learned societies: GEPS (Groupement d'Etudes et de Prévention du Suicide), SFMU (Société Française de Médecine d'Urgence), French WHO collaborating center for mental health, IAEP (International Association of Emergency Psychiatry), and AFORCUMP (Société Française de Psychotraumatologie). As a professor of psychiatry at the University of Lille (North of France) and head of psychiatry department at the Lille University Hospital, his research focuses on suicide prevention and trauma-related disorders with multisectoral approach.

**Dr. Michael Walter** is a full professor of psychiatry at the University of Western Brittany and the current department head of psychiatry at the Brest University Hospital, in France. He has also been, since 2012, the president of GEPS (Groupement d'Etudes et de Prévention du Suicide), which is one of the most famous French suicide prevention association. His research interests concern suicide prevention (especially specific and indicated prevention) and early diagnostic in schizophrenia. He has published (or been associated to) more than twenty papers in the last five years in these fields.

**Dr. Paul S. F. Yip** is the director of the Centre for Suicide Research and Prevention and a professor of the Department of Social Work and Social Administration, the University of Hong Kong. He was a vice-president of International Association of Suicide Prevention (IASP) 2009–2013. He received the Stengel Research Award for his contribution for suicide prevention in 2011. He has published more than three hundred papers in population health and suicide prevention.

# Senior Author Index

273

# Subject Index

CPSIA information can be obtained
at www.ICGtesting.com
Printed in the USA
BVOW06*1534091017
496988BV00007B/41/P